LEAVING

LEAVING

Three Generations of
an Irish Immigrant Family

A NOVEL

Gerard R. D'Alessio

Leaving
Three Generations of an Irish Immigrant Family

© 2017 Gerard R. D'Alessio

978-0-692-96755-3

Other Books by Gerard R. D'Alessio

Dr. Cappeletti's Chorus
The Giantonios: Family Matters
Iraq Dreams
The Man & In the Wake of Love: Two Novellas

Dedication

This novel is dedicated to all of my ancestors, especially my mother, who provided the inspiration for this project with stories of her childhood. It is also dedicated to all those who follow me, especially my children, stepchildren, grandchildren, and great-grandchildren, for whom *Leaving* was written.

Acknowledgment

I wish to thank my wife, Susan D'Alessio, for her constant support, encouragement, and invaluable suggestions. I also wish to thank Wendy Bernstein, my talented editor, for her perceptive and challenging comments and expert guidance.

Introduction

In 1884, 24-year-old Ellen Furlong left Waterford, Ireland, and sailed to the United States, where she would ultimately reunite with and marry her lover, John Powers. *Leaving* is the fictionalized account of three generations of their family.

The story follows the Powers family through World War I, women's suffrage, Prohibition, the jazz age, the stock market crash, and the Depression; consequently, the Powers narrative is also a portrayal of working-class urban life in Chicago from 1884 to 1933.

By its very nature, *Leaving* is, as well, the story of the heroic struggles of immigrants — including those of today — who fight daily to overcome the constraints of extreme poverty and the tragedy of early death, without the familiar and loving support of the family and country they left behind.

Much of the following account is true; however, many details have been invented or embellished.

Ellen (Furlong) Powers

John Powers

Family Tree of Patrick and Bridget (Coffey) Powers of Waterford, Ireland

Patrick Powers marries Bridget Coffey (both deceased in 1889)
Five children:

John	Bridget	Alice	Mary	Margaret
(1862-1911)	(1869-1943)	(1872-1964)	(1875-1924)	(1877-1926)

John Powers marries (1884) Ellen Furlong (1860-1892)
  Four children:
  Johanna (Josie) Powers (1885-1962) marries (1903) Theodore Arcand
    Theodore Jr. (born 1905) marries Violet
  Anna Powers (1886-1967) marries (1912) Fred Wilhelm (1879-1950)
    Mary Ellen Delpha (1906-2004) marries (1927) Joe Rio (1905-1932)
      Vincent Rio (born 1929) marries Maureen
        Six children
    Mary Ellen marries (1934) Gerard M. D'Alessio
      Gerard R. (born 1936)
    Josephine Wilhelm (1913-1994) marries (1943) John Soukup
      Four children
    Virginia Wilhelm (1917-2014) marries (1945) Joseph Turley
      Five children
  Nellie Powers (1888-1940) marries (1922) William Moore
    William Jr.
  Katherine (Kitty) Powers (1890-1969) marries (1912) Arthur Kirk (born 1889)
    Arthur Kirk Jr. (born 1912) marries Rita OKeefe
    Kenneth Kirk (born 1917) marries Evelyn Dalton
    Helen Catherine Kirk (born 1926) marries Alfred Magee

John Powers marries (1889-1903) Marguerite Hardiman (1860-1907)
Bridget Powers (1869-1943) marries (1891) John F. Powers (1865-1937)
    Margaret Jarleth Powers (1895-1985)
Alice Powers (1872-1964) marries (1892) Henry (Harry) O'Hara (born 1868)
    Thirteen children
Mary Powers (1875-1924)
Margaret (Maggie) Powers (1877-1926) marries Albert Bressler

The trouble, you see, is in the leaving,
It being so full of regret and grief.
Surely, a loss endured only through hope —
Or terrible hurt ...

1

John and Ellen

Ireland
1884

Ellen had visited the wharves many times with her family. Ever since she was a little girl, she had always enjoyed the bracing smell of the saltwater, even the stink of the mud flats at low tide. She liked the strong pungency of the old, blackened timbers and, in summer, the cool, refreshing breeze off the water.

But even so, she could not remember being on the waterfront so early in the morning. With spring barely arrived and the sun not yet high in the sky, the damp air still had a chill to it, and she was glad to be wearing her coat.

On those earlier family outings, Ellen had speculated about the passengers gathered excitedly with their friends and families, waiting to ascend the long ramp to the ships, most of which had sailed here, to the Cove at Queenstown, from Liverpool. She had wondered what it would be like to climb that ramp to a new life. Would it be like walking up to heaven? So many people were leaving their homes and friends! The very idea of sailing out of the familiar harbor into a gray and choppy Atlantic Ocean and crossing that vastness to America had always elicited in her the thrill of adventure. Today, that excitement was mixed with sadness and anxiety.

Her family had made those earlier excursions to the cove to view the scenic harbor with its ancient Viking fort and to experience the festive excitement of the big ships departing. Sometimes it had been to see someone off, to wish them farewell and safe journey. Afterwards, on the long carriage ride home or in one of the restaurants in Youghal or perhaps Dungarvan, her parents would talk of the sacrifice — the sad desperation that had made the emigration of their friends necessary.

The decision to uproot and set sail for a new country held no appeal for her parents or her younger sister, or even her older brother. But Ellen had always been fascinated by the idea. And now, here she was: two suitcases at her feet and her sister and brother at her side.

Their father had refused to come. Well, he had made an excuse — business to attend to that would keep him in Waterford. But she knew how hurt and angry he was, how he didn't want to be seen as condoning her condition or giving his blessing to her sailing away from home, away from him — even though it had been his decision that she go. Her ma, true to form, stood by him and refused to engage in any behavior he wouldn't approve of. But she had cried and hugged her daughter close when it had come time for Ellen to leave. So it fell to her younger sister, Sheila, and her older brother, Timothy, to see her off.

Excitement and anxiety tumbled in her belly like watery porridge. She'd hardly slept a wink for all her wondering and fantasizing. Even now, she felt jittery and her hands were clammy. Thank God for her gloves, so her sister and brother wouldn't notice. She knew how upset Sheila — the whole family, for that matter — was about her leaving, and she was determined to present a strong and confident appearance.

Still, she was happy with anticipation of the new life before her, brimming with possibilities and unknowns.

Ellen and John. They planned to marry as soon as possible, maybe in Boston at her aunt's, where — God willing — he'd meet her in a month's time. But perhaps they wouldn't be married until they reached Chicago, where he hoped to find work. And she would contribute once the baby was old enough — she'd learned a lot about business, spending time at her father's shop, so she knew something about keeping books. She was no dummy, nor a princess, either. Ellen wasn't afraid to work if she had to. She yearned to do something. She smiled bravely and glanced at her sister, who was looking at her with a concerned frown upon her face.

"I'm fine," she said, anticipating Sheila's thoughts. "Really. Don't look at me that way. I'll be fine. Everything's all taken care of."

"I still think Mother and Father should be here. I don't understand them. I'm sorry, but I really don't. I don't know if I'll ever forgive them, letting you go like this, all alone, across an entire ocean. I'll never understand it."

"I won't be alone when I get there," Ellen reassured her sister.

"But you will be alone for almost two weeks. Two weeks upon the water — my God, Ellen, anything could happen. There could be pirates or icebergs. You could fall off the end of the earth."

Ellen laughed. It was a sudden and unexpected relief. "Really, Sheila, you've got Mother's imagination. There won't be any catastrophes. Before you know it, I'll be in America and sending you a letter telling you all about the wonderful adventure I've had, and you won't be able to wait until you can make the same trip yourself."

"Oh, no. Not me. You'll not be getting me out there without the good earth beneath my feet."

Ellen laughed again and squeezed her sister's hand. "Don't be such a scaredy-cat."

"That's all right. I'm not headstrong like you. Look where your sense of adventure has gotten you." Sheila sucked in her breath, as if to pull back her words.

"I understand what you're saying, but I'm not sorry, Sheila. I know you think I should be. Our father certainly thinks I should be — sorry and ashamed and spending the rest of my life hiding my face and doing penance. But I'm not. I'm looking forward to having my baby and half a dozen more with John. He's a good man, a hard worker, and I know he'll take good care of me and our children. I couldn't be happier."

Timothy had been standing somewhat apart, inspecting the ship, *City of Rome,* which was barely three years old. It had three tall masts, with a shorter one astern plus three black funnels in the center of the ship leading down to the powerful engines. The sleek clipper-like ship had been built in England in 1881, and he'd read that it was 560 feet long and 52 feet wide. People said it was the most beautiful steamship ever built, and Timothy agreed. He especially appreciated that it was not encumbered by ugly paddle wheels — one on each side, like some kind of ungainly bustle — that adorned earlier steamships. This beauty had the graceful flair of a clipper sailing ship.

All together there would be more than 1,300 passengers aboard, including his sister. The steamship company claimed its accommodations rivaled first-class hotels, and that even the third-class passengers would be pleased with their home away from home. With some difficulty, he pulled his attention away to join his sisters in their conversation.

"It is true, as you say, Ellen, that John Powers is a hard worker. But he's just a young lad and merely a common laborer. He'll break his back over there earning enough wages to keep a roof over your head and food on your table. There are plenty of fine young men right here in Waterford County who would have made you a good husband and allowed you to continue a comfortable life. Sheila is right, you know, you are headstrong and stubborn. Young John Powers will have his hands full with you."

"And you and Da will be happy to have me off your hands and out of the way."

"Ellen!" Sheila screeched. "How can you say such a thing? There's not a word of truth in what you say. We're all devastated that you're leaving. You know that."

"I know full well that I'm an embarrassment," retorted Ellen. Color surged to her cheeks, bringing attention to her dark red hair. "Of course," she said, softening the set of her mouth and letting the flash of anger in her eyes disappear just as quickly as it had arisen, "I know you and Ma will miss me. I know that."

"And me?" Tim asked huffily. "Am I to count for nothing, then? A poor bastard brother banished to some medieval monastery on the isles off the Connemara, to die miserably from loneliness and neglect?"

"Ach, poor Timmy!" Ellen laughed. "My handsome brother will never die of loneliness and neglect. If you don't watch out, you'll have a brood of your own soon enough and Da will be sending you abroad as well."

"Never," he said, raising his nose to the sky. "I'm much too important to the business."

"Ooh," said Sheila. "But not so important that you can't take off on your fine mare, chasing skirts all over Grandfather's estate."

"Well," he murmured, examining his shoes, "I have an interest in our family estate."

"Yes," said Ellen, nudging her sister, "we've noticed that."

Just then, the steamship blew a loud, sharp whistle that startled those gathered on the wharf, as well as the passengers who had boarded in Liverpool the day before. Timothy picked up Ellen's valises and Sheila abruptly grabbed her sister in a strong embrace.

"Oh, Ellen, I really don't want you to go. Please stay! I'll help you with the baby, I will. Please."

Tears welled up in Ellen's eyes. "Sheila, don't. It'll be all right, you'll see. You'll be fine. You'll have a beau of your own before you know it."

Sheila laughed through her own tears. "You know it'll be a cold day in hell when Da lets me go out, seeing as what happened with you. Oh, forgive me, I didn't mean ..."

"It's all right, Sheila. I did what I wanted to do. And I'll be fine. John and I will be fine. Now remember, both of you, not one word about John following me to America and our getting married. I don't want father doing anything to spoil our plans."

"I promised, didn't I?" Sheila reassured her.

"I can't be standing here all morning, now, can I?" their brother said gruffly. "Come on you two, or Ellen will have to make a swim for it." As if to underscore Timothy's sense of urgency, the ship belched another sharp reminder into the soft gray sky.

Later, when Ellen stood at the railing of *City of Rome,* gazing down through the colored streamers at her dear sister and brother, the sorrow she had managed to keep tightly bound welled up within her. Tears streamed down her face. And then the reality suddenly hit her: She might never see Sheila and Timothy again. She might never see her mother or father again, or her grandfather's estate in Youghal, or father's meatpacking shop in Waterford, or her friends, or even this harbor, this cove, Queenstown. She might never set foot in Ireland again. Grief unexpectedly overwhelmed her.

John couldn't see the sun from where he stood on the scaffold, but he guessed it was almost 9:00 in the morning — Ellen would soon be departing from the port in Queenstown. He clenched his jaw in anger. Damn her father and his narrow-minded thinking! And his own father as well! John was still stunned by his father's fury upon learning that John planned to marry Ellen Furlong.

"Ellen Furlong? Your boss's daughter? You can't be serious! Sure, you must be joking."

When John assured him it was true, Patrick Powers had practically foamed at the mouth. John feared his father's frantic spinning about the room was partly a desperate search for something to beat him with — despite his 22 years.

Hearing her husband's ranting, Bridget Powers came running in from outside. "Jesus, Paddy, what's the matter? Have you lost hold of your senses?"

"Not me!" he shouted. "This idiot! This, our great and glorious senseless wonder. By God, you won't believe it — go on, Jacky, tell your ma your brilliant plans. Make her proud she's got a son with cabbage for brains."

"What?" she cried. "For the love of Jesus, tell me what's going on here. You!" she said, pointing at her son with a wooden ladle she'd picked up from the table, "tell me now, dammit, before I lose my temper."

John regarded his glowering parents. With a deep breath he addressed his mother. "I was just telling Da that I'm planning on getting married."

Bridget Powers looked questioningly at her husband.

"Well, go on, lad," his father goaded. "Tell her the rest of it. Tell your ma who you've set your sights on."

Bridget turned back to her son. "Well?" she said, tapping the ladle into her open hand.

"It's Ellen Furlong," he said quietly.

"Ellen Furlong! Miss Ellen Furlong? Your boss's daughter?"

John nodded. "The same," he admitted. "We've discussed it. She said *yes*."

7

"Jesus!" exploded Patrick. "The lass said *yes*. Did you hear that, Bridget? The young woman wants to marry our own beloved cabbage head. She's got less brains than he does."

"Jacky!" she howled, "you can't! You can't marry your boss's daughter. Have you no sense, lad? Are you daft? Have I raised a son for 22 years who thinks he can marry his boss's daughter?"

"Why not? We love each other."

"What's love got to do with it?" Patrick shouted. "Fall in love with your own kind. We didn't raise you to have fancy ideas about yourself. Who do you think you are that you can marry a woman of that station? It's imbecilic, that's what. You have no bloody right to be in love with such a woman as that."

"But we are in love," John answered simply. He turned to his mother, who had collapsed onto a kitchen chair. "We love each other, Ma. Can't you understand?"

"Oh, Jacky. Don't *you* understand? The Furlongs — that's another world. They aren't like us, son. They're educated. They have that fine, big house, money, horses, a carriage. They have that huge estate down in Youghal, where your Uncle Jimmy and Aunt Beatrice live as their tenants. What do you think will happen to them when her father finds out about this? They'll be turned out, that's what. And all your cousins, too. Have you no sense at all? Didn't you think?"

"I thought ..."

"He thought only with his pecker!" Patrick yelled.

His mother glared at him. "Tell me the truth, son, is she ...?"

John rolled his eyes. Sighing, he sank down at the table, his head bowed. Patrick yanked a chair out and sat down heavily across from him. John nodded slowly.

"Oh, sweet Jesus," Bridget moaned.

"You stupid bastard," Patrick hissed through clenched teeth. With his right hand he cuffed John on the head. "How far along?"

"Two months," John whispered.

Mother and father gaped at their pitiful son, then contemplated each other gravely. "I'll put the kettle on," Bridget said.

"We'll need more than tea," Patrick grumbled.

"Aye," she said, nodding, "you get the bottle and we can have a wee nip with the tea." As she filled the kettle and Patrick retrieved the bottle of Irish whiskey, John slumped in his chair like a deflated balloon.

Roused from that dark memory, John looked up and found himself on a scaffold with other men at the shipbuilding company in Waterford. Pulling his attention back to his work, he couldn't shake the memory of that awful day with his parents. Amazingly, that was only three weeks ago. Since that time, Mr. Furlong had fired John from his job at the meatpacking plant and made arrangements for Ellen to stay with his sister in Boston. Obviously, Mr. Furlong hoped that by sending his daughter abroad, he would put an end to her "engagement" and avoid a local scandal.

But despite her father's best efforts, Ellen and John managed to set their plans. She was being sent to America aboard the next ship. John hadn't the money yet to make the trip with her, so he promised to follow in a month's time. His father helped him get a temporary job in the shipbuilding company where he worked, and the family scraped together funds to help finance his voyage. Patrick wrote to a friend in Chicago, somewhere in the middle of America, asking if he could help John find a job in one of the many slaughterhouses located in that city.

So here he was on this chilly morning in early April, building one ship while his Ellen, his love, was this very moment sailing away from him on another. If it weren't for her father sending her away, they could have been married right here. They could have stayed in Waterford with their families. They could have raised their sons and daughters surrounded by cousins and aunts and uncles and grandparents. Now, he and Ellen were being banished to raise their family alone in America. His mother and father would never know their grandchildren. His four younger sisters would never enjoy their nieces and nephews.

What a sad thing it is, this business of class and honor and reputation, he thought. What a sad, sickening thing.

The very first time John noticed Ellen Furlong was the day he had started working at Edward Furlong's meatpacking business. It was February 1882, and he had just turned 20. Up to that point, he had held a variety of laboring jobs, including working the fields with his Uncle Jimmy and his cousins down in Youghal, where they rented from Mr. Furlong's father, old Squire Furlong. Although he had no clear recollection of seeing Ellen during her visits to her grandfather, she later told him that she remembered him quite well. He smiled, recalling how embarrassed he'd been that she'd taken notice of him. Still, it made them both feel as if they had known each other for a long time — that in some mysterious way their falling in love had been predestined.

Initially, Ellen's father had John doing a variety of menial tasks.

"You're a fine, strong lad, John," Edward Furlong had said. "I'm glad to be able to offer you a job here in Waterford so you can live with your family. I know you've been a good worker down at Youghal, where your uncle and my own father have spoken well of you. Do well here and mind your p's and q's, and we'll see about your learning something of butchering."

John wasn't going to hold his breath about actually having the opportunity to do some apprenticing and learn a trade. Still, he was glad to be back in Waterford, living with his family and earning a fair wage.

But that first day, he had seen her walking brazenly right through the shop and into her father's office, carrying a basket under her arm. He remembered her posture, how self-possessed she was — not arrogant or superior, but exuding natural confidence. He asked someone who she was.

"Oh, that's Miss Ellen, Mr. Edward's daughter. Don't go getting any ideas, mind, or Mr. Timothy will can you in the blink of an eye. That's his sister and their family's favorite."

"I was just asking," he'd said defensively. And for sure, he'd had no thoughts at all of courting her back then. None.

John shook his head in disbelief at all that had followed. He wouldn't have even dared to dream it.

Miss Ellen often brought lunch to her father and brother from their house, just up Hanover Street at the top of St. Thomas Hill. They lived three blocks from the shop where all the butchering was done, the sausages made, the bacon cut and smoked. The front of the butcher shop faced Hanover Street and was just off Merchant's Quay on the River Suir. The wagons that delivered the Furlong products loaded up in the cobblestone courtyard in back. The horses had to be cared for and wagons repaired, sides of meat carried from here to there, floors and tables washed down, and blocks of ice moved into the iceboxes. There was a lot to do, all right, and John often felt as if he were doing it all.

Mr. Edward's office was glassed so he could observe the operations of the shop with a glance from his desk. Young Mr. Timothy, in spite of occasional airs, wasn't afraid to get his hands dirty, and had a direct involvement in everything that went on.

Timothy Furlong took a liking to John and quickly learned that any task assigned to his new worker was usually done right the first time, and without delay. Shorter and huskier than Timothy, John was bright, conscientious, and strong, although perhaps a bit too serious. So it was that when a strong back was needed up at the house, Timothy would call on John to attend to the matter.

Often, in addition to Mrs. Furlong and the servants, the family's two daughters would be there as well. Slowly, from these chance encounters, John and Ellen made each other's acquaintance. Although Sheila was his own age — and just as pretty as Ellen — it was Ellen, two years his senior, who caught his attention.

In spite of the frustration that Ellen often provoked in him, Edward Furlong took secret pride in the fact that, like him, she was headstrong and stubbornly independent — as well as surprisingly competent, where other females generally were not. Thus, he reserved his authority over her for those occasions where it was truly important, and avoided what would have been frequent (and frequently futile) arguments by often letting her have her way. And so, it was no surprise to anyone to see Miss Ellen Furlong out and about in her horse and buggy — shopping, visiting, or enjoying a ride in the country. What might have been scandalous for another woman came to be acceptable behavior for Miss Ellen.

"I've never known anyone like you," John told her the first time they were alone together. The two had contrived to meet one Sunday afternoon north of Waterford on a narrow lane between River Road and the River Suir. He remembered that she had laughed, dismissing his comment as an attempt to impress her.

"No, I'm quite serious," he stammered. "I don't joke around. I've never known another woman with so much ..." He searched for the right words. "Believe me, I mean this as a compliment. You have a sureness about yourself. You seem solid."

Ellen burst out laughing.

"Ach," he moaned. "It's not coming out right at all."

"I think I know what you mean," she reassured him. "My family is always telling me how stubborn and headstrong I am, like a man. It's a fine thing for a man to know his own mind, but it's not fitting for a woman. Well, I don't know who came up with that idea, but I think it's a fine thing for anyone — man, woman, or child — to know its own mind and not be dominated by another's thoughts."

She punctuated her short speech with a righteous nod.

"That's what I was trying to say, only didn't have the words for it. You know who you are and what you think. You're not like some spring blossom floating in the wind. You know where you're going. That's what got my attention the first time I saw you, a full year and a half ago. I said to myself, 'Now, that's what I call a fine woman.'"

"A fine woman?"

"Those very words."

"And what does that mean, exactly?"

"Don't go getting offended on me. I meant it as a compliment."

"I'm sure you did. I'm just not sure what you mean by *a fine woman*."

"Well, I mean — admirable and respectable, with a strong character. And someone who's not going to be blown off course, someone steadfast and dependable."

"All of that?"

John looked into her eyes. Her saw her fair skin, her thick red hair pulled back tightly into a bun at the back of her head, just visible under her pretty hat, her soft brown eyes, her handsome shape. But all of that blurred and faded. In that instant he was aware only that this extraordinary young woman was gazing at him — *at him* — with intense interest.

His knees nearly buckled. "Yes," he managed, "all of that, at least, and more — only right now, I can't think." *My legs have gone weak and I think my lips are going numb,* he thought to himself. Searching for a place to sit down, he settled on leaning against the tree where the horse was tied.

"I'd say you're doing magnificently well for someone who's losing his power of speech." She said this lightly, jokingly, but her eyes still held him, and he knew she was moved.

"I know I can't possibly be the first to tell you that you're beautiful," he said softly. "But even though you are very beautiful, I confess that's not what first attracted me to you. I hope that's all right," he added. "I mean, I know that beauty is supposed to be the most important ..."

"John Powers, stop it," she said adamantly. "Don't go apologizing for what you're feeling and thinking. It is what *you* think that's important to me, not what someone else says you should think. I'm flattered that you like me, the me I am inside. There are plenty of pretty young girls, and young men too, for that matter, who don't have a pennyweight inside their noggins. Well, I do, and I'm proud of it, and I couldn't be more pleased that you find that attractive."

"Really?"

"Of course. And, I don't mind telling you, I admire your courage for telling me your feelings, even though you were afraid I might get insulted. I respect that in you, your courage."

John felt himself blushing and turned away to hide his face from her.

"Hasn't any girl complimented you before?"

"I haven't had much experience talking to women," he admitted, "other than my mother and sisters. Most girls don't have much sense, if you know what I mean — always chattering away without saying anything at all. Just a lot of silly noise."

"I know what you mean. I have the same opinion of them myself, which is why I prefer the company of men. Who wants to spend their entire day in idle gossip, discussing other people's affairs? Not me, I can tell you that."

They were silent for a few moments, then Ellen asked, "I know you work hard for my father, and my brother speaks highly of how responsible and conscientious you are. I was wondering if you have an ambition?"

"An ambition? You mean like owning my own business one day, like your father? No, I don't think I've given much thought to ambition. But if you're asking me what kind of life I'd envisioned, I'd say a life like my da's: a good steady job with decent wages, enough to have my own little place, a wife, some kiddies. Maybe enough left over to take a holiday once in a while, go out to the country, fish, teach my sons to swim. You know, someplace like your grandfather's, or even this," he said, indicating their secluded spot with the river quietly flowing by.

Ellen watched as a dreamy look settled peacefully on his face. "What about you?" John looked directly at her as he spoke. "I think you want more than to spend all your time playing the piano or carrying dinner for your father and brother."

Ellen stared at him for a moment.

"What's the matter? Did I say something stupid?"

"No," she said. "It's just that no one has ever asked me that before."

"No one?"

"No, no one. Everyone has assumed that all I could ever want is to continue being my parents' daughter, to get married someday to a suitable gentleman, to live my life exactly as my mother has — in blissful boredom."

"You want something different? What's wrong with being married and living in a fine house, with maids and servants and such?" he asked.

"And pianos and carriages?"

"Yes. Who wouldn't want such a life?"

"It's not the life you described for yourself now, is it?" she parried.

"I've got no cause for dreaming of such things. It's not who we are. It's not who I am."

"But you've a quick mind. My brother talks of how quickly you catch on to things."

"I'm not stupid. I've been to school. I can read."

13

Ellen saw that he felt defensive. "I'm just saying, you could run a business of your own. I'm sure of it."

John let out a roar of laughter.

"Well, you could," she insisted.

"Now, where would I get the wherewithal to start a business? I'll be lucky to ever even own my own cottage. You're dreaming, girl. You've got an imagination, you have."

"It doesn't hurt to dream."

"Now there you're wrong, Miss Ellen. It does hurt to dream." He became serious. "It hurts horribly. Dreams are a trap. You get lured in by something colorful and shiny and *wham*! You find yourself in a very painful place, indeed. No, it serves no good purpose to be dreaming the impossible."

"I'm not saying the impossible," she softened. "I'm only saying that, if you want something, you have to work to make it happen. Thinking of what you want and thinking of how to get it is a good thing — otherwise you might never have it."

"And what is your dream, then?" he asked.

Ellen blushed and looked away. "Well, I don't have anything against marriage and children. I want a family, of course. But I want to do something more than that, more exciting, more challenging. I want to be able to look back on my life and feel proud of something I did myself."

"Raising fine children wouldn't be enough, then?"

Her face took on a wistful look. "Sometimes I read stories about America and the Wild West, pioneer families adventuring out and building farms and ranches. I think of those pioneer women, helping their husbands build something that will last for generations. It seems to me there's an opportunity for women that doesn't exist here in Waterford. Here, we lead dull little lives."

"You have a taste for adventure, then. I see it in your face. Your eyes got all sparkly when you talked of pioneering. That's fantastic."

"You don't think it's foolish?"

"No. It's exciting, is what it is."

"My family thinks I'm foolish," she admitted, "too much the tomboy. My brother teases me and says that I'm too forceful. My mother says no man will ever want to marry such an assertive woman."

John laughed again. "Then they would be quite pleased with my three youngest sisters who would no more think of being a pioneer woman than swimming the ocean. But Bridget, now, she's the next one after me, she left last month."

"She did? To go out west? To pioneer?"

"Oh no, nothing like that. She's only 14. Friends of our family emigrated to Chicago. The missus had her hands full with all of her young ones and asked if our Bridget would like to go with them. They'd treat her as one of their own if she'd help with the babies and the household chores."

Ellen pondered for a moment. "She's going as a domestic, then? A maidservant?"

"Aye, that's what it comes to, doesn't it. Still, she saw it as an opportunity. As you say, there's not much here for a woman to dream about. Most people are just scraping by, except for families like yours."

Ellen nodded. It was true. "And you, John. Does the idea appeal to you?"

"To tell you the truth, Miss Ellen, I've never given it a thought. Going to America? The West? Indians and cowboys? It never occurred to me. I haven't read those books of yours. No, all I've thought about is what I know: Waterford, County Cork. A pint or two and cabbage soup. Maybe a train ride up to Dublin. It's all I know. Like I said, I don't have big dreams. I'm very much down to earth, I am. Very much down to earth."

They met with increasing frequency, in their favorite spot on the riverbank or south of the city, past the Clock Tower, Christian Street, and House Quay. They talked about Mr. Charles Parnell and the new popularity of his Irish Parliamentary Party. John was a strong believer in home rule, which Parnell's party was pushing for. Ellen's father was a staunch conservative and loyal supporter of Queen Victoria. Although Ellen knew that Timothy secretly supported the home rule movement, he knew better than to voice his opinion in front of their father.

Ellen, herself, wasn't so sure where she stood regarding politics, but she liked listening to John argue his point of view. He was very serious and his brow furrowed into a deep V as he made his arguments. She found herself fascinated by his black brush of a moustache bobbing up and down when his speech became animated.

It was inevitable that such sharing of intimacies would lead to a gradual increase in physical affection. In due course, they made love. Their first real sexual experience was marked by awkwardness and embarrassment, passion and wonder. But, with patience and practice, they discovered success.

Overnight, the experience changed each of them into more thoughtful and mature young adults. They began thinking seriously of a future together. Ellen could conceive of nothing other than their getting married and her father giving John more responsibility in his business. She mentioned it to no one, but the idea was fixed in her mind. On her walks about town, she paid attention to the houses, noticing decorating and landscaping ideas, considering areas where she might want to live. She knew that her parents and grandfather would want to buy the young couple a house — nothing grand, but at once cozy and large enough for a few children. In her view, she would help her new husband as he climbed the ladder at Furlong's Meatpacking Company. She'd help him make decisions about expanding and improving the family business.

John now thought of himself as a grown man. He'd had sex; he had a woman who loved him, who wanted to marry him and bear his children. He was ready to take on the responsibilities of supporting his own family. But he also began to worry about how he would provide for them. There was no room in his father's house for another person, even with young Bridget now in America. In fact, his three younger sisters were still sharing the bed that had been recently occupied by four. He hoped Mr. Furlong and Mr. Tim would see fit to promote him to a butcher's apprentice and give him a raise. Still, he fretted that Ellen's family might not approve, although she often reassured him that they would.

"Oh, don't bother about that," she'd assured him with full confidence. "My father loves me more than anything. Once he's convinced that this is where my happiness lies, he'll want to do everything he can to help."

Ellen had been regular as clockwork, so when she missed her period, she immediately suspected she might be pregnant. Several weeks later, when she detected the slight swelling of her breasts, she knew for certain, even before she missed her second period. Still, she was nervous about telling John.

At first, he'd been astonished, not understanding how it had happened, as if a conscious decision would have been required.

"How could it be?" he wondered. "We've only made love a few times. We're not even married." As if that too might have been a requirement.

But once he comprehended that in another seven months — around October — he'd be a father, he lapsed into a state of amazement. "My

God," he kept repeating, "I can't believe it. I'm going to be a da. And you, you're carrying my child. It's true, then? Is it real?"

When Ellen saw how happy John was, she put aside her own anxiety. Intoxicated by their own giddiness, they began to plan their future. They realized they would have to inform their parents as soon as possible.

That night at dinner, with everyone at the table, Ellen announced her news. "Mother, Father, I have some wonderful news to share with you. And, of course, with you too," she added lightly, nodding to her brother and sister.

Maryanne Furlong leaned eagerly toward her daughter, her knife and fork suspended in air. "And what might that be, dear? Something exciting, from the look of you. Look, Edward, how flushed with excitement our Ellen is."

Timothy barely looked up from his plate. He probably assumed that Ellen would announce she had learned a new piece on the piano or had seen a pretty hat in a store window. Sheila cocked her head in curiosity.

"I've decided I'm to be married."

"Married?" Mrs. Furlong dropped back into her chair like a stone and took care not to choke on the piece of lamb she'd been chewing.

"What?" demanded her father. "What are you talking about? I know nothing of this! I don't recall anyone asking my permission about a marriage."

Timothy looked up from his plate without changing his posture. Recalling the moment later, Ellen had an image of a turtle popping its head up out of its shell. Sheila simply gazed upon her sister with wonder. How could Ellen have been courted without anyone having an inkling about *who* it might be?

"John Powers and I have been getting acquainted, and we've fallen in love. We decided today that we're to be married."

"John Powers? You mean that young lad from your father's shop?"

"Yes, Mother."

"Ellen," said Timothy, shaking his head, "are you serious? You're not pulling our leg?"

"No, of course I'm serious. He's a fine young man. You know that. You all think well of him."

"Just wait a minute, now," Edward interrupted, finally comprehending the situation before him. "This is the first I've heard anything of this matter and nothing is happening here, absolutely nothing is going forward, until I say it is. Is that understood?"

He looked firmly at Ellen while everyone fell silent. "Now, Mr. Powers is a fine young lad. He's bright, I know, and a strong young ox as well. And he has a fine character. There's no need to persuade me of his fine points. Still, young lady, that does not mean you can go marrying anyone you please. You're my daughter, after all. You're part of this family and have obligations to others besides yourself. You know that. That's how your mother raised you. Am I not right, Miss?"

Ellen nodded, uncertain where he was headed. She had not anticipated his firm, authoritarian tone. It was so unlike him.

Her father continued, "I see now that perhaps it wasn't at all wise to have the lad up here to the house on so many occasions. Yes, I can well understand how that must have affected him, getting a close look at how we live, taking in all of our comforts. I should have realized that for such a bright and ambitious lad, it wasn't doing him any favors to become too familiar with our way of living."

"Father, that's not how ..."

"Don't interrupt me. You've had your say, now I'll have mine, you hear?"

Ellen's father had never taken that tone with her. She could not understand what was happening. She surveyed the table. Timothy and Sheila were looking down at their plates. Only her mother was looking in her direction, staring at her with narrowed eyes and tightly pursed lips. Her father took a long breath, and continued in a calmer manner.

"It's clear to me what has happened. It's as clear as this table. You've been seduced, my child. Despite the fact that you are older than he is — you were aware of that, were you not? He has taken you in, used his cunning ways like all peasants and people of lower classes, just like his ancestors."

"What do you mean?" Ellen cried out.

"Ah, Maryanne, it seems our daughter doesn't know about the wicked reputation enjoyed by the Powers clan. Well, child, let me inform you: A few hundred years ago their whole clan were pirates, plundering and thieving all over the coast down Cork way. Bloody thieves and murderers, they were. I thought young John was different, but I see now that he's just like the rest of them. He was merely biding his time until he won you over."

"Father, you can't be serious. Even if what you say about his ancestors is true, my God that was — as you say — hundreds of years ago! You can't blame him for what they did. And it isn't fair to describe him so. That's not who he is."

Her father was steadfast. "You're blinded by your own passions, child. You're young and inexperienced in these matters. You don't know how these things work. My God, daughter, look at the facts. Have you seen how he lives? Have you? These people live in hovels: thatched huts in the countryside with dirt floors, no open windows, sleeping four or more in a bug-infested bed of straw — most likely with their goats and dogs. Eating nothing but weak porridge and cabbage soup, and potatoes when they can get them. Has Mr. Powers ever brought you home to meet his family?" Edward Furlong did not wait for her answer. "Not likely, that. He'd not be wanting you to see the truth of how they live. And you? Are you prepared to live like that? Like shanty Irish?"

Ellen felt crushed, dizzy, her world spinning out of control.

"Is that how you want to live, dear?" Maryanne Furlong looked beseechingly at her daughter, "in a thatched hut with foul peat smoke burning your eyes and smelling up your clothes every day? Is that what you want for yourself?"

Ellen saw the pleading in her mother's eyes: *My God, daughter, use your reason. Use your reason.*

Ellen floundered in confusion. "But I thought you'd be happy for me, that I found someone I love, someone who loves me," she choked through tears. "John loves me for who I am. Don't you see? It's not as you say. He loves me, not all this. He doesn't expect ..."

She stopped. The truth was, she hadn't thought about it. She and John hadn't had an opportunity to talk about her dreams of the future. She'd thought about her father taking them under his wing, but she'd never shared that hope with John. Might he have had the same dream of becoming a valued member of the Furlong business and family? In fact, she'd hoped that John would share that fantasy with her. But she'd never thought about it from her father's point of view. Now, she saw how it looked to him: His innocent daughter had been seduced.

"I'm sure you believe that, dear," her mother soothed.

Sheila reached out her hand impulsively to console her sister.

"But it's not like that. It's not like you say. If anything, I seduced him, not the other way around," she admitted.

"What do you mean, Ellen? How have you seduced him?" Her father, who had softened his countenance as the potency of his argument had penetrated, suddenly looked worried.

"I mean ... I just mean it was me, not him who pursued this. I made this happen, not John. It's not his fault. You can't be blaming him."

"What do you mean, Ellen? What's not his fault?"

Ellen sat back in her chair and squeezed her eyes shut tightly, but the tears came forth and her chin began to tremble.

Oh, she thought, *how could everything have gone so horribly wrong?*

Sheila stood silently to embrace her sister, and Ellen buried her face in her sister's belly and sobbed. Avoiding anyone's eyes, Edward Furlong muttered an obscenity under his breath. Maryanne and Timothy

rose from the table and quietly left the room. Finally, when Ellen's sobbing had subsided, her father motioned for Sheila to leave the room,
leaving him alone with Ellen.

The next morning, Timothy was standing by the entrance to the
courtyard of the meatpacking business when John Powers showed up
for work. He straightened up and took a few steps toward his employee.

"Good morning, Mr. Tim."

"Morning, John. Stop a moment, will you. I need to talk to you."

"Oh?"

"It's about you and my sister."

"She's told you, then?"

"Yes."

"I see," said John.

"It won't stand," said Timothy matter-of-factly. "My parents will not
allow it. Your relationship with my sister must stop at once."

Timothy saw John clenching his fists and stiffening his shoulders.

"And, of course, as of this morning, you are no longer employed
here. You can pick up your wages from Mr. Rooney in the office, then
leave the premises immediately. You must be gone by the time my father arrives."

John was devastated. He looked at his employer questioningly. He
had thought they were on good terms.

"I'm sorry, John," Timothy said. "You've been a good worker. But it
will no longer do. My father has lost his trust in you. He believes you've
used us to get to my sister."

"And you?"

"I truly don't know. My sister tells me otherwise, but I don't know.
In any case, she shan't be marrying you. And you will have to stop seeing
her. You understand me?"

John hesitated for a moment. "I'll pick up my wages and be out of
your way," he said flatly. As he stalked through the courtyard, he noticed the workers already busy with activity. In the office, Mr. Rooney
silently handed him an envelope.

John spent much of the day in the lane by the river, waiting for Ellen
to appear. Eventually he made his way home, full of doubt and fear. That
evening, he gave his parents the news. "I've been given the sack," he
said.

His father grumbled. "I suspected as much. I'd have done the same
if I'd been in his place." After a moment he went on. "I asked at work

if there'd be a spot for you in the shipyards. I told them you're strong and handy with a hammer and saw. They'll get back to me with an answer, but it looks promising."

The following day, Ellen defied her parents' prohibition against leaving the house. As she raced her buggy to the usual rendezvous, she had no idea what she might do if he were not there.

She spied him sitting at the base of a tree, staring morosely into space. He turned when he heard the horse and buggy, and rose to meet her. "I'd about given up," he said, taking both of her hands into his and pulling them to his lips. "I waited nearly all day yesterday."

"I'm not to leave the house. Can you believe it? They treat me like a child. But I couldn't stay away any longer. I came anyway. I don't care what they say."

"Your brother gave me the sack, you know."

"Father demanded he do it. He thinks you're a pirate who's sneaked your way into his cove and stolen his precious treasure."

"I gathered as much ..."

"My parents think you're trying to get their money," she admitted gravely.

"I don't give a damn about their bloody money. It's you."

"I know. I believe you." They embraced and kissed. Then, abruptly, she held him at arm's length. "Did Timmy tell you they're sending me away?"

"Away? No, he said nothing of that. Where to? Your grandfather's?"

"No," she said, a stricken look on her face. "Much worse. America."

"America! How can they do that? I won't let them."

"It's no use, John. My father went yesterday to buy the steamship ticket. I'll be leaving in three weeks, on April fourth."

"So soon? How can he do that? There's no time for us to get married, to publish the banns. How can I afford a ticket in such a time? It's all wrong, Ellen. I don't see how it can be done."

"That's just the point," she said solemnly. "My father intends that we be separated and never marry. Oh, I never thought it would come to this. I can't believe he's done this to me."

"Not married?" John was incredulous. "But Ellen, doesn't he know of our child?"

"Of course. I had to tell him everything. I told him that I seduced you, not the other way around, but he won't believe it. He blames you for everything. Oh, John, I'm so sorry. What have I done?"

"Nothing. You've done nothing. Don't worry. We'll find a way."

He raised his burly frame from the grass where they'd been sitting. Pacing back and forth, he rubbed his face with his thick hands, stroking his bushy mustache. Ellen watched, nervously twisting a handkerchief in her hands. After a while, he sat down beside her.

"My father is trying to get me a job in the shipyards. I've got a pound or so saved already, though it isn't much. How much is the ticket for the steamship?"

"Five pounds," she said, "for third class. First class is more, but it was all booked when father bought the ticket."

"Five pounds! As much as that?" He paused to think. "No matter. I'll save every penny, work as long as possible, and follow you within a month. Do you know where you'll be in America?"

"I'll be sailing to New York and then I'm to take the train to Boston, where I'm to stay with my Aunt Margaret. I don't have the address with me, but I'll get it to you."

"With me working my arse off and you a prisoner up on St. Thomas Hill, how are we going to do that?"

"It's not right, their keeping us apart," Ellen said defiantly.

"Well, I can't very well come knocking on your front door, now, can I?"

"Of course not. But here we are. We love each other. We want to be married. I'm carrying our baby. They have no right."

"Aye, they've no right and we've no choice. What do you think will happen if you defy them and don't go?"

Ellen hung her head. "I'm to be banished one way or another. They'll not have me puffing up for all the neighbors to see. Even my grandfather's estate is too close for them. And then I'd be cut off financially as well. How would I make my way then? Big as a house? Am I to go searching for a position as a house servant? Or be a barmaid in some pub?"

"Don't talk that way. It's not fitting."

"I'm just agreeing with you. We have no choice. I have to do as my father says. I have to think of our baby."

"Yes. But we must get married. If not here, then in America. In Boston, at your aunt's."

"Yes, we will. They won't be able to stop us." She tried to sound confident.

"My father has friends who left here to go to Chicago," John told her. "They say there's lots of work there."

"Chicago? Didn't that burn down some years ago? I remember my parents talking about it. Something about Mrs. O'Leary's cow kicking over a lantern. My mother used to sing a song about it."

"Well, it's rebuilt and they have huge stockyards. There's lots of jobs, hundreds of jobs. My father can write and ask his friends to help me find work. And my sister Bridget is there. We'll go to Chicago as soon as we're married. I'll have work. You'll have the baby. We'll be fine."

"Yes. I always wondered what it would be like to travel there," Ellen agreed hopefully.

"I remember. You dreamt of being a pioneer woman."

"Wife. A pioneer's wife. And that's what I'll be."

They were both smiling now, feeling like they'd turned the tables on Ellen's father and managed to transform a dismal defeat into a pre-destined victory.

"Still," he said, "we'll have to find a way to send messages to each other until you leave."

"I'm sure my sister, Sheila, would be willing to help."

"And my sister Alice. She's just turned 12."

With the aid of their siblings, they kept in daily communication for the next three weeks. On two occasions they were able to actually meet and hold each other. But the three weeks raced by and April fourth arrived too soon. For Ellen, leaning on the railing of *City of Rome,* and for John, perched on a scaffolding in the Waterford Shipbuilding Yards, life seemed to be suspended until — some six or seven weeks later — they would meet in Boston.

John removed a thin billfold from his pocket to check that the yellow paper with the address of Ellen's aunt on Beacon Hill was still there. It was. He'd already committed it to memory.

"I don't know," Patrick Powers said, shaking his head. "It's subterfuge. It's disrespectful and it don't sit well with me at all."

Bridget Powers put her hand on her husband's arm. "But think about it, Paddy. Would you prefer that they not get married, that the poor child be born a bastard? Would you choose that for our grandchild? And don't you want your son to be an honorable man such as yourself? Accepting responsibility for his actions, as you've always taught him?"

John's father shook his head. Why was this damn woman always making things difficult? Why couldn't she just let him be the master of his own home?

Alice piped in. "I don't mind doing it, really. It would only be a matter of going to the Square every day and passing notes. I could take the bicycle."

"And I don't recall asking you for your considered opinion now, do I?" her fathered snapped.

Alice shrunk back into her seat. John held his breath waiting for his father to give permission for Alice to act as the go-between with Ellen's sister.

"It's the only way, Da, unless you can think of another idea."

Patrick shook his head. "Oh, all right. I suppose there's nothing else to be done." He turned to his wife. "You're right, of course, it wouldn't be right to let the child be born without a proper name. But I still don't like it."

John was surprised one evening when his father gruffly suggested a visit to the local pub after supper. John had been there often with his friends, but never with his father. Patrick ordered two pints and sat down with his son. "I wanted to talk to you, man to man," he said.

"Of course. I'm glad for it," John nodded.

"Well, you're on your way to having your own family now. It's a big undertaking, you know."

"I know that, Da. It's all I've been thinking about."

"I was just a year older than you are now when I married your ma. She was two years younger, just turned 20."

John took this in. *Ellen is four years older than my ma was. And Da just a year older than I am now. So we're not too young to be taking on these responsibilities.* The thought made John swell with confidence. He felt himself almost the equal of his dad — what with their drinking pints together, and talking man to man.

That expanding sense of confidence was quickly burst.

"We had no bloody idea what we were getting into," his father said, shaking his head before swallowing from his pint.

"I don't understand," John suddenly felt queasy. Was his father changing his mind and withdrawing his permission?

"Marriage is hard, son. Raising a family is hard. You see some of it, the scrimping and saving and doing without. But what you don't see, Jacky, is the worry — the great suffering parents go through. Ach, I see you don't understand a bit of what I'm saying. I don't suppose you remember too much about your two brothers."

"Just that you and Ma mention them from time to time — but no, I have no recollection of them at all."

"No, you wouldn't. You were just a wee one yourself when each of them died. Of course, that was before Bridget was born. Our little

Matthew was only three months old when he died in his sleep. He just stopped breathing. Your poor mother found him in the morning all cold and blue. What a shock that was. There was no accounting for it. He was healthy, all pink and full of baby smells. Always laughing and cooing, that one. And so to find him like that — there was no sense in it. Why would God go and do a thing like that to us?" Patrick sighed deeply.

"And then Michael died of the fever when he was barely five months old. He was a husky little brute, that one. Like you. Still, the fever took him. Those two losses, back to back like that — you've no idea what it's like. I hope you never do. It's hard, son, especially on the woman. Your ma was not herself for quite a while. That's why she's been so extra close to you. I know it's been tough on you, the way she's always hovering, not letting you be. But you've been her only surviving son. You understand what I'm saying, Jacky? That's something you might have to learn to live with. You need to know, Jacky, that being married isn't all about love and sex. And it's not just about being willing to work hard and earn a wage every day. Life can be rough and a man, when he's a husband and a father, he's got other responsibilities too. Do you understand what I'm saying?"

"I think so, Da. I see what goes on at home. How could I not, in such crowded quarters? But I know how you and Ma talk about everything. I mean, I know you're the boss and you're the one who makes the decisions, but I know how you listen to each other, like the business with Alice helping Ellen and me. Ma helped you make that decision."

"Aye, and I'm still not happy with the whole affair," Patrick admitted. "What you and Ellen did was wrong, and what you've got Alice mixed up in is wrong too. But there's not much can be done about it. It's spilt milk. Still, when I think about it, I want to beat the bejesus out of you. You know that, don't you?"

"Aye, I know."

"Well, then, do you have any questions? I mean about being married and being the head of your own household?"

John sat back and regarded his father, the thinning salt and pepper hair, the muscular build, not unlike his own. He sensed his da's loving concern and his fear that John was about to make a complete mess of his life. But John felt confident and wanted to reassure him that everything would be all right — he knew what he was doing.

"I guess I understand all right," he said slowly. "I've given it a lot of thought. But I'm not sure what you meant when you said Ma wasn't herself after my brothers died."

"Well, when Michael and Matthew died, just being wee babes, like I said, it was especially tough on your ma. For a long time, you know, she didn't want — you know — sometimes you've got to be patient with them, the women. It's not always easy, but you've got to try to be understanding, is all I'm saying. Even though you're the man of the house, sometimes you have to be gentle. Like when your sister, Bridget, went off with the O'Brians. That was hard on all of us. You know how we still miss her. It wasn't an easy decision to let her go off like that. And you, going off and maybe never coming back. You think that's easy on your ma? You think that won't break her heart to maybe never see you again, never mind your child?"

They sat silently for a while, then John suddenly left the table. He came back with two more pints and sat down, sliding one mug across the table to his father. "You know, Da, I've always looked up to you."

"Have you, now?"

"Of course. I've always admired you. Well, not always. Not when you lose your temper."

They smiled at each other and Patrick nodded. "Aye," he said, "I can get a bit hot."

"But you've always a reason. And you don't go beating Ma the way Mr. Hennessy does when he comes stumbling home from the pub almost every night of the week. And with us, I know you're just trying to teach us to do the right thing."

"I've tried to do my best, son. That's all any man can do, you know."

"I know. And you've done a good job of raising me. I only hope I'll do as good a job of it with my own son, if I'm lucky enough to have one."

"I'll drink to that," said Patrick, raising his glass.

"I've been thinking of that, of what it'll be, and I'll admit it's got me a bit scared. Of what it'll be like growing up. And, of course, what kind of a da I'll be. That's when I realized that it's a job, being a father. Like you said, there are responsibilities, more than just bringing home a paycheck. I think it's made me grow up."

Patrick looked across the table and tried to see his son objectively. He saw a strong, solid, good-looking man with wavy black hair and a moustache too big by half. It was a serious face with a determined chin and brow. "Well, then, Jacky, you'll do fine. You've been a good son and you're a fine young man. Just do what's right and try your best. That's all any man can do."

On the morning of April 16, 1884, Ellen Furlong arrived at the train station in Boston. After riding all night on the train from New York, she yearned for a long soak in a hot bath and then a good sleep in a real full-sized bed. Emerging from the station into a cool spring morning, she looked for a carriage to take her to her aunt's. And there, out on the wide cobblestone street, was a whole line of them. Some 20 minutes later, she was at her aunt's front door. She waited until the driver left before she screwed up her courage and rang the bell. A maidservant answered the door and gave her a once-over.

"I'm Ellen Furlong. I believe my Aunt Margaret is expecting me."

"Yes, Miss. Come in, Miss. I'll tell Mistress that you're here."

Ellen started to lift her suitcases. "Oh no, Miss. Leave them be. I'll take care of them for you."

Ellen stepped into the foyer of the three-story house. It was easily as large as her grandfather's house in Youghal. The maid brought the suitcases in and closed the door.

"Please have a seat, Miss, while I tell Mistress that you're here." Ellen took a seat on a fine decorative chair and surveyed the luxurious surroundings. She'd had no idea that her Aunt Margaret was so well off. Soon she heard steps approaching.

"Ah, Ellen, you've arrived already. I wasn't expecting you for another three or four days, at least."

"The ship made excellent time, only 10 days. And then I went straight to the station in New York and caught a train almost immediately. I've been riding all night."

"Poor child. You must be exhausted."

"And grimy and full of soot from the train. I'm longing for a hot bath and a real bed."

"And hungry? Shall I have some breakfast made?"

Ellen shook her head. "No, thank you, Aunt Margaret. I've no appetite at all."

"Then a bath and a bed it shall be." She took her niece by the arm and led her up the carpeted stairway to the second floor. "I received your father's letter just two weeks ago. My goodness, these new steamships are as fast as the mail packets. We're lucky you didn't arrive before the letter. Ah, here is your room, and the bathroom is down the hall."

She showed Ellen a room that contained a flush toilet and a sink with running water and a tub.

"I'll make sure you have enough hot water. Take a nice rest, and when you're feeling refreshed and recovered just come downstairs. We'll talk then." With that last statement, her voice dropped into a lower register and Ellen, even in her weariness, picked up the serious tone.

Ellen luxuriated in the hot bath. This bathroom, with its indoor accommodations and privacy, was more than even her grandfather could boast, never mind her own parents. She was sure that not everyone in America enjoyed such luxuries.

After the soak, she crawled wearily into the bed and immediately fell asleep. When she came downstairs some hours later, it was time for dinner. She found the family in the dining room.

"How wonderful that you're joining us," her aunt said. "I feared you might sleep until tomorrow. Ellen, this is my husband, Thomas Austin, and my daughter, Abby. My son, Albert, and his wife will join us tomorrow. And this is Ellen Furlong, my niece from Waterford, my brother's daughter."

Everyone exchanged greetings. This was the first time Ellen had met her uncle and cousin, and she liked both of them immediately. Her Uncle Thomas, especially, had a ready and hearty laugh and was fond of making jokes. Cousin Abby was full of questions about Ireland and her family, and her Aunt Margaret was equally curious about her own brother and father, Ellen's grandfather. It wasn't until later, after her conversation with her aunt, that Ellen realized no one had asked about the reason for her trip to America.

After dinner, Aunt Margaret led her out to the patio behind the house, where they sipped tea. "Now," said her aunt, "tell me all about your pregnancy. How far along are you? How are you feeling?"

Ellen took a deep breath and looked squarely at her aunt. "The truth of it is, I've lost it."

"What?"

"I think so. That is, I'm pretty sure of it. I am sure of it."

"You've had a miscarriage? When? How did it happen?"

"On the ship. At first I thought it was just seasickness, what with all the rolling and pitching. The weather was good, it was sunny and all, but windy, and the waves were huge. I had no idea the ocean was so enormous, so endless. The ship fought its way through the waves, constantly, one after another, and it made a lot of us sick. I don't know how those sailors do it day after day. I wanted to die. I spent most of the time lying in my bunk in the women's compartment. I couldn't even eat. God knows how much weight I've lost, between not eating and having the heaves and diarrhea."

She paused before continuing her account.

"And then, four or five days out of Queenstown, I had terrible cramps. In the bathroom I saw that I was bleeding. I couldn't look at it too closely," she said, shuddering, "but I knew it. I didn't want to know it, but I knew I'd lost her."

"Her?"

"Well, I don't rightly know. It's just the way I thought of it. You know, a girl. I guess that's what I wanted. I was just so sure of it. I called her Mamie."

"Is that your mother's name?"

Ellen managed a smile. "No, the name just came to me. Mamie Powers. That's John's name, Powers. We're going to be married."

"Oh?"

"I know you must be surprised. My father doesn't know. That's why he sent me here, so that John and I can't marry. But Aunt Margaret, we love each other and he's a good man. He's coming here in a month's time and we'll be married."

With pursed lips, her aunt picked up her cup and sipped her tea. Eyeing Ellen, she noticed the girl's chin quivering and eyes filled with tears.

"You poor thing, what a horrible way to start life in a new country, having to grieve the loss of your first child."

With that, Ellen's composure gave way and she buried her face in her hands. Margaret Austin put her arms around her niece and held her while she sobbed.

When Ellen regained control, Margaret sat down again. "I must tell you, Ellen, that I haven't said anything about your condition to anyone, not even my husband. I wanted to wait until you arrived, until I heard the circumstances. Now that you've miscarried — well, there is no *condition,* is there? As far as anyone else is concerned, you're simply here for a visit. Is that all right with you?"

Ellen nodded.

"Good. I think it's better this way. Now tell me all about your young man, this Mr. Powers."

When Ellen had finished describing all the fine qualities she saw in John, Margaret sat back in her chair. Finally, she said, "I'm going to be truthful with you, Ellen. I'm not entirely comfortable participating in this deception of my brother. He's entrusted you to my care, obviously because he disapproves of your desire to marry this young man. It would not be right for me to conspire with you to defy his wishes. I hope you understand."

"I'm not sure I do, Aunt Margaret. What is it you're saying?"

"Only that I'm not comfortable with your marrying Mr. Powers while you are living with us. Of course, if Mr. Powers shows up unexpectedly and the two of you decide to leave immediately for Chicago — well, of course, there's nothing I can do, is there? I've no choice but to let you go and then, afterward, send a letter to Edward informing him of what's already taken place." She smiled and cocked her head. "Do you understand now?"

Ellen's face broke into a wide grin. "Oh yes, Aunt. I understand, completely."

"Then, that's the way it shall be. Not a word of your Mr. Powers to anyone until we hear from him. And then we shall simply say that he's your fiancé. You weren't sure when he would be able to follow you; but now you're both determined to get to Chicago — to his sister's — as quickly as possible so you can be married there, among his family. How does that sound?"

"Yes, that's perfect. But Aunt Margaret, I have one question."

"Yes?"

"How am I to tell him about Mamie? I know he'll be sorely disappointed. He was so happy about being a father. What should I say?"

"It'll be all right, Ellen. He'll be heartbroken, as you are, as you both have a right to be. But he'll understand. His primary concern will be for you, believe me. I've gone through it twice myself. Almost every woman I know has. If you're lucky, you'll go on to have other children. I know you will. Don't worry, dear. If your young man is as you described him, he'll understand."

On May 6, John Powers boarded the *Britannic* of the White Star Line. His mother and three sisters accompanied him on the train ride from Waterford to Queenstown. His father could not afford to take the day off from the shipyard. John carried a suitcase filled with clothes and a cardboard box filled with tools, pictures of the family, and some mementos. It was the first time he or his sisters had been in Queenstown and only the second time he'd been on a train, having once traveled to Dublin for a soccer match.

The three girls were excited, but his mother struggled to put on a happy face. "You will write us," she reminded him again. "You won't forget us." John met his mother's eyes. There was no need to reassure her yet again. "As soon as you're settled, write us and give us your address. And let me know what you'll be needing, what we can send to you. And remember us to Bridget when you arrive in Chicago. You won't forget?"

For reply, John squeezed her arm and attempted a smile of reassurance. Perhaps, too, he was reassuring himself. The truth was that his belly was full of butterflies and his head full of questions: Would he be able to find Ellen in such a large country? Would he find his way, or would he take a wrong turn or wrong train and end up among the cowboys and Indians by mistake? Would he find work? Would his money hold out? Would his belongings be stolen or lost?

Meanwhile, his three sisters were oohing and aahing at everything they saw, from the train ride and their walk from the station to the wharves. The ship was massive, bigger than the one he'd worked on in

Waterford. The *Britannic* had a steel hull. Although it was a steamship, with two funnels amidships to prove it, she also had four masts rigged for sailing. Built in England in 1874, the *Britannic* was 455 feet long and 45 feet at its widest point. John would be one of 1,500 third-class passengers, each with a separate cot (the women slept in their own compartment). Three meals were served daily, all for a little less than five pounds. It was truly amazing.

Most of the passengers were already aboard when John and his family arrived. His mother gave him a firm hug and pressed some money into his hand. He picked up each of his sisters and twirled them around, then promised to write often and send them each a souvenir from America. Before he knew it, he was up the gangplank looking for a spot on deck where he could wave goodbye. From above, he stared at his mother and sisters, hoping he would not forget how they looked. The blast from the horn startled him, and he became aware that the great ship was slowly moving away from the dock. He was on his way.

Everyone around him seemed to be waving joyously, but John felt subdued. He was 22, but at that moment felt like a boy, full of insecurities and self-doubts. Nothing ahead was certain, nothing predictable, nothing known. He wasn't religious, but he looked up at the sky and crossed himself. "Jesus, help me," he said. "I don't know what the hell I'm doing." He kept waving to his family until the ship turned and he could no longer see them.

The men's third-class compartment was two levels below the main deck, with portholes that let in light and gave a view of the sky and dark green water. John found his cot and a locker, where he stored his few belongings. Around him were men of all ages, even young boys, from all over Ireland. A group of young men invited him to join them on deck.

It was surprisingly cold. The wind was bracing and he was glad when they decided to quit the railing and find a sheltered spot. All of the men were going to America in search of jobs. Some were joining family members who had preceded them; some were traveling alone or with a friend or sibling. John told them he was going to meet his fiancé in Boston, where they were to be married — and then he was going to Chicago to work in the Union Stockyards.

"Now isn't that a coincidence," said one of the lads, who introduced himself as Jimmy O'Hara. "Chicago is where I'm headed, too. My brother is there. He's been wanting me to come these past two years, but it's only now my da let me go."

John felt as if he had met an old friend.

There was not much to do except look at the flat, unending horizon and gray, gloomy sky. John had expected the voyage to be exciting, but the uninterrupted monotony made every day boring. Remaining below on his cot was at least more comfortable than being on the cold, windy deck. He was soothed by the rolling and pitching of the ship and, unlike many of the other passengers, didn't experience a moment of seasickness. But even the sensation of rocking and rolling quickly became routine and uninteresting. If it weren't for conversations with Jimmy O'Hara and playing cards with the other lads, he would have been overwhelmed with loneliness. All he could think about was his Ellen.

Her face, as he remembered it from their romantic meeting place along the Suir, appeared to him in every detail: her red hair pulled up in a bun under her little hat, a few stray wisps blowing across her forehead, the freckles on her cheeks, her soft brown eyes and turned-up nose, the lace collar with the blue and white cameo at her throat, the light blue dress that showed off her curvaceous figure, her lilting laugh. John thought he would die from longing. At night he could not stop himself from reliving their lovemaking, limited as it was. He couldn't wait to be with her again — and the idea of being married, of having her next to him each night, was the very idea of heaven. He couldn't begin to comprehend his own good fortune.

After a week, the weather calmed, the sun came out, and for the first time John understood the allure of the sea. The balmy breeze, the purity of the pristine blue sky, and the brilliance of the diamonds reflecting from the surface of the waves brought relaxation and happiness to the passengers. A few musicians produced their instruments — drums, flutes, fiddles, harmonicas — and some men brought out bottles they had been saving. The deck became a fairground filled with jigs and reels and the joyous sounds of laughter, singing, and rhythmic step dancing.

At one point, a young woman grabbed him by the hand. "Come on!" she urged. "Your legs aren't broken. Dance with me."

His initial reaction was to resist. He wasn't a good dancer and he feared making a fool of himself. The girl was pretty and he was about to be married, about to become a father.

"Come on, love, don't be shy," she coaxed. "It's only a dance now, isn't it?"

She pulled him into a circle of dancers and soon he found himself flowing along with the rhythms of the music and the beat of the Irish drummers. The whiskey he'd been drinking with Jimmy and the others melted his resistance and soon he was laughing as the girl led him along, encouraging him. She had a lovely smile that made him think of sunlight and her bright eyes never left his face.

"What's your name?" she shouted as they whirled about, the music and laughter swirling around them.

"John Powers," he yelled to her. "What's yours?"

"Nora McNamee. You want a drink, John?"

She took his hand and led him through the crowd to an old man, who was sitting in the sun on a pile of rope. "Uncle Seamus, I want to give my friend John a drink."

Uncle Seamus took in the sight of them standing before him, hand in hand like two young lovers silhouetted against the sun. "Mind, don't drink it all, Nora," he said as he pulled a bottle from his canvas bag. "And don't go inviting the whole bloody ship."

"Thank you, Uncle." Nora opened the bottle and took a good gulp. John tried to remember if he had ever seen a woman do that before. Then the bottle was in his hands and he took a long swallow. It burned going down, but left a warm afterglow. He smiled at Nora. They each took another drink before returning the bottle to her uncle.

"Thank you, sir. That was very good." He laughed. "Yes, very good indeed."

"It ought to be. It's probably the best Irish on the whole damned ship."

"Aye, you'll get no argument from me," said John.

Nora squeezed his hand. "Want to walk a bit?"

As they walked the deck, passing partying circles and accepting a drink here and there, Nora tried to engage John in conversation, but his shyness kept him from revealing much about himself. "Are you always so serious?" she asked.

John shrugged his shoulders, unsure of how to respond. "I guess," he said finally. "I've been accused of lacking a sense of humor. But I don't feel overly serious."

"What are you feeling?"

"A little drunk, I think. Mellow."

"Do you feel good now, being with me here on the deck of this ship on this bright, sunny day, sailing to America?"

"Yes, I do," he confessed.

"To me, this feels like heaven," she smiled, bright-eyed. "Everything feels so perfect — like this moment is pure happiness. Life should always be like this. Don't you feel it?"

He nodded. As he looked down into her blue eyes, her wild brown hair blowing in the wind, she stood on her toes and kissed him full on the mouth. John felt his lips responding before he realized what was happening. Her hands were behind his head holding him to her and his arms automatically circled her waist and pulled her near. Nora drew back and examined his face, then kissed him again more slowly. John felt himself melting into her, resistance fading, only dimly aware of the music and celebrating around him. In that embrace, he gave himself over to contentment, to a feeling of belonging, to the sweet, urgent desire to merge without regard for circumstances.

"I love your moustache," she whispered. "And your arms. They're quite strong."

John was silent. He didn't know what to say. The truth was, he didn't want to talk. Their eyes seemed locked on each other and, without thinking about it, without making any conscious decision, he pulled her to him and kissed her again. Her lips felt full and warm. He tasted the whiskey on her tongue and smelled it on her breath. God, he had missed kissing. His hands roamed over her back and thin waist, needing to touch every part of her. She pressed her body into his and he knew she was aware of his erection. He felt embarrassed. Someone laughed and John realized they must be making a spectacle, but part of him didn't care. Only reluctantly did he force himself to release his embrace, and allow them to separate. He let himself breathe and open his eyes. Looking around self-consciously, he realized people were staring at them, snickering then turning away.

"I guess we're putting on a show," he said.

"I don't mind. They're nothing to me. I don't know these people and they don't know me. I'm starting a new life in America. Whatever happened before doesn't count. I'm going to be reborn. I can even change my name if I want to. Don't you feel like that? Like you're starting afresh?"

"I guess." He thought of getting married, of supporting a family and providing everything for them. And he felt the pressing weight of that responsibility.

"Isn't it freeing?" she mused. "I feel like I'm getting out of prison, like I'm just waking up."

"It is a new start," John agreed, "but I feel like it's more of a challenge, something I've got to measure up to."

"My, you are a serious one, aren't you? Where are you off to then, when we land? What are your plans?"

"What are yours?" he asked, avoiding her question.

"My uncle is a playwright. I am to star in a musical he'll be putting on in New York."

"You're an actress?"

"And a singer and dancer as well. Yes, I aim to be a famous music hall star. You'll be able to say, 'I knew her before she became famous!' And you, what are your plans for your reincarnation? What are you to become?"

"What's to become of me? I guess I'll have to wait to find out."

"Well, where are you headed once we land in New York? You must have some plans."

"Oh, sure. I have a sister in Chicago. And some family friends. I'm headed there."

"Ah, that's good, now. You have some family. I'm glad you won't be all alone. But a sister won't help on cold nights, now. You'll be looking for someone to love. I can see that. You're storing up a lot for some woman."

John felt her looking at him and grew uncomfortable. "You can tell that, can you?"

"Oh, that's not difficult. I could feel you pushing through your trousers. You're all rarin' to go."

John blushed and looked away. "I'm sorry," he said.

"Oh, don't apologize. I'm flattered. It restores my confidence. I wouldn't be much of an actress now, if I couldn't get men to be attracted to me."

"Is that all it was then, a kind of a test, to see if you could get a rise out of me?"

"No, nothing like that. I like the way you look, the dark brooding eyes — so serious and mysterious — and that bushy brush you have, and the way your arms are poppin' out of your jacket. I thought you looked a little lonely. I just wanted to feel you close to me. I hope you didn't mind." She smiled. "It didn't feel like you minded. Not one bit."

John smiled now. "No, it felt good to kiss you."

"I could tell."

John looked away. He wanted this pretty woman, wanted to kiss her and hold her and make love to her. But it was impossible, wasn't it? There was no place for them to have a bit of privacy — and he was engaged, a father-to-be. How could he be thinking this way?

Yet, wasn't it like she said? They were going to start a new life, and what happened before wouldn't count. John stole a glance at Nora, who was still holding his arm while she watched a group dancing. She must have sensed his confusion.

"We have another couple of days before we get to New York. Perhaps we can see each other again," she said.

"I'd like that," he said. "But do you have to run off now?"

"I think I should."

"Why don't we just stay here a while and listen to the music?"

"Because it's not the music we want, is it? I don't think it's a good idea. But look for me later, where we found my Uncle Seamus. He's usually there. I think he paid extra to reserve that spot in the sun and out of the wind. If I'm not with him, he'll have an idea where I am."

"All right. I'll look for you later, then."

Nora squeezed his arm and reached up to give him a peck on the cheek. He cradled her head in his hand and kissed her on the mouth. At first she responded, but then she pushed him away.

"All right, then," he whispered. "Later."

Nora nodded, her face open like the sun, and then she whirled around and dissolved into the crowd. John leaned back against the bulkhead, feeling like he'd been dreaming. What was happening to him? First Ellen falls in love with him and then this pretty Nora picks him from all the lads on the ship. What was this about? Would other women perhaps also find him attractive and interesting? Might he have other choices? Is this what they meant when they called America the land of opportunity? Was it a mistake to tie himself down to one woman when he was only 22?

He looked for Nora later on in the afternoon, but found neither her nor her uncle. The next day it rained and he stayed below playing cards with Jimmy and the others. The following day, their last day of sailing, he searched with more urgency. Finally, he found her uncle near the bow.

"Ah, John, isn't it? Nora told me to tell you that she isn't feeling well. She's been below on her cot. I think she consumed a bit too much Irish, if you were to ask me. She's just a wisp of a thing, as ya know. She hasn't the capacity for it the way we do."

John felt disappointed that he wouldn't see her, yet happily reassured she wasn't avoiding him. "Just tell her I was asking after her, and that I wish her fame and success and every happiness."

"I'll do that and the same to you."

"And to you, sir. Success with your musical."

"Aye, I'll drink to that." The old man drew the bottle from within his coat and offered John a swig before taking one himself.

They said goodbye and John wandered away. He found Jimmy and they stood by the railing contemplating their new life in Chicago.

"I tell you, Jimmy, if I wasn't already as good as married, I'd stay in New York and pursue that girl."

"And a fool you'd be," Jimmy chided. "You're still a wee lad yourself, your pecker's not half grown, and you don't know what you want. This new country is going to be full of young women like her. You're in a big rush to settle down, though only God knows why."

"I admit, there's something to be said for quantity, though I don't think my father ever did it with anyone other than my own mother."

"Maybe, but I can tell you my father has. Him and Ma were always going on about that. How she didn't want it and he always did. So he found it elsewhere and then she held that against him, using it as another excuse for holding out on him. All the married men I knew in Kilkenny had a woman on the side, usually some barmaid if it wasn't their own neighbor's wife or daughter."

"That's not the way it was in my neighborhood."

"Maybe you were just blind to it. Everybody screws around. You think your marriage is going to be any different?"

"Are you saying that Ellen and I are going to cheat on each other?" John was incredulous.

"I'm saying everybody does sooner or later unless they're too ugly or too stupid — and even then, they'll find someone to do it with."

"Jimmy, you're talking through your hat. You have no idea what you're talking about. In fact, I think you know even less than I do."

"Jack, no one knows less than you do. I bet even your little sisters know more about what's going on than you do," Jimmy scoffed.

"Don't you go talking about my little sisters, now."

"I'm only saying, Jacky, that if you knew what you were doing, you'd have gotten under that girl's skirts."

"Yeah? And where was I supposed to be doing that, with everybody on board standing around gaping at us, including her uncle?"

"If it was me, I'd have found a way. If she was as pretty as you say, there's no way I'd have let the opportunity pass. And her an actress, you say? They're as good as whores anyway. Oh, I'd have found a way."

"Yeah, yeah. You're all talk, Jimmy. I bet you're still a virgin, still whacking yourself silly every night. You're going to end up feebleminded if you keep at it. In fact, I think you're halfway there."

"Oh yeah? I think someone's askin' for a fat lip or a bloody nose."

"Oh, do you now? Nah, you're too small for me. It'd be unfair."

"Blow it out your arse."

"Anyway," said John, "I won't be seeing her again."

"Yeah." Jimmy gave John a playful punch on the arm. "You want to go play some cards?"

"Might as well," John agreed. "Nothing else to do."

They entered New York Harbor early the next morning. John saw several small islands with forts on them. Jimmy pointed at one of them off to the left.

"My cousin told me about that one. That's Fort Wood on Bedloe's

Island. He said the French are building a statue to put there that will be taller than this ship."

John looked at him like he was crazy. No one could build a statue that tall. "If it's bigger than a ship, then how the hell do you think they're going to get it over here all the way from France? Your cousin doesn't know what he's talking about. Insanity must run in your family."

"No, it's true. You'll see. It's only 'cause you're so ignorant and don't read the newspapers that you don't know anything."

"Ha! And you keep up on world affairs, I see. That is, when you're not whacking yourself silly," John joked.

"You should know," his friend retorted.

John turned back to the harbor. He saw that they were heading right for the southern-most point of Manhattan Island, a place they called the Battery. That's where all the third-class passengers were to be processed. The first- and second-class passengers had only to fill out some forms on board and they were free to disembark.

They docked at 8:30 a.m. on Monday, May 19, 1884. The weather was mild and by one o'clock John was out of the Barge Office, where the processing had taken place, and on the street. He hired a carriage from a long line and told the driver to take him to Grand Central Depot, where he'd been told he could get a train to Boston.

A multitude of horse-drawn carriages, omnibuses, and even horse-drawn trains created a swarm of people and animals. All around, pedestrians, pushcarts, horses, and carriages vied for right of way on crowded streets. John was acutely aware of the oppressive stench and filth from this army of horseflesh, although everyone else seemed oblivious to it. Many of the streets, especially further uptown, were unpaved and muck-filled. He'd never experienced anything like it. Dublin was neither as congested nor as repulsive.

The hour-long carriage ride took John from the Battery, at the tip of New York, uptown to 42nd Street, where he disembarked at the train depot, a massive five-story brick building with three domed towers. Overwhelmed by the sights he'd witnessed along the route, he managed to find his way to the ticket office. The New Haven Railroad train was scheduled to leave at 6:00 that night and arrive in Boston at 7:00 the next morning.

At a restaurant across the street from the depot, John ate a sandwich while browsing through a newspaper. So far his journey was going better than he'd anticipated, but what lay ahead? He thought about Ellen and their unborn child. As he gazed out the window a young woman who reminded him of Nora McNamee passed by, and he found himself wondering where she was in New York.

When John arrived in Boston the following morning, he found an inexpensive boarding house a few blocks from the train station. Dog-tired after a night on the hard seats, he needed to shave and change his clothes before he could call on Ellen.

It was early afternoon when John climbed the front steps of the home of Ellen's aunt and uncle. He used the brass knocker on the door to announce his presence. The large brick house stood atop a hill that overlooked the Boston Commons, a large and beautiful park. A maid soon answered the door and he announced himself.

"My name is John Powers. I'm calling on Miss Ellen Furlong. Is she here?"

The maid led him through the house to a lovely brick patio surrounded by a flower garden. A handsome older woman rose from her chair and held out her hand.

"Mr. Powers, I'm so glad you've had a successful journey."

Mrs. Austin asked the maid to tell Miss Furlong that her fiancé had arrived, but suddenly John heard Ellen running down the stairs. She rushed into his arms and kissed him openly.

"I'm so glad to see you," she cried. Her eyes glistened. Embarrassed by her display of affection, John stole a glance at Mrs. Austin.

"Come, sit down," the woman urged, indicating a wrought iron settee. "Have you had lunch?" she asked.

"No, not yet. Once I'd found a room and washed up, I came right over," he told her, leaving out the fact that he'd fallen asleep for two hours.

"Then we shall have some now." She rang for the maid and directed her to have lunch prepared. "So tell us all about your adventure."

Over a leisurely lunch, John talked about his trip and Mrs. Austin told him about Boston. When they finished, Mrs. Austin suggested that Ellen take her fiancé for a walk to the Commons. It was a delightful spring day and the flowering trees and shrubs were starting to bloom.

Once out of the house, they embraced and kissed.

"I couldn't wait to see you and hold you," John said.

"Me too."

"I've been dying to ask you how you feel, how the baby's coming, but I wasn't sure I should bring it up in front of your aunt."

The couple crossed the cobblestone street and walked down the hill to the Commons. "I'm glad you didn't mention it. It's what I must talk to you about." John looked at her quizzically. "Let's wait until we find a bench and can sit down," she suggested.

John looked at her more closely. "You're looking mighty fine, Ellen, really beautiful."

She smiled and looked away. "Thank you. You're looking beautiful too."

John laughed. "Oh, do I now? You've been too long in the colonies, you have."

"You know what I mean. I'm so glad to see you. You look wonderful to me. I've missed you so much." She squeezed his arm for emphasis.

"And I've missed you. I've thought about nothing else but the two of us, our getting married, going to Chicago and setting up house for our new family." He said nothing of his constant memories of their lovemaking. An image of Nora McNamee's face appeared and he blinked it away.

Inside the Commons, Ellen spied a bench in the shade. "Let's sit there," she proposed. She took his hands in hers. "John ..."

"Yes?"

"I've had a miscarriage."

"A what?"

"A miscarriage. I've lost the baby."

"Lost the baby? How can that be? What do you mean?" he was stricken.

"On the ship coming over. At first I thought I was just seasick, but it was more than that. John, I've lost it. The poor wee thing never survived. Never even made it to three months."

"I don't understand."

"I'm sorry, John. It must have been all the pitching and rolling of the ship and my being seasick. I'm no longer pregnant."

He looked at her as if she were speaking gibberish. He staggered a few paces up the path before he turned and stared, questioning her with his eyes. She nodded and held out her hand, inviting him to return to her. Her eyes were filled with tears and her chin trembled. Slowly he walked back, shaking his head.

"You're sure?" he asked as he sat down beside her. "You're really sure?"

"Yes, I'm quite sure. I saw the blood." She paused and looked away, heaving a deep sigh. "And all of my symptoms of pregnancy are gone. I'm so sorry! Aunt Margaret is the only one who knows. She says that she's had two miscarriages herself. It's quite common. It doesn't mean we can't have other children."

"But why? I saw many pregnant women on my ship. Why should a journey on a ship be harmful to our baby? I don't understand. You must have done something wrong, something you shouldn't have."

"No, John, that's not true! I didn't do anything. I took the best care of myself that I could."

He looked her straight in the eye. "Tell me if you did something to get rid of it."

"No! How dare you think that! How could you? I would never do such a thing."

"I'm just asking, is all. The last time I saw you, you were plump with life. Now I see you, thin as a rail and I don't know what happened. I don't understand how it could happen."

"I don't know, John. It's just one of those things we have to accept."

John knew this. He knew that in his own neighborhood women had miscarriages and stillbirths. He'd seen it on Ellen's grandfather's estate with the sheep and cows. John covered his face with his hands. He recalled the conversation with his father about his two lost brothers.

Already? He thought. *Already I'm required to have such patience and understanding?*

"I'm sorry, but no one's to blame. It couldn't be helped. It was just God's will," she pleaded.

"God's will, is it? God's will took my son?"

"If it's God's will, then he must have had a reason. You can't be blaming God, John."

"Who says I can't? And if he had a reason, what was it? He didn't like the idea that we were in love? Is that it? Is it a sin for a poor laborer like myself to love the likes of you? Is that it? He's punishing me for stepping above my class?"

Ellen was incensed. She glared at him and shook her finger in his face. "Just who do you think you are, John Powers?" she fumed. "I know you're disappointed and angry. I expected as much. But the way you're carrying on — first you're blaming me. Then it's God, picking on the likes of you because you dared love your boss's daughter. Will you think for just one minute of what *I've* been through? You act like I did something wrong. This happened to *me*, you idiot! *I* was the mother. I lost a part of me. It was *my* baby. I carried her inside *me*. Can't you understand that? Can't you see?"

She stared at him, her eyes filled to overflowing and her mouth pressed into a thin, firm line.

John regarded her with comprehension just beyond his reach.

"If you love me as you say you do, then try to accept what happened," she implored him. "The miscarriage wasn't my fault. I didn't do anything wrong. I was as devastated as you. But there's nothing to be done. It happened. We'll never understand why. We just have to try again."

John dumbly nodded. Reality was sinking in. Like his da had said, there are other responsibilities that go beyond earning a wage. This woman would be his wife. They'd both suffered a terrible loss. It had happened to her as much as to him — maybe even more so. He reached out his hand to hers and clasped it.

"You're right," he murmured. "It was the shock of it. I wasn't thinking straight. I'm sorry." Ellen leaned on him, pressing her cheek against his broad back. After a while, he said, "You mentioned *her*. Was it a girl after all?"

She shook her head. "There was no way to tell. I just imagined her as a girl, like you imagined a son. It was only wishful thinking on my part."

"We'll have to keep trying until we get one of each," he said hopefully.

"Maybe two of each," she said, smiling.

"I'm sorry, Ellen. All this is new to me. I shouldn't have blamed you."

"Or God," she chided.

"Well, that I'm not so sure about."

"John, watch your tongue!"

"Why should I? The big ornery bloke, picking on poor defenseless babies." Ellen saw that he was joking — at least half-joking.

"Let's walk a bit," he suggested. "I've got to get rid of this tension."

They walked down a path in silence, Ellen holding onto his arm. After a while, he asked, "Was it painful? I mean when it happened?"

"No, not really. Not painful, exactly. I was having cramps, but they weren't too bad. I thought I was seasick. Then I noticed the blood and all. It was more sad than anything. I didn't know how I was going to tell you. I knew how much you'd be disappointed. And I blamed myself too, at first. All these other women, from Eve on, populating the world with their babies and I can't get it right. What's wrong with me?"

She paused before continuing. "And I was alone. I wanted my mother, but I had no one until I talked with my Aunt Margaret. Then I began to understand what I knew all along: Not all pregnancies work out, just like not every seed takes." She glanced up at him. "You understand?"

John nodded glumly. "Aye, I understand. Like I said, it was just the shock of it."

They walked on a ways before Ellen asked, "So with my not being pregnant, do you still want to go through with it? I mean getting married and all?"

He looked at her questioningly. "Don't you want to?"

"Of course I want to," she reassured him. "I just wondered if you still want to. I mean, now that I'm no longer pregnant, you don't have to marry me."

"Is that why you think I wanted to marry you? Because I *had* to?"

Ellen floundered. "Well, no, not exactly ..."

"Ellen, I love you. I'm looking forward to starting a new life with you. I'm looking forward to our having children together." He realized how much he wanted to be a married man, a husband, a father.

"I'll admit, I'm having difficulty accepting this — loss," he said, avoiding the word *baby,* "and I'm still angry with your parents for making us leave Waterford. But I want to be with you. I want to be married to you."

Ellen hugged him, burying her face in his shoulder. "I love you too, John. I guess I just needed to hear you say it."

"I've been thinking of nothing else, our getting married and all. Can we do it here at your aunt's?"

Ellen shook her head and pulled him along the path. "No, we can't get married here. Aunt Margaret would feel like she'd be betraying my father's trust. We have to wait until we get to Chicago, to your sister's."

"Then we'll do that straight away."

"We can leave tomorrow," she sounded excited. "We'll take the train to Chicago. My aunt already knows that we plan to leave soon. We just have to tell my uncle and cousins that we're engaged and will be leaving for Chicago to start our new life."

John squeezed her hand. "It sounds wonderful. I only wish that it would be the three of us going."

After a week of weary travel on hard straw seats on three separate trains, the couple arrived at Union Station in Chicago on June 3, 1884. It was late afternoon, but the sun was still high in the western sky when they emerged from the brick railroad station onto the wide cobblestone street. John and Ellen piled their suitcases and boxes onto a carriage and headed off to the home of the O'Brians, where John's sister Bridget was employed.

As they approached the front door of the little bungalow, they saw a red sign on the door. Knocking tepidly, John saw Bridget peek through the curtain and heard her squeals of joy. Sharon O'Brian, a stocky young woman, came to the door and John saw her expression of welcome fade into one of worry. She shouted through the door.

"Our littlest one is sick with scarlet fever and our house is quarantined. We can't let you in. George can't even leave the house to go to work. 'Tis why he's at home at all," she said as Mr. O'Brian appeared behind her. "The quarantine is to last through the week, until next Monday."

John and Ellen were crushed. After their long journey, the frustration of this unforeseen situation was a heavy blow.

With a stroke of good fortune, John remembered that he had Jimmy O'Hara's address in his wallet. They took a carriage to Jimmy's brother's apartment. Jimmy was delighted to see his friend again.

"Of course you can stay here until you find a place of your own," Jimmy said, "only be quick about it. We're sleepin' in dresser draws as it is — and that's in shifts."

Jimmy introduced them to his brother, Ed, and his wife, Janet, a thin, strawberry blonde woman with a baby girl in her arms. Ed was getting ready to go to work on the night shift at the stockyards.

"That's where I'm looking for a job myself," John said. "A friend of my da works there and I'm hoping he'll be able to help me."

"Well, I'll put in a word too," offered Ed, a tall, athletic-looking man. "It can't hurt. I'll bring an application home with me in the morning. They're always looking for fresh meat," he said, laughing uproariously.

During the next few days, John and Ellen visited his father's friend and looked for a flat near the stockyards. By the following Monday, they had found a second-floor apartment at 3412 South Halstead Street, with the ubiquitous small, wooden back porch that overlooked an alley behind their building. It was within walking distance from work, for which John was grateful — and within smelling distance, which they found unbelievably foul. John had obtained a job in the slaughterhouse, hoisting freshly killed cattle onto a chain that would carry the dead animal through a huge trough of hot water before the butchering began. It was the kind of heavy, hard work his body was designed for.

With the quarantine over, Sharon O'Brian suggested that Bridget help Ellen shop for the basics she and John would need: a used table and two ladder-back chairs for the kitchen, a tea kettle, pots and pans, dishes, cups, oil lamp, chamber pot, bed, and some bed linens.

Mrs. O'Brian was also adamant that John and Ellen marry immediately. Bridget helped them make arrangements with her church and the priest agreed to marry them that Sunday, June 16, 1884. Jimmy O'Hara served as best man and Bridget was Ellen's maid of honor. The

O'Brians surprised them with a small party. That night, John and Ellen lay in their bed for the first time as a married couple.

"Well, it's done. Are you glad for it, John? Are you happy?"

"Of course I'm happy," he said, snuggling closer and kissing her. "Why wouldn't I be happy?"

"Being married. I know not every man truly wants to be married."

"Well, I'm not every man, now, am I? I'm glad to be married to you. I can't believe my own luck. I've got a good job with a decent wage and we've got a cozy little flat that'll do for now. When we start making a family, we'll need a bigger place."

Ellen hugged and kissed him. "I'm sorry about the miscarriage."

John shook his head. "It wasn't your fault. Like you said, it happens. But I'm looking forward to getting you pregnant again."

Ellen caught his eye. "Are you, now?"

2

Chicago

1890

From their apartment window, Ellen surveyed the street below. People were bundled up against the chilly April morning, and the overcast sky hinted at rain later in the day. Ellen turned from the window, cradling the baby against the draft.

"I hope it won't rain 'til after the christening. I don't want to be rushing up and down slippery church steps with this little angel in my arms, trying to keep her dry."

John chuckled. "But that's the whole purpose now, ain't it? To get her wet. That's what the baptism is, isn't it?"

"You know what I mean. It'll be a big day and I don't want rain ruining it for everyone."

"Oh, don't you mind about that. Once we're back here, eating and drinking our fill, nobody will mind a bit of rain."

"I suppose," she said, turning back to the window, the sleeping baby in her arms. Her own sweet Katherine. In the kitchen, John's sister Mary was cooking up a small feast they would have when they returned from the Church of Holy Nativity. Thank God for Mary's help; at just 15, she was a hard worker. Ellen felt comforted knowing that all of John's sisters had immigrated to Chicago. Aside from their practical help, she felt embraced by the warm sense of family they brought with them. Luckily, Mary had the day off from the convent, where she lived and worked as a cook, and so was able to apply her skills in their kitchen on this festive day.

Ellen and John had moved from their apartment on South Halstead Street to this larger one on Lowe. It was still easy for John to get to work at the Armour meatpacking plant in the stockyards, and they had much more room. Ellen recalled their first two-room flat when they'd married six years before. Now here they were: with four lovely daughters, three bedrooms, an indoor bathroom right in their apartment, electric lights — and perhaps even a telephone before the year was out. She marveled at their good fortune.

"I'm so happy, John. Aren't you?"

"Happy? Of course I'm happy. Why shouldn't I be happy, surrounded as I am by half the females in Chicago. Christ, I can't wait until this afternoon, when I'll see another man in the house."

"Oh, you and Jimmy. All you do is drink and talk sports or politics."

"There's something else to talk about around all these females?" John quipped.

"Jimmy's brother, Harry, seems to enjoy our company," Ellen pointed out.

"Ach, Harry is just sniffin' after my sister Alice."

"They make a sweet-looking couple, now, don't they?"

"I suppose, but she's only 18 and too young to be thinking that way. I told him he'd better watch himself with her. I'd hate to have to knock his block off."

"You like being the man of the family, don't you?" Ellen smiled. "John Powers, patriarch."

"Don't tease me about that. It's a lot of responsibility looking out for my sisters as well as you and the girls. It's not as easy as you think."

"Oh, and I have it easy? Is that it, now? I've nothing to do all day but wait for your highness to put in an appearance and tell me what to do. Is that your meaning?"

John scrutinized his wife for the telltale signs of anger: her bug-eyes, flushed cheeks, and pursed mouth. Finding them absent, he relaxed.

"Sure now, you're the Queen of Sheba, you are — sitting pretty and cozy-like, just the way I've ordered it. Nothing's too good for my queen and my four little princesses."

"And don't you forget it."

"Here, let me hold her for a little while," he offered.

"Just as well. I'll help Mary in the kitchen. By the way, shouldn't Margaret be back by now with the girls? She was only going to the bakery. It shouldn't take her this long. I don't want them to get caught in the rain."

"Well, it's not raining yet and Maggie's a good girl," John reassured his wife. "She'll be back with them in plenty of time."

"I hope nothing's happened."

"Ah, you're always worrying your fool head off," he snapped impatiently.

"Time was when you'd worry about the girls. Josie is only five."

"Bejesus, don't you think I know how old my own daughters are? You don't need to be telling me such as that."

She bent to kiss his head while he held little Kitty. "I'm just all fluttery about today, is all. I know your sister is responsible and will take good care of our three girls."

"We're lucky to have her here to help, especially now with our Katherine."

50

"I know, John. I didn't mean anything."

"I know. OK, off you go now and leave me with the babe."

Ellen left the parlor and John heard the two women squealing in the kitchen. He gazed down at the little doll-like face in the crook of his arm. What a beautiful little bundle! His daughters had each been absolutely beautiful when they were born: Josie, five years ago; Anna, four years ago; and Nellie, just two years ago. In the six years since arriving in America, so much had happened. His life had been transformed in so many ways — not the least of which was the passing of his parents four years ago, and his sisters' immigration to Chicago.

John recalled the letter he'd received from Alice, telling him of his father's accident. She'd written that Da had fallen from a scaffold and died from the resulting injuries. John couldn't understand how such an accident could have happened. His father was an experienced shipbuilder and had been working at his trade for more than 30 years. How could he have possibly fallen? John suspected that something was being covered up, but Alice knew only what she had been told by the company.

Shattered by Paddy's sudden death, his mother passed only five months later. "It seems Ma just gave up on living," Alice wrote. There was no explaining it. She simply gave up.

John and Ellen made immediate plans to bring the three sisters over, but for some reason that Alice was unable — or unwilling — to explain, the authorities in Waterford saw fit to put her into a local convent school for orphans, while permitting the younger sisters, Mary and Margaret, to emigrate to America to join their family.

The nuns, in turn, sent Alice from Waterford to a convent in St. Louis. As soon as she turned 16, she moved into a rooming house with other young women. Eventually, she found a job in a local beer garden, but after a few months, John convinced her to come live with the family.

Harry had met Alice at the beer garden while visiting St. Louis, and had fallen in love with her then. He was ecstatic when he learned she would be moving to Chicago. That had been two years ago.

It worked out for the best. Both Alice and Mary were now living and working in the kitchen at the convent and Margaret, the baby of the family at just 13, lived with John and Ellen. Having Margaret in the house reminded Ellen of her own sister, Sheila, whom she missed terribly.

John smiled to himself, recognizing that he got credit for being generous, when his primary motive for having Margaret was selfish: He'd always felt closest to Maggie, and having her live with them re-created the closeness of his home in Waterford. And having another set of hands to help Ellen with the girls was an additional blessing. He loved his girls, but sometimes all those shrill voices could get on his nerves. He viewed Margaret as something of a buffer — even if she was another female.

He heard the door open and Margaret noisily herded in his little choir of angels. Josie led four-year-old Annie by the hand, but immediately let go and ran excitedly to her father.

"Da, the lady in the bakery gave us each a cookie. Look, I saved a piece for Kitty." She opened her little fist to show the squashed crumbs.

"Ah, that's very thoughtful of you, Josie, but Kitty can't eat cookies yet. She can only nurse from your ma. But I'll take it for myself if you don't mind."

"OK," she said, holding up her hand to her father, who licked the crumbs clean.

"Yum," he said, "that was a wonderful cookie. Best I've had all morning. Thank you, love."

Josie, followed by Annie, ran into the kitchen to report her good deed to her mother. Margaret lowered two-year-old Nellie to the floor and removed her own jacket. She had already set down the basket containing the pastries and cookies for that afternoon.

"The bakery was so crowded this morning, you'd think it was Easter," Margaret mused. "They were so busy that I asked if they needed more help. I thought I might pitch in on Sunday mornings and earn a little pocket money. Mrs. Bewley said she'd think about it and she'll let me know Tuesday morning. Would that be all right?"

John nodded in approval. Although he earned a good wage and was glad to help take care of his baby sister, anything more, no matter how meager, would be helpful.

"Good," he said, "maybe you'll even get a discount on what we buy there. You know, a penny saved ..."

Margaret smiled widely in exuberant self-satisfaction. With her two pigtails and fair, freckled face, she reminded him of their own mother.

"You're a darling," he said. "Now, you'd better go and help in the kitchen."

Maggie put her coat in the room she shared with Nellie and then ran back to the kitchen. John wondered where she got all of her energy — she never did anything in slow motion, but raced through life with endless eagerness. It really was a delight to have her happy energy in the household. He'd noticed that with the stress of motherhood, Ellen's light had been fading. She had gained weight during her pregnancy with Nellie and complained of fatigue ever since the birth two years ago. She never regained her strength, and this last pregnancy was a struggle. Ellen tried to put a bright face on things, but John sensed that underneath the weak smile she was plain tired. Whereas his long hours at work only made him stronger, maintaining the household and raising the girls sapped all of her strength. That was another reason he was glad to have Maggie's help with the children and household chores. But even so, Ellen rarely had the energy for making love anymore — and although he understood and tried to be patient with her, he resented it.

Lately he found himself looking at other women on the trolley car or in advertisements. Not that he would do anything, even if he had the chance; still, he fantasized about his brief encounter with the actress Nora McNamee. He'd seen her name on posters advertising musicals in the theater on State Street, but he never made any attempt to contact her — though he wondered what it might be like. He was still a young man, after all, only 28 years old and in his prime. Well, maybe now that they lived in a larger apartment and had Maggie's help, things would improve. Maybe Ellen would regain her strength and lose some weight now that the new baby was here.

A knock at the door startled him from his reverie. Before he could respond, the door opened. "It's just me," hollered Jimmy O'Hara. "I thought I'd come over a bit early to see if you needed me to run any errands, seeing as how you've got your arms full."

"Come in, come in. Make yourself to home, as if you needed an invitation. Where's your little brother?"

"Oh, Harry is still making himself pretty, something I don't have to work at so hard as he does."

"No, with your being so ugly to begin with, it would serve no purpose at all," John teased his friend.

With the commotion, the baby started to cry and Ellen came in from the kitchen. "Here, let me take her. Oh, hello Jimmy. I thought it was you."

"And how are you today? All excited about Katherine's christening?"

"I'm just hoping it doesn't rain. But aren't you here early? We won't be going to the church for another hour yet." She drew the baby to her bosom and soothed her with a bouncy motion.

"Oh, I just thought I'd get out of Harry's way and see if I could be of any help over here."

"He means he's ready for a drink, is what he means," John joked.

"Oh," said Jimmy, "you're going to have some libation to celebrate the occasion?"

Ellen headed for the bedroom with Katherine in her arms. "She might be a little hungry."

"Aren't we all?" said John.

"What is that smell coming from the kitchen?"

"Mary is cooking up a feast. I brought home a wonderful roast yesterday and we're having it with potatoes and cabbage and all manner of good things."

"All of that and libations, too? This must be heaven itself I've arrived at. I must go in and say hello to your fine sister Mary."

"And don't be stealing any food while you're in there," John admonished. "Meanwhile," he announced, pushing himself out of his chair, "I guess it wouldn't hurt for us to have a taste to make sure the whiskey ain't gone bad."

John was pouring out two tumblers when Alice and Bridget knocked on the door.

"Hi, how's my handsome brother?" asked Bridget as she gave him a kiss. "Where's my newest niece? I've got to have a look at her."

John motioned with his head. "Down the hall with her ma. And how are you?" he asked Alice, who was removing her hat and coat.

"I'm fine," she said and came over to kiss his cheek. "The O'Brians are meeting us at the church. They suggested Bridget and I come here early to see if Mary and Ellen needed any help."

Just then, Jimmy emerged from the kitchen and he and Alice squeezed by each other in the doorway. "Ah, good morning, Alice. Imagine meeting you here."

"Good morning yourself, James O'Hara. I see that you and my brother are off to an early start."

John said, "You're not hinting at a glass for yourself, now, are you?"

"After church will be soon enough," Alice admonished. "I've got to look in on Mary."

Bridget emerged from the hallway carrying Katherine. "My God, John! Ellen's exhausted. She's dozed off while nursing little Katherine. I really don't know if she's up to all this."

"Oh, she'll be fine, sis. Neither of us gets all that much sleep. She's just catching 20 winks, is all."

"Here, why don't you put down your drink and take your daughter while I get out of my coat. I'm sure Mary needs some help in the kitchen."

"Of course I'll take my daughter, but there's no need to let go of my glass. And if Mary gets any more help in there, well — you know what they say about too many cooks."

Bridget disappeared into the kitchen leaving John and Jimmy with the baby and their drinks.

"She sure likes to take charge," Jimmy noted, sitting down on the love seat and crossing his legs.

"The oldest sister always thinks she's the boss. She and Ellen are always clashing about the right way to do this and that."

"But it's your own home, ain't it? Yours and Ellen's."

"Truth is, Ellen is usually too tired to really put up a fight and I'm not going to come between them. Besides, Bridget has experience running a household, with her having been working all these years for the O'Brians, and she knows what she's talking about."

"I hear some fellow has been courting her. Will he be coming to the party?"

"Some fellow? Jesus, Jimmy, haven't you heard? She's picked a mick with the same name as myself."

"John?"

"Ha. John Powers."

Jimmy looked at his smiling friend, confused. "What are you saying, Jack?"

"Only that Bridget hasn't had enough of her Powers clan, but that she's gone and found a bloke with the very same name as her own brother."

"Jesus be damned," Jimmy said and swallowed his drink.

"Help yourself to another. And fill mine while you're up."

"Have you met him?" Jimmy asked, giving the filled glass to John.

"Only once. He's a big fellow. Tall, I mean, with glasses, and losing his hair already. He delivers milk. Has his own route. He's doing well enough, I suppose."

"Jesus. The same name as your own," Jimmy mused.

"Well, he's got a middle initial, which I lack. I suppose his folks were well off or something."

"Well, then, she'd be marrying up. That's good news." And he tossed down his drink. "What's his middle name, then?"

"No name," said John, sipping his drink, "just the initial. I guess they weren't all that well off after all," he quipped.

Ellen came back into the room. "John, don't you think we should be getting ready to go? I don't want to be late."

"Whatever you say, my lovely lass. Here, take the princess from me and I'll get my coat. All right, everyone," he bellowed, "get your things! We'll make a parade. Are you ready? Margaret, get the girls. Alice, Mary, come on! We've not got the whole day now."

Later that night, John sat in the living room drinking quietly with Jimmy and his younger brother, Harry O'Hara, a short, sinewy man. Everyone else had either left or gone to bed.

"Harry," said John.

"What?"

"I just wanted to tell you that you have a fine singing voice."

"Thank you, John. But you've already told me that three times tonight."

"Have I now? And call me Jack. Everybody should call me Jack. I don't want to be John anymore. Looks like we'll be having another John Powers about. John F. Powers."

"He seems nice enough," said Jimmy. "A bit quiet, maybe, but he puts a sparkle in Bridget's eyes."

"I suppose," John murmured. "Still, he smells like his horse."

"Ha," blurted Jimmy. "And what do you suppose we smell like when we're back from the Yards? I know I can't ever get that stink of blood and shit off me. I'm surprised Ellen lets you sleep inside the house."

"It's 'cause I'm so good looking."

"Well, it sure ain't because you can sing," Harry chimed in.

"You won't sing so sweetly with a busted nose," John threatened.

"Don't worry, Harry," said Jimmy. "You'd still be better looking than this brute."

"Mr. O'Hara, you're taking advantage of my good nature."

"And the fact that you're too drunk to get up off your arse."

"Aye, that too," John allowed. "Ah, what a fine day it was. A day worth remembering: Kitty's christening, my whole family together, my friends, my children. I only wish my ma and da could have been here to see it."

Harry and Jimmy looked at each other, then into their glasses. "Aye," said Jimmy, "it was quite a fine day."

"Well," sighed John, "I hope our next one will be a boy. I love my girls, you know, but I'd truly give anything to have a son."

"Well, you're bound to have one, you and Ellen. A bull like yourself, why wouldn't you have a son?"

John cocked his head to one side. "Who knows? With Ellen being so tired and out of sorts ..."

"It wasn't like her to conk out so early," Jimmy said thoughtfully.

"That's just it," John admitted. "It's becoming very much like her. Seems like she goes to bed with the sun. Truth is, between my working and her sleeping, I'm not sure we'll have anymore children at all, never mind a son."

"As bad as all that?" Jimmy asked, surprised. He put a little more whiskey in his glass and sat down beside his friend. Harry was having trouble keeping his eyes open and slouched against the back of his chair.

John nodded. "Aye, Jimmy. You're looking at a horny bastard."

"So much for being married, then."

Harry shook himself awake with a start. "You talking about me? About me and Alice?"

"We're just talking about poor Jacky here," Jimmy told his brother, "with Ellen being too worn out to be interested in — you know what." Harry looked at the two men.

"Let that be a lesson to you, Harry. Like my da told me, being married means you have to have patience with your woman. If you end up marrying my sister, you damned well better treat her gently."

"He's a good lad," said Jimmy.

"Never mind. You hear what I'm telling you, Harry? You'll be kind and patient with Alice or I'll put my fist so far down your throat, I'll pull your nuts up from the inside."

Jimmy almost fell off his chair laughing, but Harry was serious. "Why wouldn't I treat her well, Jack? I love the girl more than anything. I swear."

"I'm just saying, marriage ain't always the way you expect."

"I know that," said Harry. "I've been living with my brother, Ed, after all. I know it's not a dream, not like in the songs. It's hard work. Any fool can see that."

"All right, then. Just so you know what'll happen."

"I can just picture you, Harry," said Jimmy, sitting on the floor and giggling again, "with your nuts pulled up like that."

Harry grinned. "Well, I wouldn't be of any use at all to Alice, then, would I?"

"Well, lads," John sighed. "I hate to put an end to it, but we've got to get up again in a few hours."

"Aye, back to the slaughterhouse..."

The next day, Alice and Bridget came by while Ellen and Margaret were ironing and watching the girls.

"You seemed so tired yesterday, Ellen. We thought you might want some extra help," Bridget said.

"Did I look that bad?" Ellen's back straightened and her face flushed.

"No, just tired. And no wonder, with four little ones," Bridget reassured her.

"And my brother isn't much of a help, it seems," Alice added. "Though I guess men never are. My own father never raised a hand to pitch in."

"Oh no. John's really good with the girls," Ellen said. "He's always ready to take one of them." After a moment she added, "Though he's way too soft with them. It's hard to discipline the girls when he always gives in to them."

"That's true. I've noticed there was always at least one climbing all over him," said Bridget. "Still, we thought we might help with cleaning up after yesterday."

Ellen offered to put on some tea, but Bridget gently brushed her aside and headed for the kitchen. Alice said she'd take the girls for a walk. When she left with the three girls and Kitty in a pram, and Bridget returned with the tea, Ellen collapsed in a chair.

"Oh, it's good to have some quiet for a change. I often long for it. I remember sitting in a swing at my grandfather's in Youghal, and listening to the quiet. I never hear that anymore, with all the crying and screeching."

"I know what you mean," said Bridget, sitting down next to her. "Sometimes in the middle of the night I'll sit with a cup of tea. It's the only time I can hear myself think."

"Thinking about your own Mr. John Powers, I bet," said Maggie. "The two of you have trouble keeping your eyes off of each other."

"I noticed that myself," said Ellen. "Will the two of you be getting married?"

Bridget's smile was surprisingly shy. "Well, he hasn't asked me yet. He's so old-fashioned that I'm sure he'll say something to my brother before he asks me."

"So you think it'll happen?"

"Oh, I hope so." Bridget, usually so much in command, seemed young and vulnerable. "I am 21 after all, and I don't want to end up an old maid."

"Well, I think John likes your Mr. Powers, although it'll be confusing to have the two of them in the same family!"

"I've thought a lot about marrying John, of course. He'll make a good husband and father. He'd like a big family like the one he's from."

"How many brothers and sisters does he have?" Maggie asked.

"He's one of 10."

"John wants more children, too," said Ellen. "I don't think he'll stop until he gets a son, and maybe not even then. My God," she added after a moment, "I hope he doesn't want 10! That would surely be the death of me."

"My own mother had seven, but only five of us survived, John being the only son," Bridget said.

Ellen seemed thoughtful. "At home, it was only my brother and sister and myself, so I'm used to a small family. To be honest, I feel overwhelmed with just my four. I don't know what I'd do without Maggie."

She seemed near tears. "God bless you, Maggie. I don't know how I'd survive without you."

Maggie put down her iron and embraced Ellen. "Oh, I'm glad to be here, Ellen. You're like my own sister."

"And you're like mine. I must admit, I think of Sheila so often. God, I miss her so! And my brother, Tim. I'll probably never see them again."

"But they write to you, don't they?" Bridget inquired softly.

Ellen nodded and wiped her eyes. "My sister writes, and my mother. But not the men. I don't really expect it of my brother, he's so wrapped up in his own life. And my father leaves all of that to my mother. Still, I'd love to receive something from him, even a short note. Something."

Margaret returned to her ironing. "Well, if Da were alive, I doubt we'd ever hear from him. He left everything to Ma except earning a wage. She was the one who raised us. I don't know how she did it, all of us in that little thatched hut."

"Well, we all had to pitch in, didn't we, now?" said Bridget. "As young as three or four, we had our chores to do. There's no other way, is there? Children have to learn that we need each other if we're to survive."

Ellen was thoughtful. "I guess you're right, Bridget. I wasn't raised that way. I was lucky, I guess, that my parents had servants. Still, I see how important Josie feels when she lends a hand with her sisters, and Annie, too. They both want to care for the baby, and it really is a help."

"And don't they feel grown-up being able to help their mother? I see it plain as day on their faces, those little smiles of delight. Their eyes light up with pride when they're able to please you."

"I know, Maggie. You're right. I see it too. Maybe I was cheated of something growing up with maidservants. Still, I never thought it would be like this. I am always tired. I try not to let it show, but sometimes I can't keep my eyes open. John doesn't complain. He's very patient with me. But I know he's not happy. Look at me! I've put on this horrible weight. I'm always tired and never there for him anymore. I never thought it would be so difficult. God forgive me for complaining — I know I've no right. My children are beautiful and healthy and John's a good man. He works so hard. And he's so proud of his promotions, the way he's worked himself up the ladder at Armour."

"Ellen, you mustn't talk that way. You've just given birth. Give yourself time to recover. The weight will come off. You'll see. And you'll get your energy back. You're only 30, after all. You'll be fine."

"I'm sure you're right, Bridget."

Bridget patted Ellen's hand and then busied herself in the kitchen while Maggie went back to the ironing. Ellen felt guilty letting them do her work, but her aching body and fatigue made it difficult for her to remain on her feet. Guilty about her own malaise, she set about mending a basket of clothes.

Her mind wandered as she worked, recalling happier days — not only of her home in Waterford, but of the early days with John. With only Josie and Annie, she had delighted in motherhood: nursing, teaching, and playing with them. She'd had so much energy then — what had happened to her? She and John had enjoyed their lovemaking during quiet evenings when the girls were asleep; the visiting among friends, the long walks. Where had those happy days gone? Why was she always so weighted down with pain and fatigue?

In her childhood home, misbehavior and disobedience had consequences. Her mother ran an orderly household — and Ellen believed she was better off for it. It was upsetting that John didn't share her view on this. At home, he undermined her attempts at discipline. No wonder the girls behaved wildly. And the noise! Ellen had no patience for it. But John shushed her attempts at authority and took the children's side. "Leave them be. They're only kiddies. Let them have their fun while they're able." When her temper got the best of her, they'd end up in a nasty shouting match.

She felt so alone. Thank God for Maggie!

Still, Ellen was often left to her own resources. Maggie attended school three days a week, and now she'd be spending time at Bewley's Bakery as well. At almost 13, this would be Maggie's last year at school before getting a full-time job. How would Ellen manage the children and the household? Well, she'd just have to find a way. She was determined to do so. Maybe John would agree to hire a girl.

That Saturday night, John informed her that he and the O'Hara boys were going out drinking. "I've got to cut loose a little," he informed her. "It's been a while since Jimmy and I went out."

Unwilling to start another fight, Ellen fumed silently. Besides, she knew it would be no use. "When do I get my chance for a little relief?" was all she let herself say. "When was the last time we went out together?"

"Christ, Ellen, you're at home all day. You can do as you please. You're not heftin' sides of beef and getting covered with blood and guts, now, are you? How long have you been working 12, 14 hours a day, six days a week? Don't go denying me a little harmless fun now and then. You're crabby enough as it is."

Ellen glared at him. "Fine, do as you wish. You always do anyway," she stormed. The three girls turned to their father.

"Don't mind your mother. She's just in one of her moods again. Here, Josie and Annie, help me clear the table now like the good little girls you are."

When Jimmy and Harry knocked, John was out the door without a moment's hesitation. It slammed loudly behind him.

"In a bit of a rush to get out, are you?" Jimmy joked.

"Ah, the woman drives me crazy, always feeling sorry for herself, like she doesn't lead the good life."

Jimmy looked at Harry. "You see what I mean, brother?" Jimmy asked. "You sure you still want to be going through with it? It's not like it's all a bed of roses, now is it?"

Out in the street, John asked, "What are you blabbing about?"

"Nothing," smiled Jimmy. "It's just that you put on such a fine christening party that Harry here can't wait to become part of your clan."

John grinned. "Oh," he laughed, "so you've decided, have you?"

"I wanted to talk to you about it, Jack. You know how I feel about Alice. I've got a good job. I'll take real good care of her. You know I will."

John kept his head down while they walked in silence.

"What do you say, Jack?" Harry persisted. "Do we have your blessing?"

"When were you planning on getting married?"

Harry shrugged. "Alice and I haven't discussed it yet. Maybe this summer." Harry looked to his brother for support.

After a few moments, John stopped and stroked his thick moustache. "I tell you what, Harry. I think John F. is going to be proposing to Bridget soon. Bridget is older than Alice, and I'd hate for her to be the last one to get hitched. You see what I mean?"

Harry nodded.

"I'm looking forward to having you as a brother-in-law," John continued, "but I'd rather that you and Alice wait a bit. Give Bridget a chance at it. Meanwhile, save your money." As an afterthought, he added, "And don't say nothing to Alice about it, you hear? I don't want it getting out that you two got engaged before Bridget."

Harry nodded. "But when they do announce their engagement, it'll be all right with you? I mean, about me and Alice ..."

"Absolutely."

Harry laughed in relief. "That's fine. Thank you, Jack. I knew you'd come through. First round is on me."

When they were seated at a table with their pints, John relaxed in his chair. "Well, lads, I've my own bit of news for tonight."

"What's that, Jack? Ellen not pregnant again already, is she?"

"No, it's not good news. Not at all." He leaned forward onto the table. "Bad news, it is. I got the sack today."

"You what?" Jimmy almost choked on his beer. He wiped his mouth on his sleeve. "What happened, for Christ's sake? You've been at bloody Armour for years."

John nodded. "What happened was I threatened the wrong person. There's these kraut-heads up on the line where I work. Stupid bastards, especially this one, Emil. Can hardly speak English himself and all he does is make with the insults. All day long. Finally, today, I'd had enough, and I told him if he doesn't keep his yap shut, I'll do it for him."

John took a slug of his beer. "He's a big bastard, but I knew I could take him. He's with three of his buddies, so he thought he could get away with anything. He called me a dumb mick, and without wasting a breath, I clocked him. One, two, and down he was before he or his friends knew what happened."

"Jesus, Jack, who do you think you are? John L. Sullivan?" Harry was wide-eyed at the tale.

"Sullivan himself would have been proud of me. Anyway, next thing I know, I'm tapped on the shoulder by my supervisor and told to get my things. What for? For fighting instead of working, he tells me. And I told him, the dumb bozo's been running his mouth at me for weeks, but my boss says he don't care, I'm fired. What about him, I asked. That's when he told me. The stupid kraut-head is his brother-in-law."

"Shit!" Jimmy exclaimed. "You didn't know?"

"Never had any idea. You know me — I keep my head down. I don't take part in gossip. Got no use for it."

"And now you're out on your ass!" Harry said in disbelief.

"Oh, I ain't that worried. I know I'll find me another position in one of the other packinghouses. I'll go out Monday and be working by Tuesday, I'm sure. But I'm going to take a major cut in my wages."

"Aye," said Jimmy, "it'll be like starting all over again."

John nodded. "Only now I have a lot more mouths to feed."

Walking to church the following morning, Ellen carried Kitty while John minded the three older girls. Maggie was working at Bewley's Bakery. John was in a sour mood — his furrowed black eyebrows reminded Ellen of a raven's wings. He ignored her attempts at small talk. Later, she suggested he take the girls to the park while she prepared dinner. He tripped getting the pram down the stairs, and Ellen heard him swearing a blue streak. She had no idea what might have caused the black mood, but she knew that hounding him would only make it worse.

The next morning John left before sunrise, as he usually did. Everyone was surprised at 10 o'clock, when he reappeared.

"It's Daddy!" cried Josie, looking around to see if everyone heard her. Maggie and Ellen were in the living room sewing while the girls played with rag dolls Ellen had made for them.

"John, you gave me a start," Ellen said to her husband. "What brings you back home so soon? Is everything all right?"

"Aye, everything's right as rain. How about some tea? Then I'll tell you the news."

Despite his reassuring words, Ellen noticed he avoided meeting her eyes. "Maggie, dear. Put the kettle on, will you? And then, maybe take the girls into the bedroom to play."

"But you come back," he said. "I want you to hear the news as well."

Ellen checked on the sleeping Katherine, then sat down, her back straight, the cup and saucer balanced on her knee.

"Well," she said, stiffly. John saw her pursed lips, cheeks flushed above her set jaw. "We're waiting for your wonderful news. It is wonderful, isn't it? Why else would you leave work and be home before noon?"

John stared at her for a moment and sipped his tea. "You're braced for calamity, aren't you? Is that what you expect from me? After all of this," he said, spreading his arms, "that's what you expect? Calamity?"

"No need for sarcasm, John. It's plain that you're home with bad news. It's drained all your color. You look like death warmed over, you're so pale. So, out with it."

"I look that bad, do I? Maggie, do I look like death to you?"

"I don't know what to say, Johnny."

"Well," John continued, "there is a bit of bad news involved. Not a calamity, mind, but not exactly good news either. Certainly nothing any of us were hoping for. Still, it could be a lot worse." He glanced at Ellen and saw her glacial expression. "So, to get to it, I am now working for Swift and Company, starting tomorrow."

"Swift? What happened to Armour? John, what are you saying? Are you serious?"

"'Tis no joke, Ellen. No, no joke. There's nothing funny about getting the sack for standing up for one's rights."

"Sacked? You've been fired? From Armour?"

"But now newly employed at Swift."

"For how much less?" she shot back, her cheeks flaming red above her jutted jaw.

John slowly shook his head. "Oh, you are a clever lass, Ellen Powers. My God, you go right to the heart of the matter. No dancing around the bush with you."

Leaving

"How much less?" she demanded.

"It's $2," he told her dolefully.

"A month?"

John let out a heavy sigh. Silently, he leaned against the doorjamb, looking out the back door that led to the little wooden landing at the rear of their flat.

"I wish, my love. If it were only so. No, it's $2 a week — $8 a month."

"$8!" Ellen rose suddenly and the saucer fell to the floor and shattered. John remained motionless, head lowered, sucking at his moustache. He looked like an old, tired buffalo.

"My God, John, that's more than a week's wages. What are we to do? Things were tight on $6 a week, but now only $4? How do you expect us to manage on $4 a week?"

"All I've been doing since Saturday is fretting about it. We may ..."

"You've known since Saturday?"

"What I've known, Ellen, is that I got the damn boot for standing up to a foul-mouthed kraut-head. But I didn't want to tell you until I got another job. I didn't want to worry you."

"Ah, so now that you've told me, do we have good reason to worry? Now perhaps you'll tell me how we're to make do with $2 a week less. How're we going to pay our rent? Shop for food?"

"Ellen, I've got a job. We won't be out on the streets."

"But we will have to move, John. Surely that."

John sat down wearily. "Aye, probably that, yes."

"I can go to work," Maggie interrupted. "Instead of waiting for the summer vacation, I can look for a full-time job now. Another few months won't make any difference. I'm sure I can earn $2 or maybe $3 a week. Surely that would help?"

John and Ellen stole a look at each other. John pulled at his moustache with his lower lip.

Ellen nodded. "That's very good of you, Maggie. I hate to have you put an end to your schooling, but it does have the ring of common sense to it."

"So. Well." John slapped his hands on his thighs. "There, you see? Not so bad after all. And I'll be getting a raise in no time at all, I'm sure, once they've seen what I can do."

"I can start looking for a position tomorrow," said Maggie. "Would that be all right with you, Ellen?"

Ellen lowered her head and wiped her eyes. "I suppose, Maggie. Oh, God, what will I do without you?"

"You'll manage, Ellen," John said. "We'll all pitch in. Josie and Annie can help. And when Maggie and I are home from work, we'll do our bit. Right, lass?"

"Oh, of course, Johnny. I'll do everything I can. You know that."

"There, it's settled then. I'll go out this afternoon and look for a new apartment. You'll see, Ellen. We'll get through this."

Abruptly, Ellen stomped into the kitchen, holding her empty cup before her like a sacred offering. A moment later, John and Maggie heard the sharp clatter as it smashed into the sink — followed by a single brief sob. John looked at his sister and raised his eyebrows. A moment later, Ellen was back with a dustpan and broom to sweep up the shards of the broken saucer.

"Everything is always fine with you," she muttered angrily. "You're like a little boy — as long as you can go out carousing with your friends, getting into fights, no consideration for your family ..." Before they knew it, she was back in the kitchen.

John and Maggie froze in silence.

"I best be off to find our new apartment," John slunk toward the door. "I'll be home for dinner."

He kissed his sister on the cheek. "We'll be all right," he whispered. Then he winked at her. "Don't worry. Now, go to her. She needs you now."

At the end of June, they moved to a smaller flat two miles south, downwind of the stockyards. At 5144 South Carpenter, they were on the southern edge of Chicago, on the second floor of an older building not equipped with electricity or indoor toilets. The year was 1890, and the family had become accustomed to these luxuries; emptying chamber pots was a rude addition to Ellen's daily chores.

Their street, not half a block from the railroad tracks that carried livestock to the Yards, was unpaved and the wooden sidewalks were in disrepair. Mud and disappointment blanketed the flat, and Ellen was alternately lethargic, irritable, and short-tempered.

With no safe place for the girls to play, they felt suffocated in the hot, airless apartment. John left early for work, taking the trolley up Halstead Street. In spite of his earlier promises, he was too drained at night to do more than sit with the children on their equally tired sofa.

Maggie accepted a position as a live-in housemaid for a family on Lake Shore Drive, and she visited only one or two Sundays a month. Ellen took the loss very hard. It was, she said, like losing Sheila all over again. The girls, too, had become deeply attached to Maggie, and reacted to her absence with listless petulance.

In spite of the relief of one less mouth to feed, John missed his sister sorely, but kept his feelings to himself. Still, the tension served as another coal on the fire and made him more likely to flare up in response to Ellen's nagging.

"My mother didn't raise me to live like this," she yelled at John one night while she ironed. "Maybe you're used to living like shanty Irish, four to a bed and only cabbage and potatoes to eat, but you should be ashamed to have your own wife and daughters living like that."

John glowered silently, jaw clenched. He turned to face her as he walked toward the door. "And don't be taking it out on the girls. Don't be after them with your wooden spoons and potato mashers. You're their mother for God's sake. Try not to act like the devil himself."

Furious, Ellen flung the hot iron at him, but John slammed the door just in time and heard the heavy thunk as he fled.

Josie and Annie, now five and four, were assigned the cleaning and washing, but failed to attack their new duties with wholehearted enthusiasm. Ellen's temper, meant to spur their productivity, only increased their dawdling. John arrived home most nights to a raging battle among the gaggle of angry females. Once the girls were asleep in their crowded bedroom, he'd retreat once again.

"I can't breathe here," he'd say as he escaped the stifling atmosphere.

On the first Sunday in September, at a family picnic near Lake Michigan, Mr. John F. Powers proposed marriage to Bridget. The wedding was planned for the following spring. Amid the joyous mood, even John and Ellen relaxed together and played with the girls.

"Look how she won't stay still!" Ellen exclaimed about her five-month-old. "Kitty is so full of energy, she can't wait to grow up."

"And we can't wait for her to hurry up — we need her help with the laundry," said Josie, only half seriously. Everyone laughed.

"Don't worry," John reassured her, "it won't be long before I'll be getting a promotion and then we'll move out of that swamp we're living in."

"Now, Johnny, don't go getting the poor girls' hopes up," Ellen cautioned. "You're at Swifts only a couple of months. Even a good-looking brute like you won't get promoted that quickly."

"You'll see," said John seriously. "Just wait and see."

"Dreamer," she said dismissively, and turned to play with the girls.

Everyone's mood, like the weather, started to improve as they edged toward autumn. The temperature cooled and they slept more comfortably in the airless flat. John backed off on his drinking and pitched in more at night. Josie was thrilled to start school. Annie, bored without her older sister, became Mama's big girl, and took pride in doing her chores.

In the afternoon when Josie returned home, she couldn't wait to play school with Annie and Nellie, eager to show off what she had learned from the nuns. In the mornings, Annie would take over the role of teaching Nellie, and they were both learning to read with surprising rapidity.

Even the fall rains didn't take a toll. The muddy lane where they lived reminded John of his parents' cottage on the outskirts of Waterford and elicited in him a sad nostalgia.

"Sure, we didn't have sidewalks like we do here and like you enjoyed in Waterford proper," he mentioned wistfully once to Ellen, "but we were used to it and it had a charm about it."

She shook her head and dismissed his remark as the musings of an ignorant shanty Irishman. For her, it meant mud. Mud tracked in, making the floors filthy and slippery. Trying to keep the girls, their clothes, or the flat clean was a futile and thankless task.

"I don't understand you," she snapped. "You sound like you take pride in it."

In late October, Harry O'Hara proposed to Alice and they planned their wedding for the following year. The O'Haras made a party and it was the first time that the whole crowd was together since the September picnic in the park. With a neighbor watching the girls, Ellen dressed for the party.

"I can't remember the last time I felt like getting dressed up," she said to John. "We haven't been out, just the two of us, since ..."

"Since your birthday after Annie was born. You turned 26 and we went to that nice restaurant uptown."

"Yes, I remember," she smiled. "We had a wonderful time."
John helped her with her fastenings. "I'm sorry that we haven't been

able to go out since then."

She nodded. "I know. You've done your best. I don't blame you. I get annoyed with myself, too. Fine pioneer wife, I made. I can't even raise my own daughters properly."

"You can't help it if you've been ill. I know you'd like to be able to do more," he soothed her.

"If only we could afford some help ..."

"And move to a larger flat," he finished her thought, "with more windows and electricity and a toilet."

The both smiled.

"You'll see, Ellen. Things are going swell at work. All the foremen see how hard I work and what I'm capable of. It won't be long before I'm back on the inside and away from those stinking pens and making more money in the bargain."

Ellen ran her hand along his cheek. "I hope so. Your dream isn't that big. I know you deserve it."

"Ach, Ellen, you can't imagine what a sad, dirty job it is. Those poor animals; it's not like back home, say, at your grandfather's. There the animals are well cared for. They have a value. Some even have names. But here they're just shitting machines, and then chunks of red meat. The poor brawny beasts with their sad dumb eyes, all being led to slaughter. Sometimes I feel like an executioner. Sometimes I feel like one of them."

He remained pensive for a few moments. "I know this isn't your dream. Nor is it mine. But your mother wasn't the only one who didn't intend for you to live like this."

"Don't brood, John. It's not what either of us dreamed of. But I know it'll improve."

"Yes," he said, determined to make it so, "it will. Believe me. I know I can make it happen."

John embraced her buxom frame in his strong arms, feeling closer to her than he had in a long time. They remained that way for some moments, then she pulled away, blushing.

"Why, John Powers, one would think you're ready to enlarge our family."

"Aye," he said, showing his teeth. "At this moment, it sounds like a wonderful idea."

In November 1890, winter came early to Chicago, blowing down from Canada and hurtling across the lake. October's rain and mud turned first to icy slush, then to frozen ruts. Josie came down with a cough that quickly spread to everyone else in the household. John went to work anyway, afraid of losing his job if he failed to show up, but Ellen and the girls huddled in bed — or at the kitchen table, their faces shrouded by a towel over a bowl of steaming water.

The girls slowly improved, but Ellen's hacking cough persisted. Alice pitched in often and even Maggie got permission from her employers to help maintain the household. With Ellen still ill, they spent Thanksgiving by themselves, while the rest of John's family celebrated with the O'Haras.

The severe weather took its toll at the stockyards as well. Many men lost their jobs — and some even their lives — to influenza and pneumonia. In early December, John solemnly announced that he'd finally gotten his promotion.

"Starting in January, after the holidays, I'm to move inside," he told Ellen.

Familiar with her father's much smaller firm, Ellen was interested in the details of the huge, modern operation. In answer to her questions, John described the entire meat packing process — from organizing the animals in the vast outdoor pens, where he now labored, to herding the animals into the slaughterhouses. Two men took turns bludgeoning the cattle one by one with a single swing of a heavy sledgehammer. Then, when the animal's hind legs had been chained together, it was lifted up from the dirt floor. Their throats were slashed and their bodies dragged through a vat of scalding water.

Next, the animals were gutted — John's new job — then skinned. From there the chain conveyed the carcasses to the butchers, who quartered them. Other butchers farther along the line carved the quarters into steaks, roasts, and other cuts. Last, the meat was packaged and made ready for delivery.

"My new job will be the gutting," he said with some pride. "I slice open the carcass and pull out the guts. One has to be quick because the animal is being carried along on an overhead chain. You have to hurry back and start on the next carcass as soon as it appears at your position. And you have to be strong too, to lift heavy sacks of innards all day long."

Ellen grimaced at the thought.

"And the best part," John went on, "aside from being out of the freezing cold and away from all that manure and cow piss, I'll be making a dollar more a week. And that's just to start. There'll be more to come shortly. McManus, my new boss, as much as promised."

John's eyes sparkled as he smoothed his moustache and tugged at his braces.

"What a wonderful way to begin the new year," he beamed. "You'll see, 1891 will be a banner year for us. We'll save up some and, in spring, as soon as it warms a bit, we'll move to a better flat. Now tell me, Ellen, doesn't all that make you feel better? Doesn't it?"

3

1891

John started his new job in January. It was grueling work and he was huffing and puffing as he slit open the belly of one steer after another. After removing the sack holding the inner organs, he raced back to his station to start on the next steer. In the evenings he complained of a sore back after the strenuous 12-hour shift. But within a few weeks, his body had adjusted and he no longer felt the strain.

By mid-February, Mr. McManus told him that if he kept up the good work, in six months John could move to the quartering table — and earn 50 cents more a week. That evening, John rode the horse trolley down Halstead Street a happy man. When he entered the flat, shaking the fresh snow from his heavy coat, he greeted his family with a big smile.

"Where are all my princesses?"

"Momma, Da's home!" cried Josie, who had become Daddy's favorite since she started school. The first to reach his burly arms, she chirped, "Did you bring candy?"

"No, dumpling, but I've brought wonderful news."

"And what's that?" asked Ellen, wiping her hands as she emerged from the kitchen.

"McManus said I'm doing wonderful work and inside of six months I'll be on the quartering table."

"That's good news, is it?" She reached around Josie and pecked her husband on the cheek.

"Well, it is for me, not having to climb in and out of them cows all day long, getting all covered with their bloody muck. But the good news for you is that it's another 50 cents a week, another $2 a month. We're nearly back to where we were with Armour."

"Well," she said, "that is very welcome."

"Look, Ellen, we can't do anything in this awful weather, but in the spring, after the girls' birthdays are behind us, I'll find us a nicer place. I know the O'Hara boys will help us move. By June, July at the latest, we'll be out of here."

Ellen nodded. *Yes,* she thought, *it will happen.* But first she had to get through the birthdays: Annie's in another two weeks on the 27th of

February, both Kitty and Josie in March, and Nellie in May. She had promised each of the girls a small celebration. It wouldn't be much — maybe she'd bake a cake. Just the idea of it made her tired. She had been sewing something frilly and feminine for each of them, and she could do with a new dress for herself as well.

But John had made good on his promise; he was earning more and she was relieved at the prospect of a move. Perhaps to a street that was paved, a flat with electricity and an indoor toilet, a place for the girls to play outside, where they weren't in danger of being run over by horses or trains. Six more months. She could hold on that long. Maybe she would feel better by then. Maybe with spring, some of her energy would return.

She hugged her husband. "Oh, John. That would be grand. We'll all be so happy then, I know."

John took in his wife's smiling face. It wasn't often that he felt appreciated, and the visceral sensation surprised him. He returned her embrace.

"But wait, do I hear something?" He opened the door of the flat and reached down for the paper bag he'd left outside. "Why, it's a surprise! Some elves must have left it for the girls."

"What is it? Let me see!" the girls clamored.

Josie tore open the bag. "Cookies!" she shouted. "Mama, it's cookies."

"The elves brought cookies for us," squealed Annie. "Can we have one now?"

"Not now," Ellen chided. "You'll spoil your supper. We can all share them for dessert."

"Speaking of which," John said as he took off his hat and coat, "I'm so hungry I could eat a cow. What are we having tonight?"

"A nice stew," Ellen said. "The girls and I went shopping today and got some carrots, potatoes, onions, and a little beef. They helped me make the stew, didn't you, girls?"

"Mama let me cut the carrots," said Josie proudly.

"And I cut potatoes," Annie chimed in.

"And you, Nellie? What did you do? Tell your da," Ellen urged.

Little Nellie took her thumb out of her mouth. "I stirred the pot," she said, twirling her arm in a circle. "Like making mish mush."

"Well I'm very proud of you all, helping your mother make dinner. You'll make wonderful wives and mothers some day. Good job."

Josie turned six on March 25th and, a week later, the O'Haras and

John F. Powers helped them move back up Halstead to a sweet little cottage at 3738 Emerald Street. For the first time, they were renting a house all to themselves. No neighbors on the other side of the wall, or above — or worse, below them, complaining that the girls made too much noise running back and forth. They had electric lights and an indoor toilet — no more trudging to the outhouse through the rain and snow. A small yard offered a safe play area for the children, and paved streets and sidewalks allowed John an easy walk to work. It was paradise. The girls ran about, in and out the front and back doors, squealing with delight. Their own house!

Ellen beamed with pride and gratitude. She was in love again — a promise kept, and in such grand fashion: two cozy bedrooms, a kitchen and parlor and, of course, a bathroom. And windows on all sides let in the sun and fresh air. She'd be spending many evenings making curtains for all those windows, but she could not be happier.

"Oh, John. It's home! I feel it. We're home at last. Oh, I wish my sister could see it."

"Aye," he acknowledged, "it's a fine house. Well made, too. Anyone can see that. It's not a thatched hut, mind, but it'll do," he joked.

"Oh, you! All we need is a thatched hut, with the rain and vermin coming down on you at all hours."

"Mmmm," he said with a straight face, "I guess you do have a point."

"You're sure we can afford it?"

John arched his eyebrows. "It'll be a stretch, I admit, but at $12 a month, it's a bargain. I know the rent will go up next year, but by that time I'll be making more. We can do it, I'm sure. Don't worry, Ellen. It'll be all right."

"Well, it is lovely. It's not Youghal or Waterford, but it's home."

As March turned into April, Ellen worked on the curtains and John dug around the house to plant flowers and shrubs.

"It's grand to feel the dirt in my hands again, like at your grandfather's," he said, wiping the sweat with a muddy hand.

"If only we had a tree so we could make a swing for the girls," Ellen mused. "It would be perfect."

"Aye, well, maybe we can plant one."

"Sure," she said, "but the girls will be grown up by the time the tree is big enough."

"Perhaps," he smiled, "but there's always grandchildren."

"My goodness, John, don't go rushing me into old age. I'm getting there quick enough on my own."

"They'll grow up quickly, Ellen. That time will be here before you know it."

"Enough, John. I told you, I don't want to hear any more about old age."

John shrugged his shoulders and busied himself on the other side of the house. *She's right,* he thought. *She is old before her time; 31 and always exhausted. Too tired to enjoy anything, too tired for sex or a bit of fun. And that damned hacking cough! Jesus, it's been months. When the hell will it stop? And always complaining how much more she has to do now with a house to take care of — because she doesn't want the neighbors thinking we're shanty Irish. Is nothing good enough for her? And now she wants a damned swing and a fully grown tree! Jesus!*

While Josie was at school, Annie tried her best to become her mother's favorite. Five years old now, she could anticipate Ellen's needs and always offered to help with cleaning and cooking or taking care of Nellie and Kitty, now a toddler needing constant attention. Still, as hard as Annie tried, it seemed there was always something left undone or not done well enough. Exasperated, Ellen would fix her with wide, blazing eyes, hard-set lips, and an insulting rebuke. Annie took out her frustration on Nellie, who in turn began to assert herself. The resulting screaming and crying only put Ellen in a rage directed at both of them.

Little Kitty, on the other hand was a beautiful child with a sweet disposition. Always in a good humor, she rarely cried, and everyone in the family adored her.

In May, when Nellie turned three, John and Ellen made a little party. They invited some of their new neighbors as well as all of John's sisters, including Bridget and John F. Powers, whose wedding was set for the following month.

Alice, of course, brought Harry O'Hara, who invited his brothers Jimmy and Ed.

Bridget took charge as usual, and Maggie and Mary dedicated themselves to carrying out her orders in the kitchen. Ellen sat on a chair in the back yard, her beautiful dark red hair piled up on her head. With a new parasol protecting her from the spring sun, she was surprised to find herself feeling as her mother might have: the lady of the house surrounded by guests enjoying themselves, with servants (or at least sisters-in-law) keeping the party humming smoothly. Of course, their one-story frame house paled in comparison to her parents' large stone home on St. Thomas Hill in Waterford, with its fine gardens and carriage house — and it was no comparison at all with her grandfather's estate in Youghal. Still, it was a fine day and she was relaxed and happy.

John had filled the washtub with a block of ice to chill the soda pop for the children and the women. He and the other men had staked out their positions around the keg of beer, staying close at hand when a re-fill was needed. The children squirmed through the barricade of bodies for a bottle of pop, but lemonade was easily available on the table with the spread of food. A decorated birthday cake from Bewley's Bakery adorned the table, and a few bottles of Irish whiskey were stashed away to ensure a constant flow. *Ah,* thought all the men in unison, *it will be a grand birthday party indeed.*

The men talked of the current president, Benjamin Harrison, who had defeated Grover Cleveland, the popular Democrat, the year before. No one was impressed with Harrison's big spending. They talked of Jack the Ripper, who had terrorized London in 1888 and was referred to in a recent newspaper article about a series of rapes that had taken place in Back of the Yards, a section of Chicago just south of the stockyards that provided cheap living quarters for the mostly immigrant laborers. They bemoaned their long workdays: the 12-hour shifts, six days a week, for 8 to 12 cents an hour. True, talk of raises and modernization made the rounds, and it was rumored that some jobs paid over 30 cents an hour.

But despite the backbreaking, stinking work, the men were grateful. They all felt lucky to be living east of Halstead Street and not having to make due in the Back of the Yards section, which they considered a filthy swamp. Immigrants from all over Europe were crowded amid the unpaved streets, often living 10 to a room. Hardly anyone spoke decent English, and the children roamed the dirty sidewalks instead of attending school.

"I see a wide range of living conditions on my route delivering milk and eggs," John F. told the others. "This is much nicer over here. You were lucky, Jack, to find such a fine house to rent for $12 a month. Further north, closer to Union Station, this would fetch almost $15."

Lamenting the high cost of living, Ed O'Hara mentioned he aspired to get into the meat purveying business.

"I've been saving up for it," he said proudly. "In a couple of years, if my two zany brothers can keep from squandering their wages, we might have enough to get started."

"Aye," said John F., "I'd love to have my own business, too. I'd make twice what I'm making now, doing the same work. But it's so damn hard to save anything. The cost of everything is so dear, just to get by."

"And that's not even counting the cost of whiskey," said Jimmy with a sly grin.

Summer came suddenly. When the winds shifted, the foul stench of the Yards and heavy smoke from the coal plants hovered in the air, coating everything with fine dust. Ellen cleaned constantly, dusting furniture and washing the white lace curtains. At least the girls didn't have to play on muddy roads, and most of the time the prevailing breeze kept the smells and soot to the south.

John moved to the quartering table in June. With his pay raise — to almost 10 1/2 cents an hour — he was bringing home a full $7.50 a week.

The working conditions were a great improvement as well: He could stand up straight instead of hunching over to step in and out of the carcasses. He had to be quick with his knife and, with all the blood, it could be slippery and dangerous, but with practice he became focused and sure. If his skills got sloppy or careless, he recalled how his father had died: an accident on the job in spite of years of experience. That was enough to refocus on the work at hand.

Now less tired at the end of the day, he enjoyed the walk home in the warm breeze and relaxed with Ellen and the girls in the evening. Kitty began to talk, and Ellen proudly informed him of the new words she picked up every day. Not only was Annie playing teacher with her during the day while Josie was in school, but Nellie too was taking credit for Kitty's rapid verbal development.

After supper, John often puttered around the flowerbeds. Ellen didn't participate, claiming that her skin was too fair to be in the sun during the day and, by evening, she was too exhausted. But Josie, Annie, and Nellie went outside with their father, ostensibly to help but primarily to run around, oblivious to the heat.

In contrast, Ellen complained about the sultry weather. Despite windows on every side of the house, the cross ventilation didn't help.

"It's so stifling in here," she complained. "I can't bear to be touched," she would say to no one in particular.

But John received the message.

"Maybe we should move to Canada," he'd suggest, and she wasn't sure if he was joking or not.

In August, John got moved farther down the line. His new task was to separate a quarter of beef into four sections. Speed was essential and careful execution was even more crucial than before. When he got home that evening, he was all smiles.

"Well, lasses, we did it. We did it!" he announced, setting his lunch pail on the table.

"We did what?" Ellen asked. John hoisted her up and whirled her around.

"John, what are you doing? Put me down. Are you daft? You're squeezing the life out of me!"

"Well, then, I'll just have to pump you up again with some good news," he suggested, setting her down. "Not two months on the job and yet another promotion."

"Promotion?"

"Aye, and a raise, too."

"What? Another raise already? From those skinflints? You're joking, sure," Ellen shook her head in amazement.

"I'd never joke about such a thing. No, I'm serious. My boss informed me at lunch break today. He came up to me while I was leaning against the wall outside and asked me if I liked my work. I told him it's a damned sight better than pushing blood and guts around all day. So he mentioned that he's seen I'm handy with a knife and would I like to move down the line to sectioning. Well, I wasn't sure what that would mean. He saw I was wary, so he gives me a knowing smile and tells me there'd be an extra penny an hour in it for me."

He paused, to let the news sink in.

"Quick as a flash," he went on excitedly, "I'm doing sums in my head. Another penny an hour means another 72 cents a week. I'd be up to $8.64 a week, just about $35 a month. $35 a month! So I told him I'd love to have a go at it. And he says fine, I'm to start Monday. Can you believe it, Ellen? I'll be making more money than ever before and we have our house, too. Oh, things are looking up, sweetheart. Ain't life grand?"

Ellen was stunned.

"My goodness," was all she could say. "What a surprise. What a wonderful surprise."

"I've been thinking, Ellen, maybe we can begin to put a little away," John said thoughtfully. "You know, save a bit. Maybe just a dollar a month, so we'd have something in reserve if we should need it."

At first she felt disappointed and resentful, as if a gift had been given, and then suddenly taken away — she'd already imagined things she could buy for the house and the girls. But she soon realized that it was a wise and responsible thing to do. Of the five extra dollars a month, they probably should save two. If they saved $2 a month, she'd still have $3 extra.

"That's an excellent thought," she told John. "In fact, we should save $2 a month — that'd be 50 cents a week. We'll still be ahead and we'd have something in case of an emergency. After all, you never know."

"Exactly, my thoughts," John agreed.

The girls came in from the yard and clamored for his attention, which he freely gave. "How're my smart little beauties?" he beamed. "Glad to see your Da?"

While Ellen and the two oldest girls finished preparing dinner and setting the table, a thought crossed her mind: *Now, with an extra $3 a month and Kitty over a year old, perhaps it's time to have a try at giving John the son he's dying for.*

The older girls were capable of helping out more around the house, and the extra money might even pay for someone to come in now and then. Ellen had made herself unavailable to John for some time, and he had been very patient with her. She smiled to herself as she pictured the surprised look on his face when she'd approach him later that night. The thought almost made her burst out laughing, and she was delighted to discover how excited she was by the prospect.

In early September, Josie and Annie traipsed off together to Nativity Blessed Virgin Mary Catholic School. Annie was happy as a lark to share in her sister's privilege of attending school.

John was even happier. For weeks now, Ellen had rediscovered her enjoyment of lovemaking — and she was confident that this time her pregnancy would produce his wished-for son. Maybe it was the private bedroom in their own house, or the excitement of making a boy. Or maybe it was the cooler weather, or the freedom from financial worry. Whatever the reason, John was all smiles and good humor.

Ellen too, was more relaxed, free from the anxiety that putting John off might have disastrous consequences. She'd never worried that he would beat her or take up with another woman, as so many husbands did, but that he might take to hanging out in saloons, drinking up his pay. Mostly, though, she feared he would stop loving her, that they both would end up bitter and lonely. Now they reveled in their newfound warmth together.

One Saturday that autumn, Ellen took the girls on the horse-drawn trolley to downtown Chicago, where the big department stores towered above. Josie and Annie were thrilled to see the buildings soaring skyward. Amid the rushing throngs of people, horses, and carriages, just crossing a street was difficult. In Montgomery Ward, Ellen bought rubber boots to cover the girls' shoes when they walked to school in winter, and a pair of heavy boots for John. The total cost came to more than the $2 saved from the previous month, so there would be no more purchases. Scolding herself, she vowed to be more disciplined in the future. Still, they couldn't resist the allure of window-shopping. Ellen gazed with envy at the dazzling array: corsets, plumed hats, high-laced leather shoes, kitchen gadgets. The abundance reminded Ellen of her mother's home in Waterford — the fine linen tablecloths and napkins, silverware and trays, tea sets with delicate little cups and saucers, dessert plates, candlesticks. Thoughts of home made her feel sad, and she decided to write her mother and sister a letter at her first opportunity.

On the way home, the girls whined when Ellen admitted she couldn't afford to buy them the penny candy she had promised. "Don't be greedy now," she scolded. "You've got your new overshoes, after all."

That Sunday, John and the O'Hara boys rode with John F. in his milk wagon out to the country south of the city. There they spent the day cutting wood for the coming winter. Of course, the men brought a bottle with them, so it was not all work. When they got back, each man took his share of the wood. John piled it up in their small, unfinished cellar so no one could steal it.

September 1891

Dearest Mother,

I hope this letter finds you and Father well. I was so glad to hear that Father has retired, allowing Timothy his chance to show he is no longer a frivolous playboy. Timothy has involved himself with the business ever since he was a small boy and deserves the chance to prove that he can run the company competently. Of course, now that Timothy is married and to be a father himself, Father must have realized it is time for a new generation to take over. Who would have thought that our

Timmy would finally settle down, marry, and become a father? Irene is a lucky woman. I remember the Tighe family, of course, and wish them all well. I wish I could have been there for the wedding. I'm sure she was a beautiful bride and was thrilled at having a fine, big wedding at St. Michael's with all of the family there — except for me, of course.

Yes, it is painful. I must admit that whenever I think of it — of Father sending me away — it still hurts. It hurts that he won't write to me or accept that John and I are married! My God (forgive me), I have four wonderful daughters he's never seen — and you have never seen! The man is stubborn and, from my point of view, rather cruel and unjust, at least as far as I'm concerned. I used to feel so close to him. Evidently he gives no thought to me at all. Well, enough of that. I apologize for letting my emotions get the better of me.

Here is my bit of news: I am sure I will soon be pregnant again; this time, I have no doubt it will be a son. Wouldn't it be wonderful if, now that Da is retired, the two of you could come for a visit? Would it be possible? Think of it — taking a steamship across the Atlantic Ocean to New York and then traveling by train to Chicago. The voyage has improved so much since John and I traveled here in '84. Chicago has wonderful first-class hotels and restaurants that are even finer than those in Dublin. I'm sure the two of you would have a wonderful time. Chicago is such a modern city. You would be amazed. Please think about it and do your best to persuade Father.

I feel quite certain that I'll be giving birth by June of next year at the latest. Of course I'll write to you when I know, but please think of next fall as the best time to visit. Summer is insufferably hot and winter bitterly cold (I've told you about the astounding snowfalls and blizzards we are often subjected to). Autumn, on the other hand, is such a lovely time of year here in the American Midwest. All the leaves on the trees change their colors and the air is brisk. It is quite comfortable and healthy for sleeping. It would be a perfect time to see your grandson and your four granddaughters, who will be yet another year older. Maybe you could even stay for the holidays?

Yesterday I took all four girls downtown to buy Johanna (Josie) and Anna new outfits and shoes and boots. The clothing styles being shown in the stores are quite lovely. I've never seen such hats and materials. I did get a few necessities for John and myself. Even though John is doing so well (having recently received his second promotion within two months!!), we still can't afford all we need or would want. Everything is so expensive and, of course, John isn't earning what Father did.

Josie is quite the little lady and helped me so much yesterday with Nellie and Kitty. She excels at school and the sisters are always praising her. She is such a delight. Anna is also doing well at school, but is frequently in conflict with the nuns. Despite almost daily discipline, she loves school and does well. It's just that she is so headstrong and willful! She always wants to do things her own way. I have the same problem with her at home. She insists on helping with Nellie and the baby, but refuses to do as I tell her. John encourages her, of course. He is too lenient by half with the girls, letting them have their way and encouraging them to make their own decisions. Anna takes advantage of him, but he can't find it in himself to give her the discipline she needs. I, of course, have to make up for it, doing double duty, so to speak. So Anna and I often clash.

The baby is the easiest of them all, although she is frail and often suffers with a sniffle or cough. Kitty has the sweetest disposition and loves to cuddle. Everyone is in competition to hold her and play with her. She is such a ray of sunshine.

Please write more often, Mother. I miss you terribly and devour your letters when they come.

Your loving daughter,
Ellen Powers

September 1891

Dearest Sheila,

How I miss you! I was shocked to learn of your miscarriage. I hope you have fully recovered. I know how painful it must have been. You will remember I went through that myself during my crossing into exile. Of course, I was glad to know that your entire family was around you at the time. I am glad that you didn't have to undergo that frightening experience alone. And, of course, you have young Robert, too.

I must tell you straight away that I am sure to become pregnant again soon. John and I are trying for a son (and I'm enjoying the process, so there is no need to tell you that John is as happy as a clam!). My hope is that I'll be giving birth around June of next year. I just wrote to Mother and asked her and Father to visit us next fall, now that he is retired. Perhaps you could come with them and bring Robert. Please do what you can to persuade them.

My cough remains as annoying as ever, but I am certain that I do not have consumption, as you feared. Although I have some congestion in my lungs and am often weak and fatigued, I have never coughed or spit up any blood — and that is the main symptom! I am quite sure, as there are many individuals here who suffer from it. And all of them have that pale, washed-out, colorless look of the half-dead. With my fair and rosy complexion, I am the picture of health. I certainly do not look half-starved. So please don't worry. I am sure that it is only an allergy that I will outgrow soon enough. Please don't give it another thought; and of course, there's no need to worry Ma and Da about it ...

Ellen finished the letter, bringing her sister up to date on the progress of the girls and the inconveniences of living in a tiny house on a tight budget. She sat back after reading both letters again. Would she ever be able to forgive her father for sending her away in shame, banishing her from the family and the only world she knew? She imagined him on a visit to Chicago, gushing over a grandson and begging her forgiveness (maybe even shedding a few tears of shame and remorse). A smile of satisfaction brightened her face as she pictured his cheeks wet with tears, eyes reddened, lips quivering in repentant sobs.

The nights grew chillier and by mid-October it was almost dark when John returned home from the packing plant. Even in the dim light, he noticed that the flowers in the meager bed around the house had died from the cold and neglect. The vignette matched his dark mood. In a rare moment of carelessness, he had badly cut himself, almost severing his thumb. The accident was long overdue; most of the other men on the line were missing parts of fingers. The dangerous work was made more precarious by the slick conditions from blood and sweat and ever-increasing demand for speed.

The damage to his thumb, a severed tendon, would require several weeks to heal. Thankfully, because he was such a good worker, his supervisor gave him a job pushing carts, instead of turning him out onto the streets. The bad news was that he would endure a severe pay cut — five cents an hour, a full $3.60 a week — for the duration of his time off the line.

Ellen was instantly alarmed when John entered the house with his hand bandaged and his arm in a sling. First thinking he might have been in a drunken brawl or attacked by the gang of rowdies who preyed on the immigrants around the Yards, she took his news stoically, realizing how much worse the situation could have been. She was silently relieved to have already bought the rubber boots for the girls — there would be no extras for the next few weeks at least.

But her heart sank when she realized that Christmas was just two months away. In the face of another Christmas with stingy gifts for the girls, an image from her childhood flashed through her mind: pretty wrapping paper, colored ribbons and bows, and the family gathered around her parents' large dining room table laden with food and fine china and silver. She shot a glance at the square wooden table looking lonely and forlorn in her modest kitchen, the same table she and John had bought for their first flat. Poverty! She didn't deserve it!

But she bit her lip. "It'll be all right, John. We'll make do. We've been through worse." Then after a few moments, "At least your thumb will be saved."

"And don't forget my job," he added. "Damn, I'm so disgusted with myself! Just a moment's lapse, and yet everything is affected by it. Our whole lives hang by my thumb. It doesn't seem fair. It ain't right, Ellen. It ain't bloody right."

"I know," she agreed. "Is there anything I can do for you? Will you be needing clean bandages?"

"The doctor at work said he'd look at it in another week or so. At least we won't have to pay for a doctor's fee."

"But they're cutting your wages."

"Aye," he said, stroking his moustache, "there is that."

"Well," she said haltingly, "perhaps this is not the best time to tell you ..."

"What?" he asked sharply, "not more bad news?"

"Not bad news at all," she said plainly. "We're going to have a son."

He looked at her in amazement — surprise and joy mixed with wonder. How could she already know it would be a boy? "You're sure? I mean that you're pregnant?"

"Of course I'm sure. After five pregnancies, I ought to know when I'm pregnant."

"Of course. I only meant — and a boy, you said?"

"Oh, I'm sure of it," she nodded. "I just know it. I'll be shocked if it turns out to be another girl. But in my heart, I just know it. I've never been so sure of anything."

"When?" he asked.

"Near the end of June is as close as I can figure."

He drew her to him with his good arm. "Good," he said, nodding for emphasis, "by then we'll be well back on our feet. June will be good. It'll all work out. Christmas will be skimpy again this year, but by June we'll be sitting pretty. This is great news! We'll have to let my sisters know. They'll be so happy for us."

October 1891

Dear Ellen,

I was so happy to receive your letter and to hear the wonderful news of your expected pregnancy. Though, in spite of your certainty, no good will come of counting your chicks before they are hatched. Let us wait and see what happens. I pray, of course, that your wish comes true and that all will go well. But so many things can happen, as you well know, and there is no need to tempt fate.

I won't even broach the subject of a trip to America to your father until the circumstances dictate that it will be wise. At this point, he will only say no, and then it will be impossible to persuade him otherwise. You know how he can be. So we shall wait — and if you do in fact deliver another grandchild next year, that will be the time to broach the subject. Also, by then he might be more comfortable with Timothy running the business. Right now, he gets himself into a stew almost daily, fretting about what mistake in judgment Timothy might make that will bring financial ruin and disgrace to us all.

We will also have to mind how our health is, your father's and mine. His joints stiffen up in the damp weather — of which God makes sure we have plenty — and he suffers from time to time with gout. I know he won't agree to travel if he's in pain. And though I'm well at the moment, I have been suffering from hot flashes that make sleep absolutely impossible. Our comforter is on, is off, is on again. There is no end to it; though probably not as difficult to endure as your chronic cough. Do you still have it? Are you sure it's not TB (dreadful word)? I worry so about you.

Thank you for telling me about the girls. I would very much like to see them. Your suggestion for a visit next year is a delightful one, but as I said, we shall have to bide our time and see. I know your father wouldn't want me to go alone and I couldn't leave him here with no one to look after him. And, our poor Sheila! Robert would never agree to go and would forbid Sheila from going without him, with or without little Bobby.

I hesitate to mention, for you have so much on your mind already, but Sheila's marriage has not turned out to be a good one. We had great hopes for Robert. He comes from such a fine family and he receives a significant allowance from them. However, he squanders it on horses and women and carousing. It is no secret. Sheila holds her head up, but spends most of the time hiding in her house, ashamed to be seen. There is nothing she can do. He threatens to keep young Bobby if she should leave him, and she couldn't bear to be separated from the child.

Your father is fit to be tied and would murder Robert if he could get away with it. Please do not let Sheila know that I told you. She is horribly embarrassed and wouldn't want you to worry about her. I don't know what possessed me to write it down, but having done so — oh well, perhaps you have a right to know. Besides, I'm angry myself and tired of keeping this secret. I feel so sorry for that poor, sweet girl. Why couldn't she have a loving husband like you and I have? I must go.

Your loving mother

Bridget and John F. Powers hosted Thanksgiving dinner — held on a Sunday, because all the men had to work on Thursday — and announced that they were expecting their first child. Ellen and John made their announcement as well, and everyone toasted the two Mrs. Powers.

Gracious hosts, John F. and Bridget served a fine dinner of turkey with potatoes and a variety of vegetables and breads. Each of the women contributed; Ellen made three pies. The girls were delighted to see all of their aunts again. Sixteen-year-old Mary was now working as a cook for the Yacht Club on Lake Michigan and they rarely saw her; thus, the reunion for her and her siblings was especially important. The men made sure there were enough beverages to go around: soda pop and cider for the women and children and beer and Irish whiskey for the men.

"You and Bridget wasted no time, I see," John said to his brother-in-law.

The tall man grinned without removing his pipe from his mouth. "And congratulations, yourself," he answered. "How's the hand coming along?"

"To tell you the truth, Mr. Powers, I'm not sure if it'll ever be as good as new," John admitted. "It's still bound up by this cast, but the doc said it'd come off by Christmas. Then we'll see."

"Will you be going back to your old job on the line?" asked Jimmy, wiping froth from his lips.

"Lord, I hope so," John shook his head. "It's been a nightmare trying to get along on a nickel an hour less. Thank God Ellen knows how to stretch my wages and keep us from starving to death. It's been porridge and potatoes and cabbage soup and day-old bread 'til it's coming out my ears. Truth is, I need to get back on the line as soon as I can."

Jimmy nodded gravely. "Aye, it's tough all right. My brother Ed is going through the mill as well. He's determined to go into business on his own as soon as he can and he won't let poor Janet spend a penny if they don't have to. He knows it's tough on her, but he wants the three of us brothers to open a business by next year. He's got Harry and me pinching every penny as well. Says we all have to save up so we'll have enough to invest and carry us through for the first couple of months until things get under way."

Harry nodded assent. "Between my brother and my fiancée always hounding me, I feel like I'm in prison. I can't even spend two cents on the trolley — I have to walk everywhere so I can save for the business and our wedding. Oh, did I mention? We've decided on a June wedding, June fifth, 1892."

"God willing, Ellen won't deliver early," John said thoughtfully. "She's due around the end of the month, she thinks."

"Well," said Harry, swallowing some Irish, "Alice has talked to Ellen and Bridget and got it coordinated."

"And they say it's a man's world," quipped Jimmy.

"Did I understand Bridget to say she was due the beginning of April?" asked John.

John F. drew on his pipe. "Yes. Hopefully, it won't be an April Fool's joke."

"And you, John F.," said Jimmy, "does your wife have you scrimping like the rest of us poor lads? Saving up for a rainy day? Not two pennies for a glass of beer now and then?"

"Aye, it's what we've decided. As soon as I can afford my own horse and wagon, I can go into business for myself."

"And when might that be?" inquired Jimmy.

John F. shrugged and puffed on his pipe before answering. "I'd like to have it all settled before the baby comes," he said. "Then, I'd be assured of all the milk and eggs we'd need. It would be a good life — and secure."

John sensed his brother-in-law sneaking a glance his way. His heart sank. Did John F. think his job at the packing plant was not secure? Had he and Bridget been talking about him? Was everyone concerned about his ability to support his own family? He surveyed the men while draining his glass, but didn't detect any hidden feelings. *Still,* he thought, *if this damned thumb doesn't heal right, will I be able to keep up with the work on the sectioning table? Will McManus keep the job open for me as he said he would?*

"Here — give me that a moment," he said to Harry, taking the bottle of Irish from him and refilling his empty glass.

"Go on, Jack, help yourself. There's plenty, right lads?"

The talk turned to other subjects, but John's mood was ruined. He fell gloomily silent, listening as the others told jokes and stories while he drowned his sense of doom.

The women, too, had segregated themselves. Alice, who had worked briefly as a barmaid in St. Louis, was the only woman among them who had a taste for beer. At 19, she was enjoying herself immensely, singing snatches of old songs from home and doing a bit of step-dancing, which she attempted to teach to Josie, Annie, and Nellie.

"Look at her," said Bridget proudly. "She's so happy. I wish my ma were here to see her, to see us all. She'd rest in peace then, knowing we're all making our way."

Ellen mentioned that she had invited her parents to come the following fall, when the baby would be a few months old and the weather comfortable.

"They'll be coming, then?" Bridget asked.

"I'm hoping for it, but I don't know. My da invented stubbornness. He still hasn't forgiven John and me for running off like we did. But I'm praying for it."

Bridget raised an eyebrow involuntarily, then busied herself arranging the food.

Ellen nodded. She had so often told the lie — that she and John had chosen to run off and get married — that she'd momentarily forgotten: Her sisters-in-law knew she'd been pregnant and had been sent away by her father. *How stupid I am,* she flushed in embarrassment. *Well, no harm done. Bridget knows what I meant.*

"Well, I hope you get your wish," Bridget came to her rescue. "I'd give anything if our parents could be here. At least yours are still among the living, so there's always hope, isn't there?"

Mary, who considered her day off from work a miracle, luxuriated in playing with Ellen's girls. Ellen watched her wistfully. *When was the last time the hard-working 16-year-old had an opportunity to play? When indeed did I? Coming up on 32 — I'll soon be a mother of five and already feel like an old woman, like I could be their granny.*

The O'Haras arrived at the gathering — Janet cradling a bag of apples and Ed holding two large pumpkin pies. "I hope my dear brothers have left me something to quench my thirst," he shouted to the men.

"Sorry, but God helps those who help themselves," Jimmy shouted back.

"Nothing but the dregs for the likes of you," added Harry, who was already becoming a little glassy-eyed.

"How's the hand coming along?" Ed asked John as Jimmy handed him a glass of beer.

"It's coming," John said sourly.

"Well, then, I'm sorry I asked. I didn't mean to offend you straight off, now did I?"

"Ach, don't mind the old sourpuss," Harry put in.

"And what the hell do you know about it?" John glared at him. "You try feeding your family on the pittance I'm making. You think this is funny?" He thrust his bandaged hand in Harry's face.

"Relax, Jack, he didn't mean nothing by it. Was just joking, that's all," said Jimmy, trying to soothe his old friend.

"Ah, screw the lot of ya," John spat, walking over to where his girls were playing.

The O'Haras looked at each other. "What's that all about?" Ed asked.

John F. looked up from his pipe. "He's worried about going back on the line. You know how they push the production. He hasn't used that thumb in a month. If I were him, I'd be a bit touchy, too. And I don't know that I'd be putting too much faith in a boss's promise about my job."

Jimmy took his bottle of Irish and followed John to where he stood watching his girls. "Here, Jack. Have a drink." John poured some into his glass and handed it back. "Harry didn't mean nothing, Jack. We all know you're worried about your job."

John turned to look at him. "It's nice to know I'm a subject of conversation — that my friends have nothing better to do than talk about me behind my back."

"Jack, it ain't like that."

"Ain't it? You telling me that all of you haven't been speculating about my chances of getting my old job back?" Jimmy stared at him, wide-eyed. "Don't start lying to me, Jimmy."

"We're concerned for you, is all. We know you'll make it. You got a rough deal. Any of us would be worried if we were in such a tight fix."

John spoke quietly, but his eyes burned into Jimmy's. "Do you have any idea how humiliating it is? Here, I'm a grown man. Married. Four children and a fifth on the way. We've got a sweet little house with a garden — and I'm not making much more than I made back in '85." He paused. "And what happens if I can't use this bloody thumb like I did before? What happens if McManus gives me the boot? Are Ellen and me supposed to give it all up? Go back to that swamp? I tell you, Jimmy, I don't know if Ellen would make it. Hell, I don't have a bloody idea what either of us would do." He took a swallow, and looked away.

"Look, Jack, you're the most determined son of a bitch I know. You'll make it work. I know you. It'll come out all right in the end, one way or another." He waited for a moment, putting his hand on his friend's shoulder. "Come on back with the lads. Let's enjoy ourselves. It'll be all right."

John took a deep breath. "I will. Just give me a minute."

"You'll come?"

John glowered at him. "I said I would."

Before John could tear himself away from watching his girls play, he saw Ellen walking toward him.

"Is anything the matter, John?"

He shook his head.

"You look upset. I was wondering if your hand is bothering you, if there is something I could get for you."

He shook his head again and drank from his glass. "Nah, I'm fine. Just fine and dandy."

"Then why so angry? Look at me, John. What happened? It's not like you to be standing all alone, separate from your friends."

"Nothing. Really, it's just them talking, is all."

"Talking?"

"About my accident. Apparently, I'm a grand topic of conversation. Will John Powers be able to do the job on the line? Will he be able to get his old job back? Will he be able to put food on the table for his wife and children?"

Ellen had heard the same concern from his sisters. Young Bridget had offered eggs and milk. Mary, too, said she might provide some leftovers from her job in the Lake Michigan Yacht Club kitchen. Grateful for their willingness to help, Ellen feared John would be insulted by their offers. She clutched his arm and squeezed it.

"We're better off having friends who care than not having them," she suggested tentatively, "even if it feels a little embarrassing sometimes."

He nodded glumly. "I guess. Well, I'll be getting back to them then."

For the first time, he saw the lines of concern on her face. "Don't worry. I'll be fine." He leaned over and gave her a kiss. "I love you," he said, then saluted her with his empty glass. "Got to go."

The weather turned sharply colder. Fortunately, the snowfall was less than in past years, but the harsh, unrelenting wind blew through

every crack in the little house. By mid-December, the family had already used up most of the firewood John had collected, and they would soon need to buy coal to heat their home. Cheap as it was, coal was an additional expense.

Though his thumb was still in a cast, John sensed it was healing and his mood lightened. Ellen accepted help from Bridget and Mary without letting John know. "I'm a good wife, John," she reassured him, "I know where to shop for bargains and how to make a penny serve as two."

Ellen took delight in all the signs of her baby growing inside her, but because of her plumpness, it was difficult for others to notice the swelling of her belly and breasts. Morning sickness was just one more inconvenience to endure. Nellie helped her with Kitty, and the two youngest girls grew closer. Annie, however, became increasingly competitive with Josie. Unable to dislodge Josie from her pedestal, she took her frustration out on Nellie in both verbal and physical attacks.

John made sure to remind Mr. McManus that his hand was healing and he'd be back on the line "good as new." He badgered the doctor to remove the cast the week before Christmas, then begged McManus to be returned to the line.

"Give me the chance to bring the kiddies something for Christmas," he pleaded, but McManus was firm. Just before Christmas, it wouldn't be fair to dismiss the man who had filled in for him.

"I have sympathy for you, Jack, but it just ain't right and I'll hear no more about it. Christmas is a week away. The Monday after Christmas, the 28th, is when you'll come back — and you better get up to speed quick. I'll not be cutting you too much slack."

John was only mildly disappointed — he hadn't really expected to get his old job back immediately. Mostly, he was relieved to know he'd get his job back after all, and in less than two weeks' time. This was joyous news. Knowing he'd soon be earning his old wages, he would ask to borrow a couple of dollars from the O'Haras for Christmas gifts for Ellen and the girls.

But first, the visit to the doctor. The old man removed the cast that encased his thumb and extended up his forearm. He washed it, turned it this way and that, and pronounced John fit to return to his old job.

Thank God, thought John. *No more starvation wages, no more demeaning job of pushing the waste cart as if I were an imbecile. Now I'll be able to take some pride in what I'm doing.*

The O'Hara men came through for him. On Christmas Eve, John

left the packinghouse and traipsed up Halstead Street through a light snow in search of gifts. He arrived home two hours late for dinner, carrying packages and a scrawny tree. With the girls already in bed, he and Ellen put up the tree and arranged the packages underneath.

Dismissing her annoyance at John's late arrival, Ellen warmed to the spirit of the evening and felt overwhelmed by the basic goodness of the man she'd married. If only her father had been more understanding, he would have been proud of his son-in-law. She was sure of it. Instead, everyone lost out: her, John, the girls, and her parents. Well, maybe next fall her father would have a change of heart and insist they all return to Waterford with him. Maybe it was just a dream, but why couldn't it be possible? The hope lifted her up. She felt buoyant and expansive, filled with love for everyone: for John, her girls — even her wonderful parents who would make her dreams come true.

John had to work on Christmas day — animals slaughtered; meat butchered, packed, and shipped to make room for a new delivery of livestock, to keep the cycle in a state of perpetual motion. But since the bosses wanted to be home with their families too, it would be a relatively short day. John expected to be home an hour or so earlier than usual; Bridget had planned a potluck get-together at the house, and he was looking forward to seeing the family again.

The girls were speechless when they awoke to find the tree with wrapped presents beneath it. It had been years since they'd had a Christmas tree, and Josie was the only one who even remembered. No one had expected the presents — matching mittens and scarves: purple for Josie, red for Annie, blue for Nellie, and pink for Kitty. Ellen received a beautiful scarf with matching gloves. She was astonished — how had John managed this? Where had he gotten the money? She thought he'd turned over every cent of his wages to her and she knew he would never borrow. Her pleasure was diminished by a quick stab of suspicion that John had been holding out on her. It was the first thing she asked when he returned from work on Christmas Day.

"Ellen, don't fret so. It's not a big mystery," he reassured her. "I borrowed a couple of dollars from the O'Haras. I'll be back on my old job come Monday. Back on my old wages, I'll pay the lads off quick enough. I couldn't do nothing for Christmas, now could I? After all we've been through these past two months? You've done a marvelous job stretching to make ends meet. I had to do something. Don't you see that?"

Relieved, Ellen saw his point of view. "Well, we'll pay them off right away, then. We don't want your friends to think poorly of us, do we?"

"I knew you'd see the right of it."

"I'm just surprised, is all. I mean, knowing how proud you are and so much against being in debt to anyone."

"Well, it's only the lads, isn't it? It's not like I went to strangers with my hat in my hand. The O'Haras are like family."

"I agree with you. I'm glad you've got the sense to do what's necessary. It's just that I didn't think you would agree to it."

"Agree to what?"

Her face flushed and she marched off to the kitchen, flustered.

"What?" he yelled at her back. Receiving no answer, he followed her. "What are you talking about? Did you borrow money?"

"No. I would never do that. Certainly not without asking you beforehand."

"Then what?"

Cornered in the kitchen, Ellen became defiant. "Only this: If I had known that you approved of taking help from family, I would have told you, instead of trying to protect your stubborn foolish pride."

"Now you're married to a stubborn fool, is that it?"

Ellen glared at him, her cheeks flaming and jaw set.

"So what is it you haven't told me?" he demanded. "What are you keeping from me?"

"Just that your sisters wanted to help us out this past month."

"What are you talking about? How could my sisters help us out? Which sisters?"

"Bridget and Mary. It's nothing, really, John. I'm sorry I flared up. I never meant to say anything about it."

"Well, you've started something. You can't stop now. Come on, damn it, tell me what your poor husband has been too stubborn and too stupid to understand."

"Oh, John, I didn't mean that. It was just my temper talking."

"Out with it, goddamn it. Tell me now."

Ellen felt herself shrinking in size — or was it that John had become inflated? He loomed over her, his big brush of a moustache and glaring black eyes so close to her face. "Only that Bridget and Mary have been giving us some food, is all. Nothing much really — a few eggs, some leftovers from the Yacht Club. I didn't want to ..."

"My sisters gave us food? And you didn't tell me? Who knows? Does everybody know that we've been living on handouts from my little sisters? Jesus Christ, Ellen, have you no shame? No sense at all? Oh, God in heaven, what have you done? And you complain about my borrowing a couple of dollars from my friends to buy Christmas presents? Jesus!"

"John, calm down. No harm was done. Bridget just wanted to make sure the girls had their milk and eggs, that's all. Nothing really. She told me there was no need for John F. to know. And Mary just brought us some leftover vegetables a few times. John, it's all right," she tried to soothe him. "It's family, like you said. They're not strangers. How could I say no to your sisters if it was for our girls? It was just like you said, how could I not have done it? It wasn't wrong, John. Not for either of us."

In the pause that followed, in the space of a second or two, John sensed the silence around him. The girls weren't making a peep. The air itself stood still and the only sound he heard was his own breathing. He saw the glistening in his wife's eyes and realized how frightened she was. Then he felt the stiffness in his own body, his fists and jaw clenched. Stepping back, he turned away and took a deep breath. When he spoke, his voice was barely audible.

"That's all that it was, you say? Some milk, a few eggs, some left-overs?'

"Aye, John, and only a couple of times, nothing really."

"And no one knows?" He turned to face her. "No one thinks we're the poor relations living on the dole?"

"Oh God, John, not at all. No one knows except your good sisters, your own blood."

"All right, then. But next time, you ask me first, agreed?"

"Of course, John." Ellen went to him and they embraced. After a moment, she suggested they get ready to go to Bridget's. "We don't want to be late, now, do we?"

They had a wonderful time at Bridget and John F.'s home that evening. All of John's sisters were there, except for Mary, who had to work at the Yacht Club. At one point, John approached Bridget.

"Ellen told me how you helped out with some milk and eggs for our girls during this past month. I just wanted to express my appreciation."

"Oh, it was nothing, John. I'm glad we could help."

"We? Does John F. know about it?"

Bridget shook her head and smiled. "Johnny, this is a family matter, between a sister and her brother. Mr. Powers doesn't have to know everything that goes on in our family, now does he?"

At six o'clock that Monday morning, John reported for work on the sectioning table. He had been massaging and exercising his thumb since the cast had been removed, and he was confident he could do the job. Still, he took the precaution of putting some adhesive tape over the area to provide an extra element of protection, just in case.

The first day was exhausting — partly due to the pace of the work itself, but mostly because of the fear of cutting himself again. He worked deliberately, with focused attention, instead of flowing along with his usual conviction. But by the second day, when he had regained some confidence and stamina, he smiled easily when the boss came by to inspect.

"Ach, McManus, sir, it's sure good to be home again." McManus smiled and waved, and John knew all was well.

Thursday night was New Year's Eve, but John and all the lads had to work on New Year's Day, so they agreed to celebrate on Saturday night instead. Everyone pitched in as usual with the food and drinks. This time, Ed O'Hara played host, and his tiny house was filled with noise and excitement. The wood-burning stove was going full blast and everyone was warm inside and out. When the children tired early, they were piled on Ed and Janet's bed along with everyone's coats.

"I can't tell you lads how great it feels to have that dirty thing off my arm," John announced, "and to have the use of this ugly thumb again. Did I say ugly? I mean beautiful. I never knew I had such beautiful thumbs."

"We're relieved for you, Jack," said Jimmy, "but I ain't surprised. I knew you'd pull through."

"I should take your word in all things now, is that it, Jimmy? You're now the high priest of prognostication?"

"I could have told you that a long time ago," Jimmy countered, "but you were too stubborn to listen."

"Me, stubborn?" John looked around at his friends in mock protest. "Me? Saint John himself who the birds come and sing to? Me, stubborn?"

"You're thinking of St. Francis," said John F. "Birds would only visit you to shit on your head."

Everyone laughed and John joined in.

"I guess there's some truth in that, all right. During these past two months, I've felt like that's all that was happening. But '92 will be different, you'll see. This year, lads, we'll have a couple of new babies," he saluted John F. with his glass, "and another wedding — a joining of the O'Hara and the Powers families." They all toasted Harry and Alice.

"And hopefully, the opening of O'Hara Brothers Purveyors of Fine Meats," Ed chimed in.

"Really?" asked John. "The three of you have actually gone and done it? Saved enough money to quit your jobs and start up a business?"

"If all goes as planned, we hope to open up a shop on Halstead by July first, right after my baby brother marries your sister. Alice will be marrying up, John. She'll be marrying a businessman."

John shook his finger in Ed's face in mock scolding. "Now I absolutely won't hear of my sister marrying a Republican. You lads will have to stay voting Democrats. We have to put Cleveland back in the White House come November."

"Don't worry, Jack. We'll always be the common people. No damned Republicans under our roof."

"Of course," said Ed, "they'll be welcome to spend their money in our store." Ed turned to John F. "And how about you, Mr. Powers? How are your plans coming along for getting your own horse and wagon?"

John F. puffed on his pipe and reluctantly allowed a thin smile to find its way to his face. "Well, lads, I didn't want to put a jinx on it by speaking too soon — but, since you ask, I'll tell you. I think it's looking pretty good that sometime this year, I'll be able to swing it. I don't want to rush into it and end up failing for lack of sufficient funds. Bridget and me, we'll take our time. But to be honest, I can almost taste it. It's that sure."

"Well, congratulations to the lot of you," said John. "Between babies and marriages and good fortune, this will indeed be one hell of a year."

4

1892

J anuary and February were freezing cold. The wind was relentless and the drifting snow frequently made the streets unpassable. On days when the children were unable to make their way through the deeply piled snow to get to school, they passed the days at home pleasantly — except for when Annie challenged Josie's authority or picked on Nellie for being "stupid." Then the three erupted into screeching fights, which drove Ellen to distraction.

No matter how deep the snow, the men did not miss work. Even though John was earning his former wage, it seemed to disappear in smoke as the bitter weather feasted on the coal. In her attempt to limit the consumption, Ellen and the girls huddled under layers of clothing. Cold and miserable, Ellen yearned desperately for the healing warmth of springtime.

And sickness was rampant. One girl would bring it home and two days later everybody would be coughing and sneezing. Ellen felt as if her whole life consisted of wiping runny noses. Her own cough never abated, and she was perpetually tired and irritable. Meanwhile, the baby inside her continued to grow.

With money so tight, John spent Saturday nights and Sundays helping Ellen with chores and nursing the children back to health. Soon, even he felt the corrosive effects of the long, dark winter.

By the end of February, Ellen was six months pregnant. Annie turned six on the 27th and, for just one month, would be the same age as Josie. She took advantage of her new status to challenge her sister at every turn, demanding the same privileges and responsibilities.

"I'm six years old too," she declared, adopting the same bug-eyed face and arms-akimbo stance that her mother made when she was threatening punishment. Ellen grew weary of mediating these battles and often turned a deaf ear, retreating into the bedroom with Kitty in her arms and the admonition that she was not to be disturbed. There she would lie on the bed with her baby (soon to be two years old) and let the older girls work it out on their own.

Sometimes, John arrived home to a darkened house, with Ellen and Kitty still in bed while the three older girls waited gloomily for their mother to emerge from her retreat and make supper. At first, John was angry. Dinner not ready? The girls unsupervised? After a while he became resigned to it, and told Josie and Annie to help him prepare the food. Eventually, Ellen would materialize and drag herself through the motions, apologizing and attempting to excuse her negligence. Feeling defensive and anticipating a scolding from her husband, she would pre-emptively snipe until the two fell into a row. When one of the girls started crying, they'd sink into an edgy, sulky silence.

The arrival of March brought some improvement in the weather. The snow gave way to rain and wind, but the temperature was more bearable. High drifts and icy ruts were replaced by deep, slippery slush and mud. Fortunately, their street was paved with cobblestones, unlike those in the "swamps" farther south of the stockyards, and their rubber overshoes serviced them quite well. The days gradually lengthened and, in spite of frequent storms, the weak sunlight elicited hopes of spring. When they could, the girls trudged outside, and Ellen was glad to have them out from underfoot. Yet, in spite of the respite, her listlessness grew. Both she and John attributed it to her pregnancy, and predicted that her strength would return after she gave birth.

Then everything took a turn for the worse.

On the morning of March 15th — the day before Kitty's birthday — as John dressed for work he heard Ellen call to him from the bed. "John, something's wrong!"

"What is it?" he asked, slipping his suspenders over his long-sleeved undershirt. "What's wrong? Is it the baby?"

"No, I don't think so. It's just … I've got a terrible pain, as though someone is stabbing me in the chest. I can't move."

"Is it something you ate?" he asked, recalling the cabbage soup they'd eaten for supper the night before. "Could it be gas, do you think?"

"I don't know. Maybe. But I can't move."

"I'm not sure what you're saying, Ellen. Does it hurt you to move? Does it make the pain worse?"

"No, John, I can't move! It's like I'm paralyzed. I can't turn over. I can't move my arm."

"Maybe you need to rest, stay in bed a little longer."

"Yes," she said, "maybe that will do it. But I'll need Josie and Annie to help with Katherine and Nellie. Wake them and tell them they're to stay home and help me today."

John frowned. His two oldest really enjoyed school and he hated to keep them home. It was clear that Ellen was becoming more and more dependent upon them, and shunting her own responsibilities onto them annoyed him. If it wasn't one complaint, it was another. The memory of his young, vibrant wife was fading into a dismal fog. He could hardly recall that pretty colleen he first met 10 years ago. Now, though Ellen was only 32, he sometimes felt as if that young beauty had been only a dream, a figment of his youthful imagination — as misty and unreachable as Ireland itself.

John wasn't sure what to do. Ellen knew he had to go to work. Did she expect him to stay home and look after her and the children? What was the matter with the woman? All this complaining and lying about. He never would have thought her a lazy person — and yet, here she was, always trying to get out of doing her job. It wasn't right. He opened the door to the girls' room.

"Josie, Annie, get up now. Come on. Don't lollygag. I have to go to work and your mother needs you to help with Nellie and Kitty."

"But, Da, what about school?"

"There's no school for you today. You have to stay home. Maybe you can go tomorrow."

"But the sisters will be angry if we don't come. They don't like us to miss even a day unless we're really sick."

"Say you're sick, then. I'm telling you, you're to get up now and help your mother. She's not feeling well and I've got to go. I can't be late." With that he put on his coat and hat, picked up his lunch pail, and left the house.

Josie made a face and looked at her sister lying on the other side of the bed, the two younger ones in between them.

Annie blinked. "Sister's gonna rap us good."

Josie shrugged. "Won't be the first time," she sighed, and went to her mother's room. She found Ellen trying to get out of the bed, her face in an awful grimace.

"Da said we were to stay home today to help you."

Ellen collapsed onto her pillow. "That's right. I'm going to need you and Annie to help me."

"You want me to help you get up?"

"No, not just now. I've got to rest a bit first. For now, you and Annie get dressed and make yourselves something to eat. And when Nellie and Kitty wake up, get them washed and dressed and feed them some porridge."

"Are you sure you want us both to stay home all day? The sisters get really angry if we're absent for no good reason."

"No good reason?" Ellen cried. "How dare you speak to me that way, Josie! You know I wouldn't keep you from school unless it was truly necessary. I don't know what's wrong with me. It's like I'm paralyzed. Maybe it'll pass and I'll be up and about as good as new in a while. But right now, I need the both of you here. Understand?"

The rest of that day, until their father came home, Josie and Annie took care of themselves, their two little sisters, and their mother. Once the girls became resigned to the fact that they would miss the whole day of school, they began to enjoy the independence. True, their mother told them what to do and how and when, but the actual doing was entirely under their control. That was exhilarating.

Ellen tried valiantly to get up, but the gas pains never relented, nor did the extreme weakness or numbness.

When John arrived home, he saw that the situation hadn't changed since that morning. After being greeted by his four daughters, he went in to see Ellen, the girls trailing in his wake.

"Still in bed, I see," he said as he picked up Kitty.

Ellen looked from John to the girls and back again, but he didn't catch the hint. "Girls, go and set the table now. I want to talk to your father."

John put Kitty down and sent her scurrying along with the others. He closed the door behind them, then sat on the edge of their bed, taking Ellen's hand. "What's the matter, Ellen? Haven't you been up at all today?"

She shook her head. "John, I'm so frightened. I don't feel myself at all. Something's powerfully wrong. I think you should get the doctor."

"Bad as all that? How about the priest while I'm at it?"

"John, please. I'm not joking. I know how you feel about them, being quacks and lying money-grubbers and all, but I'm really frightened. Please, something's wrong. I'm in terrible pain and I can't move. I've been dizzy and nauseous all day and I can hardly breathe. The girls had to bring me our old chamber pot. I couldn't even get up to pee."

John sucked at his moustache with his lower lip. "Do you really think that old quack can actually do anything to earn his fee? It'll be at least a dollar and a half, plus whatever snake oil he wants to push down your throat. I mean, do you really think he can help?"

"Please, John, I wouldn't ask if I wasn't feeling desperate. Some of the other women say he's been helpful. Not everyone thinks he's a quack. Some swear by him. Please, put your stubbornness aside for once and do this for me. I've never asked before."

John acknowledged what she was saying. He knew he was being stubborn and stingy, not wanting to part with his pay. Truth was, he was worried about her and had been the whole day. He had hoped it was only gas pains or some minor discomfort with the baby, but now he saw that it was not so simple.

"All right," he said, "I'll go get him now. You and the girls go ahead and eat. I'll be back as soon as I can."

"Don't worry about dinner. I have no appetite as it is and the girls have been marvelous. They've done absolutely everything. I'm so proud of them. They're little women."

He kissed her, then wiped some strands of red hair from her damp forehead before leaving the room.

The four girls were in the kitchen, huddled around the stove. "Who's been tending the fire?" he asked.

"Me," said Josie. Then, looking at the expression of indignation on her sister's face, she quickly added, "Me and Annie been doing it all day."

"We took turns putting in the coal. Ma said not to put in too much."

"Your mother says you've been doing an amazing job and I'm very proud of you both. Now, I've got to go and find old Dr. Kattman, so you girls will have to be in charge for a while longer until I get back." They solemnly indicated that they understood their responsibility and were up to it.

"Have you girls eaten yet?"

"Not yet. Mama said to wait for you."

"Well, go ahead and have your supper. See if your mother wants for anything. I'll be back with Dr. Kattman as quick as I can, but it'll probably be a little while."

John headed toward Halstead Street, where the doctor had his office. Racing along the dark street, he was breathless by the time he bounded up the porch and entered the doctor's waiting room. Mrs. Kattman, who served as the nurse and receptionist, came in from another room.

"I'm sorry," she said, "but office hours are over. Doctor is getting ready to make his home visits."

"Just what I need. It's my wife. She's very ill, been unable to get out of bed all day. She's paralyzed, and dizzy and in pain."

"I'm sorry ..."

"And she's six months pregnant with our son. Please, we're very frightened."

Mrs. Kattman studied his face for a moment then began sorting some papers on her desk.

"Please, I can't go home without knowing that the doctor will be coming to see her. She's in a bad way and not naturally a complainer, if you know what I mean."

The old woman looked up at him again. "Where do you live?" she asked.

"Around the corner, 3768 South Emerald. It's not even three blocks. Won't take him but a minute to get there." He saw her hesitation, glancing toward the back of the house, where the old man was getting his rig ready.

"I'll pay, you know," he added. "I've got a good job at the Yards. I'll make it worth his while." He could tell she was reconsidering. "He could make it his first stop and then be on his way. Please."

"All right. I'll give the doctor your address, Mister ..."

"Powers, ma'am. John Powers, and my wife is Ellen Powers."

She assured him that the doctor would be there as soon as possible, adding pointedly that his fee for house calls was $2. He should pay the doctor directly at the end of his call.

Barely 10 minutes had passed when John returned home.

"Didn't you bring the doctor?" Ellen asked, fear in her eyes.

"He'll be coming shortly. He's getting his rig together. His wife said he'd make it his very first stop."

"You didn't talk to him directly?"

"No, but I gave all the information to her. She said she'd see to it. Don't worry, now. He'll be here before you know it."

As John supervised the girls and checked in on Ellen, he kept an eye on the front door, waiting for the doctor's knock. Each passing minute seemed like an hour.

"I thought you said he'd make it his first stop! Didn't even talk to him, probably doesn't think it's important, can't count on you to do anything, don't care what happens to me ..." John endured her scolding every time he passed the bedroom door.

The girls had just begun to eat their potatoes and gravy when they heard footsteps approaching. John opened the door before the doctor could knock. "Thank God you're here, Doctor. We were afraid you might not come."

"Mr. Powers?"

"Yes, please come in. My wife is just in here, in the bedroom." He took the doctor's hat and coat. "Right in here, Dr. Kattman."

The doctor sat on the edge of the bed, taking a moment to assess the situation. He withdrew a stethoscope from his black bag, placed it on her chest, and listened intently. He addressed her softly. Pains? Yes, mostly in the chest. Weakness? Yes. Fatigue? Yes. Nausea? Yes.

"And I'm unable to move my whole left side," she added woefully.

The doctor nodded silently. He inquired about her pregnancy and general health, then took a small bottle of white pills from his bag.

"May I please have a glass of water for your wife, Mr. Powers," he said without turning. John hurried from the room to fetch the glass. Annie and Josie, who had been in the doorway, scurried back to the kitchen table.

"Mrs. Powers, I want you to take this pill. Here, swallow it with the water. That's right. Now, I want you to take one pill every four hours until I see you again tomorrow evening. Understood?" Ellen nodded. "Good. Mr. Powers, your wife is a very sick woman. She has a heart condition, and the pregnancy makes her heart work extra hard. She must have complete rest. Understand? Complete rest."

"Her heart?" John whispered, but not so quietly that Dr. Kattman did not hear.

"There is no doubt, Mr. Powers. Your wife is suffering from heart failure." He saw fear and disbelief in Ellen's eyes. "Your heart is quite weak, Mrs. Powers. You've suffered a mild attack. The pills will relieve the pain and bring you some comfort, and may prevent further attacks. But I insist that you remain in bed and avoid straining yourself."

"But, Doctor," John pleaded, "she's only 32 years old! How can she be suffering from a weak heart?"

He shrugged. "Maybe a childhood illness, maybe your wife was born with a weak heart. God knows how or why. I only know what I see and hear." He closed his bag and stood up abruptly. "Now, I must hurry along." He caught John's eye. "My hat and coat and ... ahem ..."

"Yes, sir, of course." He looked at the doorway where Josie and Annie lingered. "Fetch the doctor's hat and coat, girls."

They scampered to do his bidding while John went to the dresser drawer where he and Ellen kept their money. He withdrew two dollar bills and held them out for the doctor.

"I shall be back tomorrow evening, Mr. Powers," and to Ellen, "remember, complete bed rest." She nodded mutely.

After the doctor left, John returned to the bedroom, shaking his head.

"John," said Ellen, "did you hear what the doctor said? I've got heart failure. Me. I'm 32 years old and he's saying my heart is giving out. How can that be?"

John sighed as he sat on the bed. The girls, once again, stood in the doorway. This time he beckoned to them with a nod of his head and they gathered around him. Kitty and Nellie climbed up onto the bed and nestled against their mother.

"I've been trying to figure out what we can do," he said. "Maybe one of my sisters can come and take care of you ...? Bridget is the only one who isn't working. Perhaps I can go over there tonight and ask her to come tomorrow, so the girls can go back to school."

"Oh, John, I hate to be a bother to them. She's got her hands full helping John F. with his milk route and she's almost due herself. They both get up so early in the morning, I hate to ..."

"Ellen, you heard the doctor. He insisted — complete bed rest."

She tried to move and was surprised to find that she now had more control of her body. She pushed herself up into a sitting position.

"Complete bed rest!" she cried. "Whoever heard of such a thing? A mother with four children and a husband who works 12 hours a day? He can't be serious. I'm sure I'll be fine. I'm better already. These pills are all I need."

"Don't be so damn proud," John admonished her. "You're not fine and you know it."

Annie couldn't contain herself any longer. "Are you going to die, Ma?"

"Die? Me? No, honey, I'm too stubborn to die. Don't worry yourselves. You'll see — tomorrow morning I'll be up like usual, yelling at you to get yourselves ready for school."

"Don't go counting on it," John warned. "I'm going over to Bridget's now to see if she can come over tomorrow to help out."

"John, don't. Please ..."

"There's no way around it, Ellen. At least for tomorrow. Otherwise, it's the girls doing everything themselves. Do you want them missing school?"

"I'm sure it won't be necessary. See? I can move. And there's no more pain."

"I'm sorry, Ellen. I'm not a fan of that old quack, but he seemed to know what he was talking about. And, as you yourself point out, the medicine he gave you has worked." Suddenly he realized that the doctor hadn't charged him for the medicine — which made him respect the doctor even more. "That proves he knows what he's talking about. And that means you're staying in bed — at least for tomorrow."

He put on his hat and coat, pausing near the stove to dunk a piece of bread into the soupy mix.

"I'll be back in a couple of hours. Girls, take care of your ma and the babies, then get yourselves to bed. Josie, listen for your mother in case she needs you."

On Halstead Street, John waited for a trolley to take him south, then he walked the mile in the dark to John F.'s house. Ellen was right, of course. Bridget and John F. kept farmer's hours and they might already be asleep. *Besides,* he thought, *Bridget is due to deliver within three weeks or so herself. Can I really ask this of her? I know full well how much she helps John F. prepare for his morning route. Ah, if only it had been simple gas pains. Or a pulled muscle, maybe, from lifting the girls or a basket of laundry. Or maybe it was the baby. Funny, the doctor barely paid any attention to the fact that she was pregnant, only referring to it after he'd made his diagnosis. Probably is a quack. Heart failure. How could that be? And even if it was — which is ridiculous in the first place — how could he know? Taking her pulse? Listening to her breathe with that stethoscope?*

He passed by the shabby apartment where he and Ellen had lived, with the falling-down outhouse and no electricity. A light spring rain started as he walked west to his sister's house; by the time he arrived, he was soaked through and chilled. John F. and Bridget lived in a small bungalow, with only a single step to their front door. A light was on inside. John knocked and heard John F.'s footsteps approach from the inside.

"My God, Jack, what are you doing here so late? What's wrong?"

"May I come in, John?"

"Of course, man — come in, you're soaked."

"It just started up when I got off the trolley," he said as he entered the small front room. Bridget emerged from their bedroom, her hair down and brushed, wearing a heavy robe.

"Johnny, what's the matter? Why are you here so late? My goodness, you're sopping wet."

"Aye, Bridget. It's a heavy mist outside."

John F. went to the stove and stirred up the fire, adding a bit more coal.

"What brings you out on such a night? Something must be wrong. Is it Ellen?" she asked. "Is it the baby?"

"Aye," he said as John F. brought a chair from the kitchen. They waited for John to continue. "I hate to ask, it probably being nothing at all, but the doctor ..."

"You've had the doctor?" asked Bridget, knowing of her brother's disdain for the entire profession. *Ghouls,* he'd called them.

"Yes, I fetched him this evening. Ellen's been in bed all day. The two older girls stayed home from school to take care of her and the babies."

Babies, he thought. At two and four, not quite babies anymore — especially with a new one on the way.

"The doctor said she has a bad heart. *Heart failure,* he called it. He gave her some pills. She said she's feeling a bit better — she can at least sit up now and move her arms and such."

Bridget turned to her husband with a look of fright.

"Will she be all right, then?" asked John F.

John shrugged. He became aware he was still wearing his hat and coat, and stood up to remove them.

"I don't know," he slowly replied. "The doctor said he'd come again tomorrow evening. Until then, he said she should have complete bed rest. He doesn't want her to exert herself at all." He let the words hang in the dimness of the room, which suddenly felt claustrophobic.

"I want to help," Bridget said. "Do you want me to go back with you tonight?"

"Oh, no — God, I hadn't even thought of that. I just hoped that maybe you could come tomorrow morning to look after her and the two little ones. I hate to see Annie and Josie missing more school and having to take care of everything on their own. And I can't miss work, not after what happened with my thumb. It'd be out the door for me, I've no doubt."

Bridget looked questioningly at her husband, who nodded grimly. "You can go after we get the wagon loaded. I can take you to Halstead before I start my route."

"Are the trolleys running that early?" she asked.

The two men looked at each other.

"They don't start until six o'clock in the morning," said John. "What time would you be leaving here?"

"Not later than five," said John F. He put his hands on his knees and sighed. "I guess," he said, looking to his wife, "we might get an earlier start. Then I could bring you all the way up to their house."

"Then, that's what we'll do," Bridget agreed. She turned to her brother. "It's settled then, Jack. I'll be there about five o'clock to get

110

the two oldest girls off to school, then I'll look after Ellen and Nellie and Kitty."

John lowered his head and let out a long sigh of relief. To his complete amazement, his eyes filled up with tears. He started to say *thank you,* but the words caught in his throat and he began to sob. His sister leaned over to him, but he waved her away.

"I don't know what's come over me," he finally managed to say.

John F. got up to find his pipe. Bridget put her arms around her brother.

"It's just that ... I didn't even want to ask for your help. Ellen insisted that she'll be fine by morning, with the pills and all. I didn't want to impose on you."

"I know, Johnny. But we're family. We're all we've got. We've no mum and da now, do we? Just each other. Everything will be fine, now. You'll see. I'll be there in the morning even if Ellen's as fit as a fiddle. It's no bother for John and me. We're glad to do it. I'd not have it any other way."

Nodding, he smoothed his moustache then stood to embrace his sister. John F. returned to the room, drawing resolutely on his pipe.

"It's all set, then, is it? We'll be there before the sun rises."

John nodded. "I should be going if I'm to make the last trolley."

Bridget fetched her brother's hat and coat and accompanied him to the door.

"Thank you again, both of you," he said at the door.

John F. dismissed it with a wave of his hand. "We'll see you in the morning," was all he said. Bridget gave her brother a final embrace and John stepped out into the dark, steady drizzle. Walking toward Halstead Street, he felt lighter, relieved, and realized how worried he had been.

Everything will be all right now, he thought to himself. *Everything will sort itself out. It'll all be fine and dandy by this time tomorrow night.*

As he approached Halstead, he saw the lamps on the horse-drawn trolley racing northward. There was no way to catch it. *Damn!* Three or four miles would take at least an hour in this weather. He hunched his shoulders against the increasing rain and began the long trek.

There were no sidewalks this far south, and walking through the mud was slippery and arduous. It was in the early hours of the morning when John finally stepped into his dark house. With everyone asleep, he made an extra effort to be quiet as he removed his wet coat. His work clothes were soaked through, so he draped them over chairs in the kitchen and placed his shoes under the stove. He added some more coal to the fire, hoping that everything would be dry in the morning. Still wearing his damp long johns, he crept into the bedroom and saw

111

Josie snuggled up in bed with her mother. Her arm lay protectively across Ellen's pregnant belly, as if giving comfort to her new brother-to-be as well.

Six years old, he thought, *and already the little mama.*

He found himself some dry underwear in a pile of unfolded laundry and silently withdrew from the room. He would sleep on the small sofa, rather than wake Josie and send her back to the bed she shared with the three other girls. Throwing a blanket over himself, he closed his eyes and surrendered to fatigue. The tension began to ebb. Tomorrow, he told himself, Ellen will be better.

He dreamt of home, of Waterford: the thatched hut along the River Suir, the smell of burning peat, the chatter of his sisters throughout the house, his mother scolding them for ignoring their chores, the sound of a horse clip-clopping by. Was he still dreaming? Was it the iceman? The turfman with his wagon full of dried peat? The milkman?

John awoke with a start. Bridget was already coming up the front walk. The sky was beginning to turn from black to blue. He threw back the blanket and hurried to the kitchen to retrieve his trousers. Still damp, but they'd have to do. He'd just pulled the suspenders over his shoulders when he heard Bridget stepping onto their small front stoop. He rushed to open the front door before she knocked.

"They're all still asleep," he whispered. Bridget nodded. John waved to his brother-in-law as he turned his wagon back south to his milk route.

"When do you have to leave for work?" she asked him.

"What time is it?"

"Just a little after five," she answered.

"Not for another half hour. That's when Josie and Annie get up. The big one's in there with her ma. I'm not sure who's watching over who."

Bridget smiled. "Why don't you get yourself ready while I put breakfast together?"

He nodded and strode off to the bathroom, once again thankful for indoor plumbing. After washing and shaving, he returned to the kitchen, where his sister was heating water for tea and porridge. He was glad for the warmth of the stove to ease the morning chill, but wondered briefly if his sister was a mite too generous with the coal. He rummaged in the icebox and took out a hunk of cheese and an apple, and added a piece of bread for his lunch.

"You start on your tea and I'll go wake the girls," Bridget said.

He smiled absentmindedly at Annie's whining complaint when Bridget nudged her awake. Then his sister went to the front bedroom to wake Josie. He was sipping his tea, thinking of his brother-in-law's fine horse and wagon, when he heard her call.

"John!" Bridget shouted. "Come quickly! Now!"

Out of his chair in one fluid motion, he froze in the bedroom doorway. His sister was standing over Ellen. Josie was sitting up in bed, rubbing her eyes. Even in the dimness of the early morning light, he saw the cold, bluish white of Ellen's face, like marble in moonlight.

John lifted Josie out of the bed and set her on the floor, where she passively followed Bridget back to her own bedroom.

John waited for them to leave the room. He touched Ellen's lifeless face and felt its cold stiffness. How? When? How long had his little girl lain in bed with her dead mother beside her? How long had he slept in the next room with her here, dead in her own bed? Had she been alive when he came home last night? Had Josie fallen asleep next to a mother already dead? He thought of the baby — his son! —and put his ear to Ellen's belly. There was no sound. No gurgles, no thump-thump of a heartbeat.

He stroked her stiff, lifeless face in disbelief. Stricken, he sank into the bed, the life leaking out of him too. He shook his head in despair. Nothing made sense. His head was a jumble. He had no thoughts, no bearings.

Bridget returned and he was only vaguely aware of the girls standing in the doorway behind her.

"John," said Bridget, "you must fetch the doctor. And the priest. John, do you hear me?"

"Aye, the doctor and the priest." After a moment, he raised his head. "Bridget, it's Katherine's birthday."

Bridget swallowed. "Don't worry about that now. I'll tend to the children. Go." She gently helped him to a standing position. "Get moving," she said softly. "There'll be lots to do."

John let himself be steered out of the house. He took a few steps, stopped, and looked around. Suddenly he felt very alone. Dawn was breaking and the eastern sky was lightening in a soft array of delicate pinks and lilacs and oranges. He shook his head and glanced around to get his bearings. *The doctor,* he reminded himself, and set off in that direction. *And the priest.*

"Oh my God!" he exclaimed out loud, halting in mid-stride. "Work.

I've got to let McManus know I can't come in." A sense of urgency pierced his numbness.

Arriving at Dr. Kattman's house, he noticed a light on in the kitchen at the rear of the house. He went around back and knocked lightly on the door. A young woman, the cook, answered the door. "Yes?"

John was afraid that he'd lost control over his mouth, and it took him a moment to muster the physical strength to make his lips and tongue move.

"It's my wife," he began. "I need the doctor to come. He saw her last night. He came to our house. My name is Powers, John Powers. My wife's name is Ellen." The cook stared at him strangely. "She died. She died last night, or maybe sometime early this morning. We found her, my sister and I, when we went to wake her this morning."

"Your wife died?"

"Aye," he said. "Can the doctor come? My sister is at the house with my girls. I've got to go fetch the priest and let my boss know I can't come in. I can't go into work, now can I?" He glanced at her as though asking for permission.

The woman nodded blankly.

John thanked her and then turned. *First, McManus,* he thought, *and then the priest. I can't lose my job too,* he thought, as he rushed toward the Yards.

Bridget stood over her sister-in-law in a state of disbelief. She touched Ellen's cheek — and then felt foolish. *It's obvious that she's dead. There's no need to be checking.* She leaned over and put her ear to Ellen's belly. Then she closed her eyes and shook her head. When she stood up, she said a brief prayer and crossed herself while holding her own protruding abdomen protectively.

"Come," she said to the girls, "your ma's asleep now forever. Her poor soul's in heaven with God and the angels. Come and say goodbye to her." She helped the silent girls, scared and confused, climb onto the bed and crawl to their mother.

"Now give her a nice hug and kiss and tell her goodbye." One by one, the girls did as they were told.

"Did Mama die?" asked Nellie.

"Yes," said Bridget.

"But how could she die? How could she fly away to heaven while I was holding on to her all night?" Josie asked.

Bridget shrugged. "I don't know, sweetie. But it wasn't your fault.

It was just her time. God wanted your ma with him, I guess. I don't know."

"Did she die 'cause I was bad?" asked Annie. "She said I'd be the death of her."

"No, honey, that's not why she died. She was sick, is all. Her heart gave out. It had nothing to do with you, understand?" The girls looked up uncertainly. "Now, Josie and Annie, go get dressed and help Nellie and Kitty while I tidy up in here. Your da will be back soon with the doctor and the priest. We don't want them to think this is a pigsty, do we?"

John found McManus right away, standing at the outer door, hands on hips. As soon as he spotted John, he began shaking his fists. "Where the hell ya been, for Christ's sake? You're late for the line. You know better'n that, Powers."

"I'm sorry, Mr. McManus. It's only because my wife died during the night and ...

"What? You say your wife's died on ya?"

"Just this morning, when we went to wake her. She was already stone cold."

"Jesus."

"I got here as quick as I could to tell you that I can't come in today. I just came from fetchin' the doctor. And now I've got to get the priest."

McManus nodded. "Jesus, Powers, I'm sorry for ya." He put his hand on John's shoulder and dropped his head for a moment.

"Look, today is Wednesday. I'd like to give you the rest of the week off, but I cannot do it. You understand, Powers? I can double up today and tomorrow, but that's all. I need you back here Friday morning. Understood?"

John nodded.

"And don't forget, every day there are dozens of men asking for work. They'd kill to have your job at half your pay."

"Aye. I know. Thank you. I'm in your debt. I'll be here, don't you worry. Friday morning, bright and early." He attempted a smile, but it came across as a grimace.

"And Powers ..." John stopped and turned back. "My condolences."

John nodded, then hurried away.

Two days. Well, I'm lucky to get that. McManus is all right. He has a heart. Been through some tough times himself, I suppose.

John's limbs were shaking, yet his body felt heavy and leaden, his chest constricted. *How am I to go on without her? Without my Ellen? No Ellen, no son.*

He plodded along, putting one foot in front of the other. Self-consciously, he wiped the tears from his cheeks with his sleeve and tried to focus on the decisions that lay before him. *Who's to watch the girls while I go to work? Who's to keep house, and do the washing and mending? The food shopping and the cooking? How am I to manage that? I'll have to pay someone to come in. A housekeeper. But how am I to do that? I can hardly afford things as they are, never mind paying someone wages. Maybe for just room and board? Would it be possible? Someone to live in? But where would she sleep? There's no room in the bed with the girls as it is. Maybe one of my sisters, he thought. Not Bridget. She'll be having her own baby in a few weeks. Not Mary. She'd never give up her job at the Yacht Club. And Alice will be marrying Harry in a couple of months. That leaves Maggie. Sure, she wouldn't be 15 for another two months, but she'd lived with them and taken care of the girls before. They'd love to have her back, especially now with Ellen gone. Maybe Maggie, then. She's got a good job with that family on Lake Shore Drive. Fancy digs, that. Nice family, and she likes them well enough, and their kids. Still, Maggie might do it, for me and the girls.*

At the Church of the Holy Nativity, John knocked on the rectory door and asked to see Father Fagan. The housekeeper showed him into the front parlor and told him to wait until the father came back from the service. The furniture was too fancy to sit on, especially with his damp clothes, so John stood by the window, looking onto the street through the white lace curtains.

He kept imagining Ellen, her pale face made even whiter by the deep red of her hair loose upon the pillow. *Jesus,* he thought to himself — *poor Josie, sleeping next to her like that.* He shuddered. He remembered Ellen sitting in her buggy in the narrow lane by the River Suir, where they used to meet. He remembered the first time they made love there, and found himself getting sexually aroused.

Embarrassed, he chastised himself. *Imagine, my wife just died and I'm getting excited for her — and in a priest's house at that. Christ, what's wrong with me?*

In the study, Father Fagan greeted John warmly. He had known the couple since they were first married, and he was visibly shaken upon hearing the news of Ellen's death.

"We must go right away," he said. The priest summoned his carriage and they rode the two miles back to the house. The funeral service would be the following afternoon, and Father Fagan gave John the name of a funeral director who would give him a reasonable price for the burial.

While John was out, Bridget washed Ellen's face and fixed her hair. She tried in vain to move her sister-in-law to the center of the bed, but Ellen's dead weight was too much for her. Instead, she busied herself tidying the room. Then she closed the bedroom door and focused her attention on the girls.

They were still in shock, not fully comprehending the finality of the events. Kitty, of course, understood only that something serious had happened. Nellie envisioned her mother flying to heaven to visit God and the angels who lived there. She knew her mother wouldn't be back soon. Heaven must be a long way off, she surmised, and wondered if she too could one day grow wings and fly above the rooftops like the angels.

Annie still feared she was to blame for the tragedy. Even though she understood her mother was dead, she still expected her to emerge from the bedroom and scold her. "*Now, have you learned your lesson this time?*" she'd ask, wagging her finger. Annie decided that if she behaved especially well, she might escape responsibility for the bad thing that happened. She vowed to be good for as long as it took.

Josie had a somewhat clearer understanding of the concept of death. It meant that her mother would no longer be there for them; she would no longer make breakfast, clean their clothes, brush their hair, yell at them to wash their hands and brush their teeth or stop giggling when they should be sleeping. She wondered if Da would get them a new mother. Children at school told of getting new mothers or fathers as well as new sisters and brothers. She wondered who the new mother might be. She also wondered if Dr. Kattman would give Mama some medicine that would make her well again. Why else would Da go fetch him?

Bridget answered the door when Dr. Kattman arrived. Josie saw them close the door to Ellen's bedroom behind them, and she was sure her mother would walk back out with them. With that confidence, she assumed responsibility for watching over her younger sisters.

Annie was especially nurturing to Nellie, whom she so often bullied. For Nellie, this confirmed that something really out of the ordinary was taking place. In her mind, doctors meant delivering babies, and she waited expectantly to hear the wailing of her newborn brother. Josie engaged Kitty in playing with a doll.

Dr. Kattman took a perfunctory look at Ellen, placed his stethoscope on her abdomen briefly, and shook his head. Sighing, he pulled a death certificate out of his bag. Born: Ellen Furlong, 1860, in Waterford, Ireland. Parents: Edward and Maryanne; siblings: Timothy and Sheila. Date of death: March 16, 1892. Cause of death: Heart failure complicated by pregnancy. Name of second deceased: Unborn baby.

When he was done, he picked up the small bottle of white pills by her bedside, briefly glancing at the label. He looked at Bridget.

"I might as well take these, if you don't mind. I'm sure someone else will be able to use them."

When he and Bridget returned to the front room, the three older girls examined them with wide eyes. Dr. Kattman expressed his condolences and left. Josie ran to the bedroom door and found her mother lying still in her bed, just as before.

"Didn't the doctor give her some medicine to make her better?"

"No, sweetheart. There's nothing to be done. Your mother's gone."

"Nothing? He isn't going to make her well again?"

"No, honey. All the life is gone out of her. She's passed away and is no longer with us."

Josie peeked back into the bedroom and saw her mother there. How could her mother be there but not be with us? "He could if he wanted to," she mumbled and stomped off to her own bedroom with Kitty and Nellie in tow.

Just then they heard Father Fagan's carriage stop in front of their house. Annie opened the door and ran out.

"Da," she shouted, "the doctor was here, but he didn't give Mama any medicine to make her well again."

John helped Father Fagan down from the carriage. "Annie," he said, "your mother has died and gone to heaven. There's nothing the doctor could do, nothing any of us can do, to bring her back."

Annie stared at Father Fagan. It was the first time she'd seen him outside of the church, with its confusing rituals, secret language, ringing bells, and swinging incense. The father had obviously made a special trip to their house to whisper some magic words and grant life after death to her mother. She kept her joyful conclusion to herself and ran back into the house shouting, "Father Fagan is here with Da."

The priest nodded solemnly to the gathered family and disappeared into the bedroom with their father. Again, the door was closed — proof of some ceremony only for adults to witness. Listening to the mumbling behind the door, Annie smiled to herself. But when the two men emerged, Ellen remained lifeless and inert. The girls peeked in and stared intently at their mother's eyes and lips, half-imagining slight movements.

Slowly, over the next few hours, they gradually came to understand the finality of death and its cold loneliness.

When Father Fagan left, Bridget made a pot of tea. She and John sat down at the square wooden table. "I've been thinking," she said, "perhaps one of your neighbors has a telephone and will let you call Maggie or Mary at work. Or maybe one of the shops on Halstead has one you can use. We've got to tell them what's happened."

Still numb, John nodded. "Aye," he said after a few moments, "there's the apothecary on Halstead. I'm sure I can use their phone. There's none of the neighbors we know that well. I hate to ask ..."

He didn't know the name or address of the people Maggie worked for on Lake Shore Drive, so he called the Yacht Club and asked for his sister Mary. She was stunned, not wanting to believe it could be true.

"Oh, Johnny!" she cried, "I am so sorry. I'll be there as quick as I can," and promised to contact Maggie's employers as well.

John walked north toward the center of the city to find the funeral director Father Fagan had recommended. He could have taken the trolley, but the walk gave him time to think. He needed to be alone. On the way, he passed a saloon. It was empty except for a few down-and-outers who hung around for the free food, hoping to con someone into buying them a drink. John threw back a shot of Irish, then left to avoid the clinging attention of a poor drifter — though what he really wanted was to get sloshed.

Not yet, he told himself. *But tonight I'll get good and drunk. I deserve it.*

At the funeral parlor, he was astonished to learn the cost of a burial. He opted for one of the least expensive, knowing he'd have to borrow the payment. He had no money saved and owned nothing of value to sell. Ellen had no jewelry other than her wedding band and cameo broach, and he couldn't sell those. She'd be buried with both of those pieces.

The brooch, with its Wedgwood blue background, featured a delicate white portrait of a young girl. Back in Waterford, Ellen always wore the piece at her throat. It seemed to set off her smiling face beneath the dark red hair and charming little hats. She hadn't worn it for a long time. These past few years had been hard for her. Would it have been different if he'd known she had a bad heart?

Immediately, the guilt overwhelmed him. *Jesus, Ellen. I'm sorry if I was impatient with you. Maybe we shouldn't have had all those girls.* But how could he wish away any of his daughters? Still, if they'd had only one or two instead of four — and certainly this last baby. That's what did her in. Getting pregnant this last time. *All for trying for a son. Please, Ellen, forgive me. How was I to know?*

The funeral director said his staff would be at John's house later that afternoon to set Ellen in her casket in the living room. The following afternoon, they would move the body to the Church of the Holy Nativity and then to the cemetery, where Father Fagan would conduct a graveside service. Finished with the arrangements, John departed feeling more hopeless than ever. It was so businesslike. There was nowhere to escape the relentless finality of it.

He chose to walk home, knowing he'd have the opportunity to stop in another saloon for a quick one. He was bursting to unload the awful news. "I've just lost my wife and son," he yearned to say. It didn't matter who, just to say it out loud to another human being. He stopped in the first saloon he passed and ordered a drink. When the barkeep poured out the whiskey, John blurted: "I've just lost my wife and son."

The bartender stared at him. "That's right," said John, tossing it down. "My wife died this morning — actually, during the night. Heart failure. She was six months pregnant with my son." The words choked and his chest heaved.

"Jesus," said the barkeep. "Here, have another on me. Both wife and son? Jesus."

John could only nod, afraid he'd start blubbering. He tossed back the second drink then stumbled to the bathroom, where he let the tears come. Afterwards, he washed his face and returned to the bar. "One more," he said.

"Here's luck to you," said the barkeep, pouring whiskey.

John left a coin on the counter and cradled the shot glass in his fingers. *I've got to get a hold,* he said to himself. *Can't go bursting out in tears every time I open my mouth.* He took a sip, savoring the burn. *I'll have to go over to the O'Haras and tell them. I need to be with Jimmy and Harry and my sisters.* He wanted to be surrounded by them, feel their arms around him, embrace the gentle, soothing sounds of their voices. He ached for it. He finished his drink and waved to the barman before starting his long walk home.

With John out handling arrangements at the funeral parlor, Bridget made the decision to send Josie and Annie to school. It would be easier if they were out of the house when the people from the funeral home came for Ellen. She wrote a note to the nuns explaining what happened, and sent the girls off.

"But we'll be punished for being late," Josie protested.

"I don't think so, girls," Bridget reassured them. "Now fetch your things and get a hurry on. And don't worry," she said when she saw Annie's questioning look, "I'll be here when you get home and so will your father. Now, off you go."

She shooed them out the door and watched as they ambled reluctantly, and then began to run. When they were out of sight, she went to Ellen's closet and chose an outfit for her to be laid out in. It was when she picked out a corset and bloomers that she collapsed onto the bed next to Ellen's body, sobbing in grief.

After two more stops along the way, John arrived home to find John F.'s horse and wagon in front of his house. As he approached, one of his neighbors called to him. John had seen her before, but only knew that she lived across from him with her husband and children.

"Excuse me, I don't mean to intrude, but I noticed a lot of activity at your house today. Has something happened?"

John frowned in his attempt to focus. "Yes, Mrs. ..."

"Sullivan," she said, "Ann Sullivan. I've spoken with your wife on occasion. We've become friends. Is she all right? I know she's been tired lately."

"Well," he said hesitantly, "Ellen died this morning."

The woman's hand flew to her mouth — she gasped, then crossed herself. "Lord have mercy," she said. "How did it happen?"

"It was her heart, the doctor said. Heart failure, he called it."

"When will you be having the service?"

"Tomorrow afternoon, at Holy Nativity." He fidgeted. "The funeral parlor people will be here soon to lay her out ..."

"Yes, of course. Well, if you need anything, we're right here," the woman reassured him.

"Thank you, Mrs. Sullivan. That's very kind." As he turned and went into his house, he sensed that she continued to stand there watching.

Well, he thought, *that's one way to let the whole neighborhood know.*

John F. was sitting at the table drinking tea with Bridget, each one with a little girl on their lap. Nellie ran to her father and he realized how good her little arms felt around his neck.

"You're here early," he said, addressing John F.

"I was worried about Bridget," his brother-in-law said, reaching into his vest pocket for his pipe, "what with her being due in another few weeks."

"Aye," John agreed, sitting down with them. "Where are Josie and Annie?"

"I sent them off to school," Bridget explained. "I thought it better that they not be here when the people from the funeral home come."

"They should arrive soon," he told them, then glanced at John F. "Would you like a drink?"

"Not now. Maybe later."

"I just remembered," John said. "I've got to go tell the O'Haras."

"Do you want me to give you a ride?"

"Thank you. My feet are killing me for all the traipsing up and down Halstead Street since this morning. I'd be much obliged."

John F. turned to Bridget. "Is that all right, or should I stay here with you?"

"I'll be fine. Go ahead and take John to the O'Haras."

The two men stood. "Would it be all right if we took the girls with us?" John asked.

"Fine with me," John F. said. He glanced at Bridget and she nodded.

"Yes, I think it will do them good to get out. I'll get their jackets." Soon the two men were sitting up on the driver's bench, John holding Kitty on his lap and Nellie squeezing in between the two men.

Nellie wondered if they would be bringing the whole O'Hara clan back in the milk wagon for a big party. *Maybe,* she thought, *Mama will wake up for that.*

Janet O'Hara saw the horse and wagon pull up in front of her house and heard the squealing of little girls. She rushed out to greet her guests.

"What a wonderful surprise," she said, "but why aren't you two busy working at your jobs like proper Irish husbands?" Her wide grin was meant to disarm them, but she knew how unusual a midday visit was.

John climbed down from the wagon and, still carrying Kitty, approached Ed's wife. "I've come to tell you ... Ellen died during the night. Heart failure."

Saying the words aloud let loose another torrent of tears. Janet embraced him. Stunned, she let John cry on her shoulder while she tried to absorb the news. After a minute or so, he straightened and wiped his face with his large handkerchief.

"I'm sorry," he said.

She gave a little shake to her head and glanced quickly at the girls. John F., who stood holding Kitty, bowed his head and turned away so as to not embarrass John.

Janet turned to John F. "Bridget?"

"She's at their house, waiting for the people from the funeral home."

Janet reached out to kiss each of the girls. "What can we do to help?" she asked John.

"I don't know. I haven't thought about it. I just wanted you to know. We're having the funeral tomorrow afternoon at Holy Nativity."

"And she'll be laid out at home until then?"

John nodded and looked away. Nellie was tugging at him, clambering to be held. He felt comforted by her little body clinging onto him.

"Maybe you'd all like to come over," he said to Janet.

"Of course. Is there anyone else we can notify?"

"No, I don't think so. I reached Mary at the Yacht Club. She said she'd telephone Maggie where she works."

"All right then," Janet said, "we'll see you this evening after the men get home. We'll let Alice know, of course." They embraced again, and the men and girls climbed onto the wagon. John F. smoked his pipe while he drove back to Emerald Street. John held his two little girls tightly to him all the way home.

Soon after they returned, a horse-drawn hearse pulled up in front of the house, with two men and a woman on the driver's bench. The men carried a coffin into the house and leaned it against a wall in the front room. The scene reminded John of pictures he'd seen of Egyptian tombs with mummies in them. They went into the bedroom to prepare Ellen's body for the wake.

Noticing how tired his wife was, John F. suggested he take her home.

"It's all right, Bridget," he said. "Mary will be here soon. Maybe she or Maggie can stay over and help out with the girls tomorrow morning."

"We'll be back tomorrow," Bridget said, "after my John finishes with his route." Watching his brother-in-law escort Bridget to the wagon, John almost laughed at how awkward she was, with her big belly, climbing up to the driver's seat. Suddenly his eyes blurred as he remembered Ellen's own ballooning, and how it altered the way she moved.

He made some tea for himself and the girls, and gave them each a piece of bread with sugar on it. Pouring a little whiskey into his own cup, he tried to imagine what the people were doing in Ellen's room. The fact that two men were helping to bathe and dress his wife was unsettling, and he felt his jaw tighten. He tried to ignore the thought, knowing it was a necessary task they performed every day.

Still, it felt like an invasion, a violation of Ellen's and his privacy. They were still in there, in her bedroom, when he heard Josie and Annie come up the walk. As the front door opened, he saw they were accompanied by a nun and he quickly stood to greet her.

"Mr. Powers? I'm Sister Frances, one of your daughters' teachers. Mother Superior asked me to come home with the girls to express our condolences, and to see if there was anything we might do to help."

"Ah, thank you, Sister. No, there's nothing I can think of."

"Will you have someone here to help with your daughters?" She nodded toward Nellie and Kitty. "I see you have two more little ones. You'll have your hands full, taking care of four little girls, and getting these two young ladies off to school every morning."

"Aye, Sister. I'm hoping one of my sisters will be able to help out."

"That would be prudent. We'd hate for anything to interfere with their schooling. They're both doing so well." Sister Frances smiled down at Josie, who was still holding one of her hands, and exchanged a knowing glance with Annie, who was attempting to pour herself a cup of tea.

"Still, if there's any way we can help, Mother Superior wants you to know our prayers are with you. We also have a connection with St. Joseph's ..."

John, puzzled, tilted his head.

"The orphanage. We've placed a number of children there under similar circumstances. Some of us teach there as well."

Orphanage? An orphan asylum? For his girls? What was it with these women? Half-women?

"Thank you, Sister. I really don't think that will be necessary. I'm sure my family will provide all the help we'll be needing."

"Yes," she said, "that would be ideal, wouldn't it? Well, then. Goodbye girls. Goodbye Mr. Powers. We will pray for your family."

John mumbled his thanks and watched her leave. With the click of the latch, John suddenly felt very alone. All four of his daughters were there with him — his complete and total responsibility. He thought of all the work to keep the household running smoothly: cooking and shopping and cleaning; bathing and dressing the girls, brushing their hair, waking them up and putting them to bed, bringing them to church, ironing their dresses. Ironing! He saw them watching him and realized they were frightened.

They're wondering if I'm up to it — and they know I'm not. There's no way I can do it all. When would I work? He looked at the clock and longed for Mary to arrive.

The people from the funeral home opened the bedroom door.

"Mr. Powers," said the man in charge, "we have your wife ready now. Is there a specific place you want us to set up the casket? I assume you want it in the front room, perhaps toward the middle, so people can gather around? Or would you prefer we place it against one of the walls?"

Still holding Kitty, John accompanied the man to the front room. They chose a place along one of the walls, and set up sawhorses with wide planks of wood draped with black cloth. Then they laid Ellen's body into the coffin and placed it on the draped platform in the living room. The woman arranged some flowers and ferns around the coffin.

"There, now, Mr. Powers, what do you think?"

John approached the coffin. Ellen's head rested on a white lace pillow, her red hair combed and luxurious. Wearing her good black dress, the cameo broach at her throat and plain wedding band on her hand, she loosely held a rosary and cross upon her chest. They had done a good job of applying makeup to give her face some color. The woman John saw in the casket looked peaceful and in repose.

"You've done a fine job," he said. "She looks beautiful."

One of the men wrote out an invoice and handed it to John, explaining that they would be back on Thursday in time to take them all to the church.

"We'll have the same hearse that's out front now to carry the casket, and two carriages to take members of the family. After mass, we'll be going to Mt. Olivet Cemetery."

Payment for the full cost of the burial service, $7.50, would be due when they arrived at the house. John agreed, although he still didn't know where he was going to come up with such a large sum — almost his full week's wages — in addition to the rent — $12.00 — due in less than two weeks. And then there was the wake itself, with the food and drink that needed to be bought. Shaking his head in despair, he felt a tinge of shame for being angry with Ellen for causing all these problems.

John sent Josie and Annie into their room to do their homework, and Nellie tagged along behind them. Kitty wouldn't leave her father's lap, so he sat at the table, drinking his fortified tea and clutching the warm comfort of her little body. Eventually, he realized he'd have to get supper ready for himself and the girls. He turned on the lights in the front room and kitchen and looked for something to eat. Potatoes and carrots and onions. Bread, cheese, a few eggs, and some milk.

John was in the process of making soup when he heard a horse and carriage stop in front of his house. A smile broke out on his face when he saw the carriage driver hand a valise down to Mary. John opened the door and shouted to her, "Mary, my darling, am I glad to see you!"

They embraced. "How are you managing?" she asked, feeling like the older sibling. He looked so drained and tired.

"All right, I guess. A bit overwhelmed, actually. There's so much to do. I don't know how Ellen handled everything."

Mary nodded. "I can stay through Sunday, John, but then I've got to get back."

"I understand," he said. "I'm so glad to see you …"

The girls were standing at the front door, the three older ones calling out, "Aunt Mary! Aunt Mary's here. Have you come to stay with us?"

"Only for a few days," John answered. Then to Mary, "I'm surprised you took a cab. Why didn't you take the trolley?"

"My boss said that if I'd stay at work for the afternoon, he'd give me the money to take a cab to your house."

"You must be well regarded," he said, thinking it would be a cold day in hell before McManus would shell out a penny on his behalf, never mind a carriage ride across town.

Mary gave a quick little smile, then turned her attention to the girls. They exchanged kisses and hugs. For them, 16-year-old Mary was more like an older sister than an aunt. It was obvious to John that they were eager to cling to her, to feel the vibrancy of her body, the strength in her arms, her warmth and feminine smell.

"I was just starting to make some soup for supper," he said, as they entered the house.

"Oh, I can do that for you," she offered. When she saw Ellen's casket, she immediately crossed herself. Gazing upon her sister-in-law, she sighed, "Oh, Ellen, how sad." The girls held onto her while she looked at their mother. "Oh, girls, I'm so sorry for you." This statement brought forth quiet tears from Josie.

"Where should I put my things?" Mary asked her brother, who had picked up Kitty.

"I guess in the girls' room. I'll have a couple of them sleep in with me so you'll have some room."

"I want to sleep with Aunt Mary," Josie said quickly, wiping her eyes. All of her sisters chimed in.

"We'll sort all that out later," he said. "For now, take your aunt's things into your bedroom." Mary took off her cape and hat and headed for the kitchen.

The others arrived after supper: Ed and Janet O'Hara with their daughter, Jimmy O'Hara, as well as Harry and Alice. Mary Powers said Maggie would arrive the next morning. The O'Haras brought food and whiskey and the women found a place to set out the dishes.

Mr. and Mrs. Sullivan and their children came from across the street, as did a few other neighbors. Most everyone brought food. It was the first time John had met some of them, and he didn't even know their names — although a few had occasionally borrowed coal from each other. Two of the men went back to their houses and returned with a table and some chairs to accommodate the crowd at the wake. All had known death in their own families: miscarriages, young children and siblings dying, as well as parents. They knew the hardship that John and his girls would soon be facing.

John confided in his sisters that he would need another $6 by to-morrow afternoon in order to pay the funeral expenses. "I've only a dol-lar and a half until I get my pay on Saturday," he admitted dolefully. They quietly told the guests who had gathered, and before long, Ed O'Hara came up to John. "We've taken up a collection among us, the family as well as your neighbors. It's for the funeral expenses."

John lifted his eyes from his drink.

"Take it, man. It's done in kindness and respect. There's none of us could pay for a funeral on our own. No one has that sort of savings." He handed John a small paper bag. "It'll be enough for tomorrow, so now that's one less thing you have to worry about."

John took the bag, feeling the weight of the coins. Mixed with em-barrassment and shame came a great relief.

"Thank you," he said. Then he pulled himself up straight. "Listen, everybody." He held up the bag. "I want to thank all of you, on behalf of my little girls — and myself — for your generosity." He paused, but nothing more came forth. Ed patted him on the back and a few others offered assurances that they understood what he was going through.

As the evening wore on, the Sullivans and other neighbors headed home, leaving only his two sisters and the O'Haras. Ed's daughter, Mary, was asleep in the bedroom with his own four little ones. The adults sat in the kitchen, avoiding the body in the other room. Tired and bleary from drink and emotion, they were unwilling to separate from each other.

"That was a fine thing you all did, taking up the collection," John said humbly.

"You'd have done the same," Ed said, speaking for the rest of them.

"Aye, I hope I'd have had a few spare coins to contribute. And these neighbors — I don't even know them, never saw half of them. And look, we're sitting on their chairs, eating their food ..."

"It could just as easily be us," Janet said. "Remember when you and Ellen first arrived in Chicago and came to our house? How we were quarantined? We were afraid we would lose our Mary. But we were also afraid that one of us, Ed or me, would die. It was scary as hell, that was."

"Aye," said John, "all I can think about is what I'll do now. I mean after tomorrow, with the girls and all. How am I to manage?" They avoided answering, glancing around and considering the severity of John's predicament.

"I'd be glad to help, Johnny," Mary broke the silence, "but I've got to get back to the Club on Sunday night. They're counting on me."

John said, "I know, Mary. We've all got commitments. We all need to be somewhere. But I can't be turning them out on the street to sell newspapers — or worse yet, themselves, like so many of those poor children we hear about: orphans, beggars, abandoned children. Christ, if only my mother and father were here. I've never missed them so."

"What about Ellen's parents?" Alice asked.

"What about them? They wrote her off for marrying me. They've never shown any interest in the children. Not any of them. Never once. Bastards!"

"Still, Johnny," Alice persisted, "this is different. This isn't about you or her, this is about your girls, their own granddaughters. Surely, they might consider taking them in."

"Or helping out financially," Jimmy added. "From what I remember, Ellen's da was loaded."

"Oh, they've got the money all right, but they've no heart at all. Besides," John said, slamming his glass onto the table for emphasis, "they don't deserve the girls. Turning out their own daughter like they did, just for marrying one of their hired help, smashing her dreams and ruining her life. All this," he said, gesturing to the coffin against the wall, "is their fault."

"It wasn't for *marrying* you that they turned her out," Alice reminded him.

"Well, whatever. It amounts to the same thing. They turned their back on her, on her plans for the future, on us, our children — their dear little granddaughters! The hell with them! Let them choke on their bloody money."

"This wasn't exactly the dream Ellen had in mind, was it?" Alice pointed out.

John stared at his sister. "No, it wasn't. She thought she was the apple in her da's eye, that he'd buy her a house in Waterford, let me work myself up in his business, like his own son, Timothy. But he made rubbish of that, didn't he? Bloodless bastard."

"Still, they should be notified that their daughter died," Janet said.

"At least notify her sister," added Alice. "Lord, how they loved each other!"

"Aye, Jack, it's only right," Jimmy said.

John looked at his friend. "Jimmy, don't tell me you expect me to be writing such a letter to my dear in-laws."

Alice laughed out loud. "The last thing they'd be wanting is a letter from you, saying that their daughter had died. They'd blame it all on you for sure. No, I'll write to them. I'll know how to do it."

"God bless you then, but I'll have no part of it," John muttered.

"Fine, I'll be glad to do it. And, maybe, at least for the next few weeks until Harry and I get married, I can help you with the girls, too."

John did a double take. Everyone stared at Alice in surprise, especially Harry. John continued to look at his sister questioningly.

"Why not?" she asked. "Harry and I aren't getting married until June 5th. I'll be quitting my waitressing job soon anyway ..."

"You're quitting your job? Why on earth would you do that? Won't you and Harry be needing your wages?"

Alice smiled sheepishly and looked at Harry. He sighed in resignation. "Truth is, I'm already two months pregnant. In another month I'll be starting to show. It won't do for me to be working in such a rough place as that tavern when I'm pushing my belly around in front of me. It just won't do. Me and Harry agreed. I'll be doing some seamstress work from home, so I'll still be making something."

Janet and Mary congratulated her and Harry's brothers gave him knowing grins.

"Jesus, Alice, have you no shame?" uttered John. "And you, Harry, you couldn't wait another couple of months?"

"Look who's talking," she answered back. "You're a fine one to be calling a kettle black."

"She's right, Jack. Fair is fair," said Jimmy, a big grin plastered on his face.

"And what would you be knowing about it?" John flared. "You, who's never even been in love, never went with the same woman more than a couple of times, just being with floozies who hang about in the saloons. What would you know about how it is to lose a wife, the mother of your own children?"

"Jesus, Jack," Jimmy said, "are you saying I don't know what it's like to lose somebody I care about? How about my own parents? How about my own sisters, dying of fevers and consumption, with hardly anything to eat, practically dying of starvation back there? You think you're the only one who's ever suffered?"

"Ah, you're all drunk," John said, as if to dismiss the whole conversation.

"Well," Alice said, "I'm not as drunk as you are. And besides, who else is going to watch my nieces? Mary already said she can't do it and Bridget is just about ready to pop. There's no way she can take care of them."

Janet turned to Mary, "Mary, why can't you do it? Is your job in the kitchen so important that you can't give it up to help your only brother and his girls?"

At 16, Mary was the youngest there, and so the least accustomed to drinking Irish whiskey. In fact, she had never had so much to drink.

"I am helping my brother," she managed to say. "I'd do anything in my power to help anyone in my family."

"So, why ..."

"Because," she said, drawing out the word, "because it's my whole future there at the Club. It's not just any old job." She looked at Alice, "Like being a barmaid. I'm learning a skilled trade. I'm to be a chef someday. A chief cook. I'll be able to go anywhere I want and earn good money. Don't you realize what an opportunity I have there? I'm learning to cook great dishes. I'm not just boiling potatoes or cabbage and stew, but great dishes, like from France and Italy. I can't give it up. I've worked too hard to give it up."

Glassy eyed, she looked around at the others. "If it was just any old job, I'd dash it in a minute — you know that, don't you? But this is my career; it's my whole life. You can't expect me to chuck it all away now, can you?"

"Nobody's expecting anything, Mary. I already said I'd do it for the next few weeks or so." Alice looked at John. "That'll give you some time, at least, to see what's to be done."

John remembered Sister Frances and St. Joseph's orphan asylum. *Christ,* he thought, *it won't come to that. Hopefully, Maggie will be able to come through.*

"We'll see," John said. "Maggie will be here tomorrow. Maybe she'll be able to help out."

His remark was met with shrugs and nods. Mary knew how her younger sister, only 15, loved her position. Of course, everyone cared about the little ones; they'd just lost their mother, after all — and a new brother as well. Still, they had their own lives to manage, didn't they?

130

Ed O'Hara stood up. "We'd best be going. We'll be here tomorrow for the procession to Holy Nativity."

"You'll all be pallbearers, then?" John asked.

"Aye, Jack. Each of us and John F."

"And if George and Sharon O'Brian show up, then George will make the sixth," said John.

He went with Janet to retrieve her little Mary from the back bedroom. When he pushed open the door, he saw them all in bed, the five girls — his own four clustered against the older girl like pups around their mother. His eyes filled up.

"Just look at them," John said. "So sweet." *What's to become of them,* he wondered. *Poor motherless things.*

After everyone left, John and Mary lifted Nellie and Kitty, limp as rag dolls, and carried them into his bedroom to sleep for the night.

"I'll see you in the morning," he said, kissing Mary's forehead. "Thank you for being here." She kissed his cheek and turned to her room.

When John had stripped down to his long johns, he slid into bed, curling an arm around his two littlest angels. Just then he remembered: *Today was Kitty's birthday. Two years old and we all forgot. Not even a toast in her name.* He gently leaned over to give her a kiss. *God,* he said to himself, *I hope I can do right by you girls. I'll do my very best. You can count on that.*

Despite the bright blue sky and sweet smell of spring, the next morning dawned under a somber haze. Clinging to their father and Aunt Mary, the girls were reluctant to approach the open casket without encouragement and support. They gazed at their mother and whispered tentatively to her, unsure of what to do. Afterward, they studiously avoided the casket, as if it weren't there at all.

Mary took care of the girls, dressing them, brushing their hair, and consoling them. Meanwhile, John sat dazed at the table. After drinking some tea, he walked outside, leaving the front door open behind him. Wandering around the house, he looked at the dormant bushes, mumbled to himself, gazed skyward now and then, and eventually went back inside to sip again at his tea.

Later in the morning, Bridget and John F. arrived in the milk wagon. Sitting at the table with John, Bridget helped compile lists of things to do, items to be bought, tasks to be seen to. John F. let the girls sit in the wagon and pretend to drive. They were the first to spot Maggie walking from Halstead Street, lugging her small cardboard suitcase. The girls clambered down and ran to greet her. At the sound of all the squealing, John and Mary looked out the front window.

"Ah, it's Maggie," John said, a nervous churning in his stomach. *I wonder if she'll be willing to stay.* The alternative seemed depressingly bleak.

John F. carried Maggie's valise inside and John embraced his favorite sister at the doorway. When she saw the coffin, she whispered a quick prayer and crossed herself.

"Oh, John, I'm so sorry for you and the girls." Josie put her arms around Maggie's hips and squeezed. The other three girls attached themselves to Mary and Bridget and watched.

"I'm sorry I couldn't be here last night, but I came as quickly as I could."

"You're here now. That's all that matters, that we're all together."

Maggie hugged her sisters. "Where's Alice?"

"She'll be coming shortly," Bridget said, assuming her role as the eldest. "She'll be coming with Harry and his brothers."

It wasn't much longer before the hearse pulled up in front of the house, followed by two empty carriages. It was decided that Mary and Maggie would accompany John and his daughters. Bridget and John F. and Alice and Harry would ride in the second carriage.

George and Sharon O'Brian had sent word that they and the remaining O'Haras would follow in an additional hired carriage. Everyone had agreed it wouldn't do for John F.'s milk wagon to be part of a funeral procession.

The casket was carried to the hearse. A few women and children from the neighborhood gathered quietly to watch. Finally, the procession set off at its slow pace toward the church. The girls enjoyed the ride but knew enough to hide their excitement, realizing this was a serious occasion. Taking their cue from the adults, they were on their best behavior. Kitty sat on Mary's lap and Nellie on Maggie's; Josie and Annie squeezed in on either side of their father.

Father Fagan said the mass; because he knew all of the Powers family, he was able to make the service personal and meaningful. When the words had all been spoken, the pallbearers solemnly carried the casket out and slid it into the hearse. The procession reorganized, they followed as the hearse made its way south to the new cemetery at Mt. Olivet.

It was on that long ride that John appealed to Maggie.

"Mary has to get back to her job at the Yacht Club and can only stay until Sunday," he began. "Alice has agreed to stay for the next month or two, but then she'll be getting ready for her wedding. So I'm hoping that starting sometime in May, you'll be able to come and be with us, like you were once before. Otherwise, I don't know what we're to do."

It was clear that Maggie was torn. How could she say no to her own brother at a time like this? Did she have any right to demur? As the youngest of John's sisters, she had the fewest rights. Wasn't that the truth of it? Yet, it would mean giving up her position, saying goodbye to Mr. and Mrs. Gallagher and their two children. Could she do that?

"For how long, John? For how long would you be needing me?"

"How long? Why, until they're grown. Until they're old enough to take care of the house and themselves. I don't know, lass ..." He looked at Josie and Annie beside him. "What would you think? Another five, six, seven years?"

He saw the panic on Maggie's face. "Jesus, you'd still be a young woman. You're barely 15. It's not like I'm asking you to give up your life, you know." Then he softened, "You know how much we all love you."

Maggie hugged Nellie closer as she turned to gaze out at the passing fields. What her brother said was valid, but at the same time she didn't want to be parted from Mr. Gallagher. He was so kind to her, like a father — even better — always giving her little things and making arrangements to take her and the children on outings. She knew he did it as much for her sake as for his own children. He gave her books to read so she'd be better able to guide the children. Could she really give all that up?

"Oh, Johnny, this is all so sudden," she responded quietly. "I have to think about it."

"Maggie, they've no mother. We're all alone. We need you. There is no one else."

Maggie saw the girls looking at her, pleading wordlessly with their eyes. Tears welled up and, for the first time, she felt Ellen's passing as a personal loss — not just for Ellen and her brother's family, but her own painful loss.

"Johnny," she said, clutching at Nellie, as if somehow the child could protect her, "I know how it is, I do. And I want to help. I will. But I've got to talk to my employers. I can't just leave them."

Guilt and fear suddenly overwhelmed her. She wanted to tell him that the Gallaghers were her family, the only family she had belonged to for these past two years. But she remained quiet.

"I've got to talk to Mr. and Mrs. Gallagher. I can't promise. Let me talk to them first."

What more was there to say? John wondered. *She knows how much we need her, how much the girls need her.*

"Well, darling, you know how we're all depending on you. I don't know what we're to do otherwise."

"I understand," Maggie said. "I know. I'll talk to them as soon as I get back."

"Well," he said, trying to reassure himself, "Mary will be here until Sunday and then Alice will take over until sometime in May, so you've got time to get it all straightened out over there by the lake."

As soon as he said the words, he regretted alluding to the fact that Maggie worked for wealthy people and lived in a fancy house on Lake Shore Drive — as if the reason she might not want to come was because she didn't want to give up the good life. Then with an actual physical shock, he realized: That was *exactly* the kind of life Ellen had given up when she chose him.

Maggie didn't respond. She and Mary made eye contact and she knew that Mary understood her conflict.

In the other carriage, Bridget and Alice were also discussing the fate of the young family. "What will happen to those girls if Maggie doesn't agree to come?" Bridget asked her sister.

"John said one of the nuns from their school suggested St. Joseph's."

"The orphan asylum?"

Alice nodded gravely.

Bridget stole a look at her husband. He closed his eyes for a moment, then shrugged and looked away.

"It's better than being on the street," she said, "but that's about the best that can be said for it. We're four of us sisters. There must be something we can do."

"Perhaps you and I could each take in two of them," Alice suggested, looking questioningly at Harry.

"Jesus, Alice, how can you suggest that?" John F. said with exasperation. "You're going to be having your own baby, as is Bridget," he said, gesturing to his wife. "Where are those girls supposed to sleep? On the floor?"

"I think it's better for them if they stay together," Harry volunteered. "I'd hate to see them separated."

"Harry has a point," said John F. "My own mother died when I was a lad. It was just me and my brothers after that. That's what kept each of us going. I can't imagine what it would have been like if I'd have had to go it alone, without them."

Bridget sighed. "It's true — we've no spare room. If we weren't having our own, it would be different, but under the circumstances ..."

"It's got to be Maggie, then," said Alice. "We'll have to convince her that she has to do it. Maybe we can help her out from time to time, to give her some relief."

They nodded. Yes, they would let Maggie know she wouldn't be alone. They'd pitch in when they could — but they were counting on her to keep the family together.

At the gravesite, Father Fagan said a prayer and read from the Bible, and then the coffin was lowered into the freshly dug grave. Annie and Josie stared numbly, showing no outward emotion. Who could imagine the frightful thoughts and images that might be terrifying them? What horrible ideas of death and afterlife informed their young minds: What would happen to their mother under the shoveled dirt? What did "dust to dust and ashes to ashes" really mean? Was Mama going to burn in hell? Were they being sinful and disloyal for entertaining such questions? Nellie and Kitty began bawling at the scene.

The adults were quick to support each other as well as the four girls. The men hoisted them up and carried them. John, too, came in for his share of support, but his friends had difficulty expressing themselves in words. His sisters embraced him and they wept silently.

As they turned away from Ellen's grave, Bridget and Alice took Maggie aside. It was up to her, they asserted, to keep the girls together at home. The extended family would be there to help as best they could, but they were counting on her. All Maggie could do was nod. It was impossible to tell if her eyes were red from grief — or from considering her own predicament.

Back at John's house, neighbors and friends filtered in and out throughout the day. Later in the evening, only family and Jimmy and Harry O'Hara remained. It was agreed that Maggie and Mary would stay until Sunday, and Alice would come early Monday morning to get the girls off to school. She would stay at the house, sleeping with two of the girls, until sometime in May when, hopefully, Maggie would come to live with them.

John, of course, would return to work in the morning. Starting on Monday, he could expect Harry to be a regular visitor in the evenings, now that Alice would be living there for a while.

The next morning, Mary and Maggie packed a lunch pail and sent John off to work, then got Josie and Annie ready for school. The girls basked in their attention. Ellen had often lacked the energy to brush and braid their hair or see to it that their clothes were washed and ironed. When they left for school, they skipped down the street hand in hand. Maggie and Mary turned their attention to Nellie and Kitty.

Despite the solemn circumstances, John's sisters enjoyed doting on their young nieces, perhaps imagining what it would be like to care for their own little ones someday. Maggie's pleasure was slightly diminished by her sadness at losing the security of her job with the Gallaghers. If only she could find some way out of her dilemma — having to choose between her brother and nieces and her new family, the Gallaghers.

The new routine in place, it became clear that John and the girls had come to assume Maggie would be with them on a permanent basis. For their part, it was no longer a matter of *if*, but *when*. Inwardly, however, Maggie clung to a hope that an alternative might be found that would allow her to stay with the Gallaghers. Although she continued to say she still needed to talk to them, that was discounted by John as being a mere formality. In his mind, all Maggie had to do was give her notice.

Sunday afternoon, John and the girls said a sad goodbye to Maggie and Mary and watched as they hurried toward Halstead Street to catch the trolley. The girls begged John to be allowed to go outside to play and, after seeing that they were dressed warmly enough, he let them run screaming into the yard. Closing the door, John realized he was alone for the first time since Ellen's death. Mary had prepared food for the next few days — the icebox and vegetable bin were full — so he had no immediate chores to distract him. Standing in the front room, he examined the space around him. The sparsely furnished room was eerily silent. With an empty hollowness in his heart, he walked aimlessly into the kitchen and poured himself a glass of whiskey.

Sitting on his front stoop, he was glad for the overcast March day. The chill rawness reminded him he was alive. He envied the girls, distracted by their play. He felt nothing but the weight of responsibilities. How would he keep it all together?

As he sipped his whiskey, John contemplated the future. Maggie would come in two month's time to care for his girls. He thought of his own mother and how wonderful it would be if she could be here now for him and his girls. At least Alice would come in the morning, thank God — although in a few weeks she'd be gone too, back to her life with Harry. And in another half year she'd be raising a child of her own.

But young Maggie could be with them for a few years, and he took great comfort in that. Still, with Ellen's death fresh in his mind, he no longer took life for granted. Disaster could strike at any time. And Maggie was only his sister — she wasn't committed to him and the children the way a wife would be. He couldn't depend on her the way he had with Ellen. Life provided no guarantees, so there would always be the fear that some malevolent fortune could suddenly take it all away.

Just like that, he said to himself, recalling the catastrophe that had befallen them all when a little slip of his knife almost put him out of a job altogether.

That was rough, he remembered, *yet nothing like this.*

And then he recalled his father's death. How had that happened? A moment of carelessness, a brief distraction that changed everything — a single pivotal moment upon which whole lives hung. With his father's death, life had changed. His mother died of a broken heart and his orphaned sisters were sent in desperation to John, to be their savior. Now, who was in danger of being orphaned? He drained his drink and went inside to refill his glass.

When the sun began casting its long shadows, John called the girls inside. Most of their pent-up energy spent, they reluctantly washed up. John asked Josie and Annie to lay the table as he set out the meal his sisters had prepared for them. This was now the fifth day they had sat down to supper without Ellen, but the first as just the five of them, with no aunt or uncle or neighbors.

Josie broke the heavy silence by reminding her father she would be seven on the coming Wednesday. John calculated quickly that it would be one week since her mother's death. Neither Josie nor Kitty will ever celebrate another birthday without being reminded of when their mother had died.

"Are you hinting at a celebration, then?" he asked her.

Josie shrugged her shoulders. "Maybe we could have a cake," she suggested. "Aunt Alice could make one. I'd be glad to help."

John smiled. "I don't think a cake would be too much to ask," he said.

"What about Kitty?" Annie blurted out. "She didn't have anything for her birthday."

"I know," her father said.

137

"It's not fair," she insisted.

"You're right, Annie. But, two wrongs don't make a right. Not celebrating Josie's birthday won't make up for missing Kitty's, now, will it? Would you have us forget all our birthdays just to even things out?"

Annie retreated into a sulky silence, her attempt at depriving her sister of an occasion defeated.

"We can add Kitty's name to the cake, Da. I wouldn't mind," Josie offered.

John looked at his oldest with pride, avoiding Annie's glare. "Then, that's what we'll do. And, it's a very grownup idea if I do say so."

So, in three more days, Josie would turn seven and, once again, officially be a year older than Annie. Her brief stint as Josie's peer was fast disappearing and, like some annual celestial event, would not return for another year.

John had the three oldest clean up while he went to the living room. With Kitty on his lap, he sipped at another glass and read to her from a newspaper. When the girls were finished in the kitchen, he had them make sure they were ready for school in the morning.

"Now, when your Aunt Alice arrives in the morning, we must all do our part to make her stay here a pleasant one. You'll all have to help her, just as you helped your ma and me. You understand? Your aunt is doing us a kindness, so we all have to pitch in."

In the morning, just as John was getting ready to leave, Alice rode up in a cab with Harry. John gave him a hand with Alice's trunk. "My God, sister, have you come with all your worldly goods?"

"I am going to be here for almost eight weeks," Alice explained, somewhat offended.

"I'd have to rob three houses to have enough to fill a trunk like this," Harry chimed in.

"Oh, you men," she smiled. "You'd always wear the same worn-out things if it were left to you."

"Well, if I was as pretty as you, maybe I'd pay more attention to my appearance," Harry answered with a wink. As soon as they had wrestled the trunk inside, John hurried off. As Harry went on his way and Alice entered the house, the girls were just beginning to stir.

Over the course of that first week, Alice, John, and the girls gradually adjusted to the new arrangement. It was an interesting process of discovery, especially for John and the two oldest girls. Alice was much more energetic than Ellen had been. Perhaps she was motivated to be as helpful as possible during her relatively short stay. Or maybe she hoped to assuage the loss John and the girls had suffered. At any rate, she fell into a routine: cooking, washing, ironing, cleaning, and shopping, as well as managing the delivery of ice, coal, and milk. She handled it all with an energy and a diligence that neither John nor the girls were accustomed to. She even had the strength to brush the girls' hair, embroider their names on their clothes, and play games before dinner.

Josie and Annie bragged to their friends at school about their aunt. "She sewed my name in my coat. See? And she plays with us, too." John was surprised by his sister's domestic skills, although he knew she was spending more on food than Ellen had, with less than spectacular results. Still, he realized that he had accepted Ellen's lethargy as normal and was surprised to discover a different reality. A woman — a wife — might have more energy and interest in life than Ellen had. If he were ever to marry again, he would keep this in mind.

As expected, Harry came most evenings to visit Alice. Much of the time he arrived early and stayed for supper, though on those occasions he usually brought a bottle of Irish, or a bag of potatoes, or some candy for the girls. He and John often made a serious dent in the bottle. Alice would join them for a glass, but Harry and John were developing a serious taste for it. Even when Harry wasn't there for the socializing, John would go through a few glasses by himself.

23 March 1892

Dear Mr. and Mrs. Furlong,

It is with a heavy heart that I must write to inform you that your daughter, Ellen Furlong Powers, passed away a week ago today, on 16 March 1892, of heart failure complicated by pregnancy. Please accept our sincere condolences on the loss of your daughter.

As you may know from Ellen's letters to you, she was six and a half months pregnant. I am sorry to tell you that the baby, which Ellen strongly believed would be a boy, also died. The funeral was held this past Sunday at the Church of the Holy Nativity and a mass was said by Father Fagan. We buried Ellen in the new diocesan cemetery at Mt. Olivet, a few miles south of where she lived. Ellen left behind her husband, John, and her four daughters: Josie, whose seventh birthday we celebrate today; Annie, who recently turned six; Nellie, who is four; and Kitty, whose second birthday was, unfortunately, on the sixteenth of March, the day of Ellen's passing.

Ellen had been feeling poorly for quite some time, and suffered from a persistent cough. She was constantly fatigued, which she thought was due to her pregnancy. On the day before she died, severe pains confined her to her bed. John summoned the doctor, who gave her medicine which seemed to help. Josie slept with her mother that night as John had gone to fetch our sister, Bridget, to care for her the following day.

Ellen passed away in her sleep.

My younger sisters, Margaret and Mary, obtained leave from their employment to care for our nieces, as John had to return to work. On Monday, I left my own employment and am now living here with John and the girls, keeping house and caring for them until I must leave to prepare for my own wedding at the beginning of June. At that time, my sister, Margaret, will take over from me on a permanent basis. She will be taking care of John and your four granddaughters until they are old enough to no longer require her care.

I tell you this not only to acquaint you with the circumstances of your daughter's unfortunate and unexpected death, but to make you aware that your granddaughters would benefit from whatever financial help you can provide. My brother, John, has been a hardworking husband and father these past eight years and has done his best to provide for his family. Ellen was a wonderful wife and mother and will be sorely missed, not only because John and the girls loved her dearly, but also because of all she did to keep the family functioning during hard times.

John has a decent job at the stockyards and makes a good wage. However, the cost of living is high. The two oldest girls go to parochial school and expenses are incurred. There are no savings to fall back on in the event of further misfortune.

It goes without saying that my brother is unaware of my writing of this matter, for his own pride would never permit it.

Ellen often spoke of you. It was a great source of sadness to her that she was separated from her family and she was looking forward eagerly to your visit this autumn, when her new son would have been a few months old. It is a tragedy that her passing has made a family reunion impossible. Yet, in spite of Ellen's passing, a visit from you would be a blessing for your granddaughters and for you, I am certain. As you may

know, both of my parents are gone. It is a source of deep disappointment
to my brother, my sisters, and myself that none of our children will know
our parents. This is why I believe it is especially important that Ellen's
children have an opportunity to know you, their grandparents.

Ellen held an abiding love for her brother and sister, which, I am sure,
was reciprocated. Please convey our sincerest condolences to Sheila and
Timothy for us. I'm sure they will miss her as much as we will.

On behalf of my brother, my sisters, and my nieces,
I remain,
respectfully,
Miss Alice Powers

By early April, Alice was growing increasingly concerned about John
and Harry. "I've got no problem with the need for a drink at the end of
a hard day's work or for a special occasion," she said one evening after
supper, "but you fellows are taking this bottle of Irish a little too far
down the road, don't you think?"

Harry was embarrassed that his fiancée was scolding him in front
of John. "Alice, what are you saying? Are you criticizing us for having a
wee drink?"

"No, Harry. I've no problem with a wee drink, not even with a few,
given the right occasion. But the two of you are making a nightly habit
of this. You're finishing half a bottle or more of an evening, and that's a
lot more than a wee drink."

"My God, Alice," said John, "my wife just died. We're still in mourning here. Don't go getting sanctimonious on us. You of all people."

Alice looked at him in disbelief. "John Powers, please don't treat
me as if I were feebleminded. I've been working in saloons too long not
to know blarney when I hear it and trouble when I see it. I'm telling
you for your own good, just as our own da would if he were here — you're
seeing too much of the bottom of the glass and don't even bother to tell
me otherwise. I know what I'm talking about."

Neither of the men had ever seen Alice so steamed up and assertive.

"Alice," John tried again, trying to sound calm, "if you're concerned
that I'm turning into a lush, then let me remind you: I haven't missed
a day of work since you've been staying here with us, and for years before that, come to think of it, except for Ellen's funeral. So don't go act-
ing as if you're my ma, 'cause you ain't. This is my house, after all, and
Harry and I'll have a goddamned drink if we want it."

"Jacky," she said, "do you remember Mr. Hennessy, back in Water-ford?"

John reared up. "Jesus Christ, Alice, you're not comparing me with that drunk?"

"No, not exactly. I'm only saying he wasn't born that way, spending all of his time in the pub, coming home, beatin' his wife and kids. It took him a while to get like that."

"Oh Christ, Alice, you don't know what you're talking about. This is foolishness, damned foolishness. You're in serious need of a drink your-self, I'll tell you that. Jesus, comparing me to that old bum, Hennessy." He started to laugh and when Alice tried to interrupt him, he raised his hand to silence her. "Harry, you're going to have your hands full with this one. She'll be leadin' you around by her apron strings for sure if you let her."

Harry took his cue from John and put his hand on Alice's arm to re-assure her. "Don't worry yourself, love. We're not overdoing it. There's nothing to be upset about."

"Don't go sweet-talking me, Mr. Harry O'Hara," she threatened. "I've seen more than my share of drunks and you better believe I won't be marrying one."

She saw the look of shock on Harry's face and softened her tone. "I couldn't bear it if either of you ... I love you both so dearly ... I just want you to keep it under control. It's a sneaky business the way it takes over your life. I'm frightened, is all."

"Well, sister, I love you too, though maybe not quite as much as Harry does," John laughed, "but you worry needlessly. Just give me a bit of time to get accustomed to things as they are now. I've no intention of becoming a drunk. Besides," he smiled, "who can afford to drink like this every night?"

Alice regarded Harry. "Then maybe you can stop bringing a bottle over. Or maybe just some beer will do instead?"

Harry nodded and gave her a smile.

They heard a clippity-clop outside and Alice got up to look. "It's John F.'s horse and wagon."

She opened the front door and both men came up beside her, ex-pecting to see John F. himself. Instead, a young man climbed down from the wagon. John recognized him as a neighbor's boy who sometimes helped John F. on his route. The lad shouted out to them as he jogged up to the stoop.

"Mr. Powers sent me to tell you that his wife gave birth this after-noon to a baby girl named Margaret. Both baby and mother are doing fine."

"Wonderful!" they cried.

"Do they need any help?" Alice asked.

"No," said the boy, "my mother has been there all day and my sister will be helping as well."

"And you'll be giving Mr. Powers a hand with his milk route?" asked John.

"Yes, sir, I will." He turned to leave. "Well, I guess I'll be getting back. He just wanted all of you to know."

They thanked him for bringing the happy news and asked if he thought the Powers family would welcome a visit on Sunday.

"Mr. Powers said he was sure you'd ask and that yes, of course, you'd be welcome."

"Then tell him our clan will be there after church and we'll bring our own refreshments," John laughed.

When they returned inside, John broke out his bottle. "Well," he said, "we must celebrate our first niece and drink to her health."

Alice joined in whole-heartedly. It was as if the previous conversation had never happened. She was thrilled for her big sister, whose first pregnancy had been easy. Perhaps that would auger well for Alice, too. They drank to Bridget, John F., and new baby Margaret, and made plans to visit the next day.

"The girls will be excited," said Alice, "their first cousin."

"And Maggie will be proud," said John, "the first niece named after her."

"Actually," Alice corrected him, "I think it's his mother's name."

"Still," John smiled, "she'll be proud as punch, believe me."

The next morning, John and Alice brought the girls to church. Later, they took the Halstead Street trolley and then hired a cab for the rest of the trip, since John and Alice could not carry the two little ones as well as all the food and drink they'd brought. Hiring a cab was an extravagance, but John and Alice were almost as excited about the new baby as Bridget herself — and, of course, the girls were thrilled to be in the horse-drawn carriage.

When the O'Haras arrived that afternoon, the women congregated inside while the men spilled out of the snug house and did their drinking leaning against the modest cottage. They teased Harry about being next to become a father, and the likelihood that Jimmy could become one too — though without the benefit of marriage. Then the talk moved to work and the O'Haras' plan for a meat purveying business and John F.'s plan for his own route — both stalled for lack of funds. Everything costs so dear, they complained, it's near impossible to climb up a bit.

Although Harry had respected Alice's request to stop bringing whiskey to the house, John began frequenting one of the saloons just outside the Yards for a couple of shots after work. He had plenty of excuses: mourning the loss of his wife, or celebrating the birth of his niece, or relaxing from his hard day. Alice noticed he was getting home later, but when she asked him about it, he tossed it off as just shooting the breeze with a couple of the lads after work. At night, he supplemented what little Harry now brought with some of his own, and while Alice cleaned up after dinner, the men would go for a short walk, taking a few pulls from the half-pint bottle John carried in his jacket.

But John never missed a day at work and never drank during working hours, so he refused to believe his drinking was a problem.

7 April 1892

Dear Alice,

I hope my letter finds you well. Whenever I think of you, I still picture that sweet 12-year-old with pigtails and freckles, riding her bicycle to our meetings in Waterford. And now you are planning your own marriage. My heart is full of good wishes for you.

Needless to say, it is also full of grief. I am torn between wanting to thank you for writing to my parents and wanting to rage and cry out. How could such a thing happen! Ellen was so strong and vibrant, so full of confidence and gumption. How can she be gone at such a young age?

I remember the last time I saw her, the morning she left for America. I was so much in awe of her strength and her courage. I wanted so much to be more like my older sister. I would have sworn she was indestructible; and now, to hear of her death … It will take a long time, if ever, for any of us to fully accept it.

Still, I must thank you for writing to let us know. My mother gave me your letter. Of course, my parents know nothing of the role you and I played in bringing my sister and your brother together. Even now — perhaps especially now — they would never forgive me. In fact, it shames me to admit to you that my father blames John for Ellen's death. My mother, ever dutiful, will never contradict him, despite the fact that she does not share his belief. I think he blames himself but will never own up to it.

So, for that reason, he would never consent to visiting America or even acknowledge that he has four granddaughters there. What a shame that my mother and father will never see them, nor will the girls ever know their grandparents.

I dream of coming to America myself. I would love nothing better, believe me. Unfortunately, I have not married well. My husband is a hateful, disrespectful, vengeful man who derives sadistic satisfaction from humiliating me. He has made my life a hell. I would leave in a minute, only I know that he would keep my son, Bobby, from me if I left him. I love my son dearly, yet it is my love for him that keeps me chained to this life.

My sister once predicted that someday I would want to come to America to join her. At the time, I protested vehemently. Now, what I wouldn't give to be able to steal away with my boy and escape from my husband's control. Alas, it is impossible. I cannot even enclose some meager amount of money in this letter for Ellen's girls, for I have none of my own — not a shilling.

As much as I grieve for my sister, I grieve even more for my little nieces whom I will probably never see. My heart goes out to them. Hopefully, someday I will be in a position to help them. Meanwhile, please know that I am grateful that you and your sisters are in their lives. Give my sincerest condolences to John and to my nieces. Let them know of me and of my love for them. I am heartsick over my inability to do more for them at this time.

It occurs to me that you may be wondering why I have not mentioned my brother. Timothy is completely engrossed in his own life. He is a husband and father, but the truth is his life is the business. As long as my father is alive, Timothy must toe the mark. I fear he will not be his own man until my father is gone.

Needless to say, regarding Ellen's death, he takes my father's position of blaming John and even blaming Ellen herself. In a word, he is self-centered and seems to have no interest in anything not directly concerned with the business; that is, he is exactly like father.

Alice, I must go. I feel a closeness to you, as if we were true sisters; hopefully, we shall continue to write to each other. I am overcome with

sadness for all of us. Please be well and do write.
   With much warmth and affection, I am
   Mrs. Sheila Duffy
      P.S. Perhaps it would be best that you address future correspondence
to me in care of my mother.

Alice didn't receive Sheila's letter until almost two weeks later. She read it while sitting on the front steps, enjoying the warmth of the morning sun. The mail had arrived as she was hanging wash, Kitty and Nellie playing nearby. She recalled the pretty teenager she'd conspired with, the delicious sense of secret adventure. How romantic it had seemed to her at the time: her brother in love with the forbidden Ellen Furlong, sailing across an ocean to live in another country in order to pursue their love for each other — a love misunderstood and condemned by Ellen's narrow and prejudiced parents. How exciting it had all seemed then, only eight years ago.

It suddenly dawned on Alice that she was now the same age her brother was when he ran off to marry Ellen. And what seemed like such a romantic adventure at the time had gone terribly awry. Alice looked at her two motherless nieces playing in the yard, and the basket of wash needing to be hung, and the kitchen to be filled with the sounds and smells of her preparing dinner. There was nothing romantic about getting married and starting a family, she thought to herself, giving her belly a fond rub. It was just the hard, unending work of staying alive one day at a time. She understood the men's desire to drink away their troubles, but she was determined, once she and Harry were married, to put a stop to his growing habit, even if she couldn't control her brother's.

That evening, after the girls were in bed, she showed Sheila's letter to her brother. John read it, shaking his head in disbelief.

"What a pig-headed bastard the old man is. How can he behave like that to his own blood?" He passed the letter to Harry, who sat across the table. While Harry read, John continued his rant: "How can a man write off his own daughter like that? As though she never existed? And granddaughters? Just throwing away four lovely girls? His own blood, his own family! And he's supposed to have loved Ellen? Can you imagine? She actually believed she was his favorite, the apple of his eye. What a bloody bastard."

Harry finished reading and silently gave the letter back to Alice. "I could never do that," he said. "What a terrible thing. The man's not

146

human. He don't deserve to live, that one."

Alice put her hand on his arm. "I know that about you, Harry. I know you could never be so cruel, so unfeeling."

"Well, to hell with him, with all of them," John swore. "I'm not surprised. It's not any different from before, is it? He wrote her off eight years ago. He didn't care about her happiness, only about his own reputation and what the neighbors and businessmen would say. He hasn't changed."

"I feel sorry for Sheila," Alice said. The two men nodded and murmured agreement.

"And her brother turned out to be a prig too, didn't he? Just like his old man," Harry said.

"Christ, what a family," John said with resignation. "That Sheila's the only one with a heart. My da would never have done this. Never."

"That's true," Alice agreed. "He was a hard man sometimes, but he cared about us all. He wanted us to be happy. That's what was important. Besides, Ma wouldn't have let him abandon any of us. She was strong, she was — not like that spineless woman Ellen had for a mother."

"Sounds like she has no mind of her own," Harry put in.

"Ellen was different — she had her own opinions about things." John turned to his sister, "She was a bit like Ma that way."

"And they both had a bit of a quick temper, too," Alice added, smiling at some memory.

"Aye," said John, and he too retreated into his own reverie.

By the beginning of May, Alice had managed to carve out a couple of hours each day to use her treadle-operated Singer Sewing Machine. Janet O'Hara and Sharon O'Brian brought her some fabric and she honed her sewing skills making a few things for the house and some simple clothes for the girls,. The practice prepared her for the seamstress work she would be doing from home starting in two weeks, and it helped her brother save money.

In spite of the lengthening days, John showed no interest in getting back to gardening. Instead, he spent the time after work sitting on the front stoop with Harry and Alice, watching the girls play until their bedtime; and soon after he would retire as well.

Maggie sent a message that she would not be able to leave the Gallaghers on the 16th of May, as she had planned, due to something important that had come up in the Gallagher household. But, she assured them, she would be there on Wednesday, May 25th. Alice was disappointed; she had been looking forward to making some final additions to her trousseau. But another week or so wouldn't make that much difference, and perhaps she'd work on that instead of on more things for John's household.

As May progressed, the days grew warmer and the girls anticipated the end of school. Alice was excited about the prospect of finally being able to live with Harry. He found an apartment and was on the lookout for some second-hand furniture. And, it now looked likely that he and his brothers would be able to quit their jobs at the Yards and open their business by the end of June. Similarly, John F., spurred on by the birth of his daughter, was also planning to start his own milk delivery business about the same time. Spring, the time of rebirth and new beginnings, was filling their spirits with hopeful energy — all, except for John, who remained disheartened.

Friday, the 23rd of May, started out well, with everyone in the household looking forward to Maggie's arrival on the following Wednesday. This would be their last weekend with Alice. They had grown quite close and the girls would miss her, but they were equally excited to have Maggie join them. Everyone shared this mixture of sadness and joy. John left for work feeling rested, and even took a small measure of enjoyment from the warmth of the morning sun as he walked to work. The two older girls awoke with anticipation of the easier discipline and increased socializing that marked the end of the school year.

At work, John was concentrating on the task immediately in front of him. Suddenly, he became aware of a growing commotion behind him — scuffling, swearing, and grunting. Pausing to look up, he saw his co-workers staring wide-eyed at something just behind his shoulder, then raising their hands in alarm and shouting.

Later, John remembered it as if the scene had happened in slow motion. He recalled an immense pressure crushing his back before the force of it had time to reach the front of his body. He remembered thinking he must let go of his knife so he wouldn't cut himself or anyone else. Smashed against the massive metal table in front of him, the air squashed out of him, his legs were swept out from under him and a great, heavy weight — what turned out to be two brawling co-workers — fell on top of him, crunching his body awkwardly under them. His jaw struck the steel table as he fell, the doubled mass of men landing fatefully on top of his trapped and twisted legs.

Other men pulled the brawlers off him and McManus immediately had them both thrown out of the building while John was still sprawled on the floor. He thought his jaw was broken, although it proved not to be. Once he recovered from having the air knocked out of him, he became aware of a sharp pain, like a stabbing knife, with every breath. His ankles and legs throbbed, twisted awkwardly beneath him. Immediately, his face swelled and he had trouble forming words.

When McManus returned, he examined his employee. "Jesus Christ, man, look at you," he cursed. John tried to move, but McManus put a firm hand on his shoulder and told him to remain where he was. "Don't move — looks like your leg might be broke. We'll get you a stretcher."

"Broke?" John managed to mutter.

McManus looked him in the eye and nodded. "Sorry, Powers. Damned rotten luck. Don't move. I'll be back."

As soon as McManus disappeared, John let himself lie back on the blood-covered slaughterhouse floor. Tenderly, with one hand, he felt his swollen face, then his ribs, concluding that some must be broken. He raised himself up and saw the grotesque angle one of his feet formed with his leg. The pain was intensifying as the swelling increased. He laid back on the floor and shook his head in disbelief. *Jesus,* he thought, *what now?*

His boss returned with a couple of men and a stretcher and they carried him down to the main floor and out to the courtyard.

"We'll have an ambulance here for you soon, Powers," McManus said. "I'll send your pay around to your house." John looked at him questioningly. McManus shook his head. "There's nothing I can do. You're broken to pieces. It'll be weeks before they put you back together again, never mind your being able to stand for 12 hours." He shook his head. "There's no way around it. I can't keep your job open for you." He looked away. John knew there was no use in pleading.

McManus turned to him again. "When you're all mended, I'll see if there's anything I can do. But I can't be promising anything, you understand." Then he added in his gruff voice, "But I'll do what I can." He squeezed John's shoulder and walked back inside.

With great effort, John called him back. "Please," he mumbled through his swollen mouth, "send someone to tell my sister what happened, so she'll know where I am and won't worry herself sick." McManus gave a brief nod, and returned to work.

It seemed like an eternity before the horse-drawn ambulance arrived. At the hospital he learned the extent of his injuries: a dislocated and badly bruised jaw, some pulled and strained muscles, two broken ribs, one severely sprained ankle, and one leg broken just above the ankle. Casts were put on both legs and he was admitted to the hospital to recuperate for a few days at least.

That night, Jimmy O'Hara came to visit him. "Harry's helping Alice with the girls," he said, "so they sent me." Jimmy looked around the ward and then patted the inside of his jacket. "I brought you a little pick-me-up — figured you could use it."

"God bless you, James," John managed to whisper. "Give it here, then," he said, gesturing impatiently with his hand. After taking two good pulls from the bottle, he sighed. "Thank you and all the saints in heaven. Lord, but I needed that."

Jimmy regarded his friend. "You look a mighty wreck, lad. Like you fell off a building."

"Or had one fall on me."

John recounted the events, and how the two brawlers had been immediately thrown out of the building and blacklisted. The swelling on his bruised face made his speech slow and garbled.

"Do you even know what they were fighting about?"

"Don't know and don't care. I'm just mad as hell they had to pick that spot to do it in. Goddamn it, Jimmy, what am I to do now? Everything's lost. I'm a damned failure."

"What are you talking about? What have you failed at?"

"Everything. Can't you see? It'll be weeks before I'll be able to work again. What am I to do in the meantime? How am I supposed to pay my bills? My rent? Food?"

Jimmy shrugged, "Well, of course it won't be easy ..."

"Oh, Jesus, you're a master of understatement, you are. 'Won't be easy,' my arse. It's impossible! Christ, I had such plans once upon a time. Just like you do, you and your brothers. Your own business, being your own boss. I remember once, when me and Ellen first started seeing each other, she asked me if I had any ambitions. I told her no, just to earn a decent wage and have enough to have a little cottage, like my ma and da, raise my kids — you know?"

Jimmy pictured Ellen as a young bride.

"I had it there for a little bit," John said morosely, "until Ellen died."

"That wasn't your fault, Jack. Nothing you could have done about that."

"Maybe. You never know. Looking back, I might have ... I don't know, maybe got her to a doctor earlier. Maybe not tried to have another baby."

"But you didn't know, Jack."

"Now, look at what a mess everything is. No Ellen, no job."

"But you'll get your job back, surely."

John shook his head. "Ah, Jimmy, don't you understand? I'll be off my feet for weeks. McManus can't hold my job for me. When I'm all healed, sure, I can go ask him for work, but you know as well as I do that I'll be right back to square one — seven or eight cents an hour. Where the hell am I going to get another job paying me 12 cents an hour? I got four girls, damn it. What's to become of them? Where are they supposed to live if I can't pay the rent?"

Jimmy took a pull from his bottle, then offered it to John. "I don't know, Jack. I hadn't thought about it. I didn't realize until I got here how banged up you are. I guess I just assumed everything would be the same as before."

John shook his head. "If only that were so. Lord Jesus, what I wouldn't give for that. But it won't happen. Ah, shit, Jimmy. I'm done for. I give up. I can't do this any more."

"What're ya talking about? Giving up? How the hell can you do that? You just said it yourself — you've four kids. You can't give up on them."

"What am I supposed to do, then? Rob a bank? Jimmy, I'm going to lose the house, my home. I'll have no place to keep the girls or be able to feed them, never mind myself. I'm no use to them, none at all. Christ, I couldn't take care of Ellen and now I won't be able to keep my girls. They'll end up in that orphan asylum the nun spoke to me about, living on the dole."

When Jimmy glanced up, he saw the swell of tears in his friend's eyes, overflowing and streaming down the bruised cheeks. He spotted a towel near the bed of a sleeping patient and handed it to John. "Do you know how long they're going to keep you here?"

John wiped his eyes and shook his head. "I'm not sure — at least a few days, they said. I'll get out sometime next week, I suppose."

Jimmy thought for a moment. "I don't see why you couldn't stay with us."

John gave him a quizzical look.

"Yeah," Jimmy said, nodding his head as the thought coalesced. "Sure. Harry will be moving out to his own place soon enough. That would leave the sofa empty. You could stay there. No reason why not."

"And sponge off you O'Haras? How could I pay my way, Jimmy? I can't expect you and Ed to keep me in my accustomed manner, now, can I?"

Jimmy smiled. "Jack, it wouldn't be forever, now would it? A few weeks, you said. So, you'd lose a little weight, maybe."

John shook his head, "I couldn't do that."

"Well, then, you'll work for your room and board."

"Work? How in hell am I supposed to do that?" he said, nodding his chin at his two immobilized legs.

"Well, my brothers and I will be starting up the business soon. I'm sure there'll be things that can be done from a chair — filling out forms and keeping track of things. We couldn't pay you, of course. We're all to be on starvation wages for a while ourselves, but it would be a help to us, I know. I'll speak to Ed about it when I get home, but I don't see why not."

John raised an eyebrow. "I wouldn't want to be a bother."

"And Janet can stretch the food. There's no end of people can be fed on potato soup," he laughed. "And, you could help with watching her kids."

John stroked his moustache. "Maybe it could work," he drawled, surprised at the hint of hopefulness in his own voice.

"And if the girls have to put in a few weeks in the orphanage until you get back on your feet, well, it's not the end of the world, now, is it?"

John considered the offer: two months at the most until he was back on his feet and could find a paying job and a cheap apartment to rent. It wouldn't be the same as having their cozy house, but nothing would ever be the same again anyway. They'd never have their mother back. But maybe in another three or four months, he could have his family together again. Then, Maggie could come as planned and everything would be — what? Well, at least they'd be together. He'd be a father, doing what he was supposed to do as head of his family.

"All right," he said, "you speak to the others about it. If they're willing, then I'm willing. But it'll only be for six weeks or so, until I'm on my feet again."

"Of course. You think we want your smelly old farts stinkin' up the place? The sooner you're out, the better."

"All right, then. Let's drink to it."

"Aye," said Jimmy, "a fine idea, that."

5

Gary, Indiana

Wednesday, September 20, 1911

Ann looked around the gravesite at her sisters gathered there with her: Josie, with her husband, Theodore Arcand, and their five-year-old son, Teddy Jr.; Nellie; and her baby sister, Kitty, with her fiancé, Arthur Kirk. Kitty and Arthur, a sandy-haired man with a thin moustache and glasses, were planning to marry in February. All four sisters had traveled by train to Gary, Indiana, from Chicago; the funeral parlor had provided carriages to the cemetery.

On the other side of their father's grave were Aunt Bridget and Uncle John and their 19-year-old daughter, Margaret. Aunt Mary, a spinster at 36, stood at the foot of the coffin with Aunt Maggie and Uncle Albert, the Bresslers, who were childless. And there were prosperous Aunt Alice and Uncle Harry O'Hara, with their three youngest boys (the six oldest had remained home to attend school).

One would think that nine children in 19 years would take its toll on a woman, but Alice, at 39, still had black hair and a trim figure, as well as her high energy level. Indeed, it seemed the children kept her young. Of course, Harry's success allowed her a full complement of live-in help. Annie wondered what it would be like to work for Aunt Alice and Uncle Harry. Would they be as picky or as exploitive as the people she had worked for as a housemaid?

Ann thought of her own little girl, Mary Ellen, now five years old and still in St. Joseph's, where Ann herself had spent half her childhood. She dropped her head, feeling guilty and ashamed and avoiding other peoples' eyes.

At least my mother had the decency to get married after she got pregnant, but here I am, 25 and single with a daughter pining away for me in that awful institution. Ann shivered involuntarily and Josie put her arm around her sister. Feeling unworthy of solace, Ann bristled and shook it off.

Josie, her husband and son beside her, was thinking how sad it was for her father to be gone before young Teddy really had a chance to know him well. When she and Ted married eight years ago and moved back to Chicago, she had not seen all that much of her father, who had remained in Gary. The thought flashed through her mind that now he would be here eternally.

The fact was, they had grown quite distant since Ma died. Even living with him and Marguerite for four years hadn't rekindled the closeness they had enjoyed when she was younger. And now he was gone forever, same as Ma. Well, Ted's parents were still alive, so Teddy would have one set of grandparents at least.

She felt Annie shudder and instinctively put her arm around her younger sister. Surprisingly, Annie stiffened and shook her off. But, maybe not too surprising after all. You never knew about Ann — she could be so touchy, so sensitive, so quick to take offense. But two minutes later, she'd be joking and you'd never know she'd been angry. Just like Ma, Josie smiled.

Aunt Bridget caught Josie's eye and gave her a wink. What a sweet woman! No one had tried as much as Bridget to pick up the slack for their father and provide some sense of family. And her daughter, Margaret, was a sweet young woman — pretty and bright. She was the first girl in the Powers family to graduate from high school. Josie glanced sideways to her three sisters. Kitty had graduated from eighth grade, while the other three had reached only sixth. Well, that was common enough — even her own mother, intelligent as she was, had only gone through eighth grade back in Ireland. And Dad had only four grades of learning. I suppose he did his best, she sighed.

Bridget looked across the grave, the priest's murmur hovering vaguely in the background like the drone of a swarm of bees. She felt sad for her four nieces and Josie's little boy, who would never know the grandfather they were burying that day. Oh, little Teddy probably knew what the old man looked and sounded and smelled like, but he'd never have an understanding of the man — how hard he worked at the most basic tasks to provide for his family. *Well, didn't he?* She glanced quickly around as if seeking confirmation from her sisters. *God,* she thought, *how does Alice do it? Nine — and only four killed poor Ellen.*

As the priest wound down and swiftly crossed himself, they returned their attention to the present. Harry hurried to take charge of the situation, reminding everyone to meet back at the funeral home. From there they'd walk to Ferguson's Inn, in the center of Gary. Alice invited Mary to ride with them in their automobile.

"We'll just hold Tommy and Francis on our laps," she assured her sister.

"How good of Uncle Harry to do this for all of us," Josie said to her sisters as they returned to their carriages.

"Well, he's the only one who can afford it," said Annie, an edge to her voice.

Josie's husband, Ted, jumped to his defense. "Well, Mr. O'Hara has worked hard for every penny. You wouldn't deny him that, would you?"

"I'd call working hard what he used to do: working in the Yards, like my father did when we were little girls. Not driving around once a month in his fine touring car, collecting rents."

Ted was about to reply, but Josie gave his arm a subtle squeeze and he swallowed his words. He wasn't going to get into some squabble with Ann, who could flare up at the drop of a pin.

"I liked what the priest said about Father," Kitty chimed in. The others looked at her questioningly. "Like what he said about his being a hard-working and God-fearing person who tried to be good and do good," she explained.

"I must have missed that part," said Ann.

"Well, I'm sure he tried to do the best he could," Nellie soothed.

"He should have tried harder," Ann spat out.

"Anybody know anything about this Ferguson's? I'm hungry enough to eat a horse," said Arthur Kirk, Kitty's fiancé.

Ted Arcand spoke up. "I hear it's quite good. I think someone mentioned that Mr. O'Hara had a room reserved for us. I'm looking forward to it, and a good drink, too."

"Well, with Aunt Alice and Uncle Harry, you can be sure there'll be drinks," Kitty said brightly.

Mary took the O'Haras up on their invitation and squeezed into their five-passenger touring automobile with them and their three young boys.

"Well," she said, "there certainly is a lot more room than in those little runabouts one sees so much of in the city these days."

"It's the latest model and it ought to be swell; it cost over $3,500. With all of our children, we need the larger car," Harry explained. "It's a necessity. I understand that some companies are coming out with a seven-passenger model within the next couple of years, but so far this is the biggest one available. We always have to leave some of the children at home. If Alice continues to get pregnant, I'll have to start strapping them onto the roof or the running board."

Mary rolled her eyes at his joke. "Harry, will your brothers be meeting us at the restaurant?"

"Yes and no," he said. "Jimmy is taking the train from Chicago and should be at the funeral parlor by the time we get there, but Ed is busy minding the store, so he and his family won't be coming."

"What a shame," Mary said. "Our brother thought so much of Ed and Janet. Too bad they can't make it."

Alice turned to her younger sister. "Did you know that Ed and Janet's daughter, Mary, just gave birth to her third child? Her second boy. Janet is staying with them to help with the children. So Ed is a bachelor for a couple of weeks. And then with the business ..."

"No," Mary said, "I had no idea. So little Mary is a mother for a third time and here I am a 36-year-old maiden aunt. I guess my own nieces and nephews are the only children I'll get to know." At that, she pulled two-year-old Francis onto her lap. "But it'll be good to see Jimmy again. I'm glad he's going to be there."

Harry and Alice exchanged a quick glance. "Yes," Harry said, "I'm glad he can make it." Mary heard what sounded like annoyance in his voice.

"I hope you won't be disappointed by the fare at the restaurant," Alice said.

"Oh, no," Mary laughed, "it's such a pleasure not having to prepare it myself, it almost doesn't matter what it is."

"Still, you must be used to the finest cuisine."

Mary smiled at what she perceived as a compliment. "That's true, but sometimes when you've dined so often on lobster, a good Polish sausage tastes wonderful."

"I think it'll be a step up from that," Alice said, a little miffed. But she attempted to make light of it by adding, "At any rate, we've all had our fill of boiled potatoes and cabbage, that's for certain."

"Yes," agreed Mary, "it's wonderful that none of the children have had to go through that. I think of those days sometimes." Alice nodded and each sister turned inward, recalling their earlier deprivations.

Bridget, John F., and their daughter, Margaret, rode in the first of the two horse-drawn carriages. With them were Josie and Ted Arcand and their son, Teddy. Puffing on his pipe, John F. engaged Mr. Arcand, a foreman at Armour and Company, in conversation about current events, crime, and what he thought of President Taft.

"He's no Teddy Roosevelt, that's for sure," said Ted, "but you have to give him credit, going after U.S. Steel the way he did."

Bridget changed the subject. "John and I are so proud that Margaret just started college. I don't know what I'll do with my time now that she's no longer living at home. John doesn't need me to help in the business the way he did when he first started. He's employing people to do all of that now."

"I'm hoping to be a mathematics teacher," Margaret said in response to her cousin's inquiring look.

"That's wonderful," Josie said, "A teacher," she added in admiration, "imagine that." She turned to her aunt, "Can you even conceive any of us ever having such a notion? Graduating from high school? College? A career as a teacher? And in mathematics, no less." They laughed at the preposterousness of it all.

"Well," Josie sighed, "you should both be so proud. If Da had lived to see it, he'd have been proud too." Imagining her own son's future, Josie squeezed Teddy's hand. "I know Da hated that none of us could continue with our schooling."

In the second carriage, Ann and her sisters listened while Aunt Maggie regaled them with stories about the frustrations of working as a seamstress and her dream of someday opening her own dressmaking business.

"Your Aunt Alice did seamstress work at home when her first two boys were still babies," she reminded them. "My, how she hated that! I hope I have better luck starting my own dressmaking business."

"I remember," Annie said, "that's when we first went into St. Joseph's."

"Yes, that's right," Maggie said, looking surprised that any of her nieces actually did remember. "Well, anyway, I'd like to start my own business since it doesn't look like Al and I are going to have any children. It would be nice to be able to create something of my own."

Kitty asked Ann why her beau, Freddie Wilhelm, hadn't come to the funeral service. Ann shrugged, saying he couldn't get time off work. Fred drove a milk route for a dairy company, just as Uncle John had done (indeed, Fred's horse looked like the same tired horse John F. had used back then). Uncle John had his own company now and no longer delivered for someone else. Maybe someday Fred would own his own route too, Ann mused.

Nellie asked Ann about her daughter, Mary Ellen.

"It's too bad they wouldn't let her come to her own grandfather's funeral."

Ann made a face. "Goodness, Nell, don't you remember how strict those old crows were? Them and their routine; nothing so important that it's allowed to interfere with their damned routine. It still infuriates me to think of it."

"How does Mary Ellen take to it?" asked Kitty.

Ann shrugged. "Same as we did, I suppose. She puts up with it. Has she any choice?"

Neither sister was sensitive enough to perceive that Ann didn't want to talk about her life in front of Arthur Kirk and Al Bressler.

"Are you and Freddie planning on getting married next year?" Kitty persisted.

Ann's first impulse was to shake her head in disbelief. Kitty was so obtuse sometimes. But that came from being naive and gullible — she was so sweet-natured that she couldn't imagine anyone taking offense at anything she might have to say. Ann glared at Kitty, but then saw the look of sincere interest on Kitty's face.

"We are talking about it, but we haven't decided on anything definite yet."

"So he's asked you? And you've said *yes*?" Nellie asked excitedly.

Now Ann broke into laughter. "My goodness, Nell, you'd think you were the one getting hitched."

"Well?" Nell and Kitty said in unison.

"Well, yes, as a matter of fact, to both your questions."

"Then you're engaged!" Nellie squealed. "Oh, Annie, I'm so happy for you! But I can't believe you never said anything to Kitty or me, what with the three of us living together."

Kitty reached over and gave her sister a hug. "Congratulations, Annie. We're so happy for you. Freddie is so sweet. I know you'll be very happy together."

"Now, see, that's just the reason I didn't want to blab about it. Here you are already making plans and everything. We've just decided this is something we might do if everything works out."

"What do you mean?" Kitty asked. "You're both working. What's the problem?"

"Well, just things — like, for example, if I'm to continue working, where we might live, whether we're to have children, and so forth. And there's the matter of religion. Fred's a Lutheran, you know. Besides, he's only just asked me and he wants to put some money aside first. My goodness, give us some room to breathe so we can see where it is we're going."

"I'm sure that you and Fred will work it all out soon enough," Arthur put in. "Kitty and I went through the same kinds of questions, didn't we?" he asked, turning to his fiancée. Aunt Maggie and Uncle Al, who had been listening with great interest, nodded knowingly to each other.

"Can we tell the others?" Nellie asked. "They'll be so happy for you." Ann blushed, her face turning almost as red as her hair. She shrugged, as if to say, *why not? Cat's out of the bag.*

"And Mary Ellen," Kitty began tentatively, "is that one of the things to be decided too? I mean, would Fred be willing to let Mary Ellen live with you? I understand that not every man ..."

"Oh, no," Ann reassured her, "Fred's adamant — he wants to adopt her as his own as soon as we're married. Nothing's more certain than that."

Kitty patted Ann's hand, then squeezed it. "I'm so glad for you and for Mary Ellen. I know it hasn't been easy for you."

Ann compressed her lips to suppress a tear. She didn't enjoy being reminded of what she'd been through: six-and-a-half years at the orphanage, the next four years back with Da and his new wife, Marguerite — that French bitch — and then the horrible experience with that awful family in Gary, where she got pregnant with Mary Ellen. Then these last five years working as a housemaid again, putting up with the same nonsense and abuse with rich bitches looking down their noses at her, like she wasn't worth anything. God damn their eyes.

Jimmy waited outside the funeral home to greet everyone as they spilled out of their carriages. Annie watched as Uncle Jimmy made the rounds, kissing and hugging and shaking hands. It had been a long time since she'd last seen him, probably at one of the many birthday parties or communions that Uncle Harry and Aunt Alice were constantly hosting.

He looked old in spite of his ruddy complexion. Well, he was pushing 50 after all — almost as old as Da — and all the drinking and carousing had taken its toll. Still, he was a charmer — always a funny story, and that magical way of looking at you directly in the eye, as if only the two of you existed. At least for that minute, until he went about making his rounds, draining drinks and glad-handing whoever else was there, like the two-bit politician he aspired to be.

Uncle Jimmy was a rascal, her da's best friend and "partner in crime," as they liked to say. Ann deliberately hung back so she'd be the last one he noticed.

"Ah, Annie, my darling little redhead, the spittin' image of your dear mother. How are you holding up?" he asked as he embraced her and gave her a kiss on the cheek. She smelled the aftershave lotion on his closely shaved skin and already the sweet smell of whiskey on his breath.

"I'm fine, Uncle Jimmy. I'm glad you made it."

"Wouldn't miss it for the world. How could I, your da and I being like brothers?" he said, twisting his first two fingers together to show her what he meant. "Where there was one of us, there was two. God knows how I'm still alive and he's not. It's almost like we were married, we were that close. Well, maybe not *that* close," he laughed, and took her arm as the others started to walk to the inn a couple of blocks away.

"Where are you living now, Uncle Jimmy? Are you really back in Chicago?"

He hemmed and hawed and did a little tap dance around the question. "Oh, you know how it is, darling. I'm here and there, back and forth. I never know where I'm to lay my handsome head from one night to the next."

Ann shook her head in mock scolding. "Uncle Jimmy, when are you going to grow up and settle down?"

"Never, lassie. Never, if I can help it. Life is too much fun. Life is for the living of it and not to be squandered on those who have no interest in it. No, there's too much enjoyment lying around for the taking for me to be settling down. Look where it got your poor old da. Twice married he was and twice as unhappy as me, the poor sod. God rest his soul."

Reflecting on the four years Da was married to Marguerite, Annie had to agree. But then she recalled those early years that, in her mind, defined happiness: sitting on her father's lap while he read the papers, helping Ma in the kitchen, playing outside with Josie and Nell. "Settling down seems to agree with your brothers," she said.

"Aye, that's true. Both Harry and Eddie, happy as clams, aren't they? Well, like you said, maybe it's just that I never grew up. Taking on all those responsibilities like they do. No, that ain't for the likes of me, I'm afraid."

Ferguson's was charming — a large inn with a wrap-around porch furnished with settees, rockers, and small, cane tables and chairs. Its original sprawling lawns and gardens had been drastically reduced in size by the encroachment of the city, where workers from the steel mills now made their homes. Inside, the vast carpeted rooms were quietly elegant, with airy French doors opening onto the veranda and views of the attractive landscaping.

A private dining room reserved by Uncle Harry was already set up: one table for the three O'Hara children plus young Margaret Powers and Teddy Arcand, and another for the 14 adults. With everyone seated, that table, too, was divided by age and generation, with the aunts and uncles at one end, headed by Uncle Harry; and the other end assigned to Uncle Jimmy, flanked by his four nieces. Near one of the French doors was an open bar.

When drinks had been poured, Uncle Jimmy stood and raised his glass to his brother Harry, at the far end of the long table.

"Here's to my brother and his lovely wife, Alice, with deep appreciation for providing such a fitting occasion to celebrate the passing of our dearest friend. We are truly one large family. I don't know if the O'Haras belong to the Powers clan or if it's the other way around. By any measure, we are all one intertwined muddle of souls, and poor departed John Powers — too poor to have ever afforded a middle initial (*everyone laughed and looked at John F., who broke into a smile*) — was, at least on occasion, one of the most muddled. He was also one of the most loved. Wherever he is, I hope he will hear the music of our laughter and taste the salt of our tears. Again, deeply felt thanks to you, Harry and Alice, and to all of us, my loving condolences on the passing of John Powers. We shall all miss him terribly. Now let us have a fine Irish wake to send him on his way."

To that, he raised his glass and emptied it, as did most of the men. The women sipped at their drinks, except for Alice and Mary, who knocked theirs down in one gulp.

"Are you determined to die the same death my father suffered?" Ann asked her uncle.

Jimmy turned to answer her. With a smile playing about his lips, he asked, "Is it my liver you're worried about, or are you trying to pick a fight with me?"

"Why would I want to fight with you?" Ann asked innocently.

"Because you're angry at your da for leaving you, and I'm as close to being him as you can get."

Ann flushed and straightened up in her chair.

"I'm angry at him for going and leaving me behind," Jimmy admitted. "Why shouldn't you feel the same?" The smile stayed on his face but Ann's eyes glowered.

"Come on, lass, it's only natural. It's nothing to be ashamed of."

Ann knew that her sisters were looking at her and Uncle Jimmy.

"Well, you're half right, at least," Ann admitted. "I am angry at him, but not for dying. I'm angry at him for having been such a drunken fool, wasting his life the way he did." She saw the look of shock on her sisters' faces.

"Well, don't look at me like I'm some kind of idiot. What I said is the truth. You all know that."

"That's not the way I think of him," Kitty said.

"Nor I," said Nell, "not a drunken fool at all."

"Like the priest said, he was a good man who tried to do good," added Kitty.

"Well, you two were always his favorites. I'm not surprised you're standing up for him."

"Annie," interjected her uncle, "it's true your da did his share of drinking, as any true Irishman should, but he was no drunken fool."

"Jimmy O'Hara, how can you say that? Really! He died of liver disease for God's sake. How do you suppose he did that? From sippin' a glass or two of an evening? He drank too much, too much of the time. That's why he got that cirrhosis or whatever it's called. That's why he couldn't hold a job, why he always got into fights, why he married that monster, Marguerite, and why even she left him. Don't give me that 'boys will be boys' malarkey. He was a drunk, an alcoholic, a lush — and that's why he died. And that's what's going to happen to you too, you fool, if you keep at it."

There were tears in Ann's eyes as those around her sat shocked and silent. The aunts and uncles at the other end of the table didn't hear this exchange.

Jimmy laid a hand on her arm. "Annie, what can I say? Perhaps you're right. Maybe my love for your da has blinded me a little to some of his failings. Sure, he could put away a few too many and sometimes when he did, he had no patience for the stupidity of others, or their foul manners or their outright hatred of us Irish. And maybe he was a little quick to knock some sense into them. And, I'll agree, marrying that woman was a mistake from the beginning, but he did it for you girls. Never forget that. He wanted desperately to get all of you out of that asylum and he thought marrying her, and her money — yes, I'll give you that — and making a new home for you was what he needed to do. And Marguerite didn't leave him because he drank. She left him because there was no love between them. None at all. Never was. But he married her anyway. For you. That's the kind of man he was — he would do anything for his daughters. No, Annie, he was no drunken fool at all. Not your da. He was a brave and desperate man, but no drunken fool."

"If he loved us so much, then how come it took him six-and-a-half years to get us out of that place? He didn't need to find us another mother. All he needed to do was to hold a job and pay the rent on a place for us to live. We would have settled for that privy he used to refer to as the swamp out on the Southside, as long as we would have been together."

"Annie, it wasn't that easy. You were just a little girl. You don't remember how it was then. Jobs didn't pay 12, 15 dollars a week like they do now. It wasn't so easy to find work that could pay enough. And remember," he said, gesturing to his left, "these two were hardly more than babies. Who was to look after them if he was working 12 hours a day? You and Josie? You were what — six, seven years old yourselves? No, sweetheart, you're not being fair to your old man. It wasn't like you say."

"Annie," said Kitty, leaning onto the table, "I don't know about Marguerite, since I didn't live with you during that time, but my recollection is that Papa always worked. I mean, I know sometimes he'd be out of a job, but never for very long and it seemed as though he was always working, either in the steel mills or at something — often with you, Uncle Jimmy."

He nodded in agreement.

Josie spoke up for the first time. "You're both right. Da usually was working, like you said, Kitty, but we have to admit, his work history was very unstable. He was never more than a laborer, finding odd jobs here and there, low paying, temporary. Enough for a room and some drink, like Annie said, but not much more. Look at what he was laid out in. That suit ..." She shook her head in disgust and Ted put his arm around her for support.

"And Annie," Josie continued, reaching for her sister's hand, "I don't mean to be starting anything by saying this — I'm just making the point that sometimes things are difficult and we can't always do as we wish. Look at your own daughter, for example. Of course you want to have her with you, but Mary Ellen's been at St. Joseph's herself for five years."

Josie thought Annie might strike her if she weren't holding onto her hand. Still, she could see how her sister fumed at this sensitive topic.

Nellie turned to address her youngest sister. "Kitty, you were lucky you didn't have to live in Gary with Pa after he married Marguerite. Such a cold house it was. Marguerite obviously hated our being there. But the only way she could have Da was to take us. He'd insisted on that. The fact is, she bought him and we were part of the deal. You were the lucky one, getting to live with the O'Brians instead."

Kitty shook her head in disbelief. "And I was always so jealous of the three of you. I imagined you had it just like in the old days when Ma was alive, that you had something I was deprived of. I always wondered: Why didn't my father want me? What was wrong with me that the three of you got to go with him and I didn't?"

Josie said, "If the O'Brians hadn't rescued you from St. Joseph's before Da got married, you would have been with us. But I think he knew how it would be and he probably figured you were better off with

George and Sharon and their two little ones than being exposed to the hard misery we shared."

"If only it had been like it was before Ma died," Nell said. "I don't know, if I had to do it all over again, whether I'd choose to stay at St. Joseph's or live with Pa and Marguerite."

"What was so bad about her?" Ted spoke up from across the table. There was a moment of silence in which the three older girls looked to each other. Who would go first? What was the worst thing anyone could say about Marguerite?

Jimmy broke the spell. "First thing you must keep in mind," he started, accepting another drink from the waiter, "was that Marguerite Hardiman was a widow. Not exactly wealthy, mind you, but fairly comfortable. She was French, from Canada, where she had been married to some well-to-do. He was killed in a fire, burned to death, and Marguerite was — how shall I say — disfigured in the blaze. Her face, and she was a fairly attractive woman to look at, wasn't damaged, but her body was severely burned and she carried those scars with shame — and I know, a great deal of anger. No, I never saw them myself," he said with a smile and a wink, "but your father told me all I'd ever want to know."

He took a pull from his drink before continuing. "She lost two little girls in that fire." He paused and looked down at the table. "I think she moved down here after that to be with her mother who — would you believe it? — died soon afterward, so she found herself in a foreign place all alone. She was desperate for companionship, but who would want her, with that tortured body? She met me and your da in a pub here in Gary after we'd come down here for jobs in the steel mills."

Jimmy smiled to himself. "She could hold her liquor, I'll give her that. Anyway, she and John hit it off well enough and they eventually came to an agreement. She'd provide a home for you three girls, who were still in St. Joe's, and he would ... ahem ... be her husband."

Jimmy shook his head and drained his glass. "But it never worked out. She was cold and cruel, always belittling him, always angry and crabby. Ach, how John used to complain to me." He turned to Josie and Ann. "That's why he made the two of you quit school and go into service, so you could escape that witch. It wasn't because he didn't love you or didn't want you. He knew how unhappy you were and it tore him apart inside. I know — he poured it out to me on many occasion."

"But even he didn't know the half of it," Ann added, "like the way she used to punish us. Remember?" she said arching her eyebrows at her sisters. "The punishment details: scrubbing the floors, the walls, the cement steps outside the back porch, the front sidewalk ..."

"The way she'd make us kneel on raw rice for hours on those cement steps," Josie said, nodding her head for emphasis.

"And standing on our toes, leaning against the wall with our fingers, and whipping us across our legs if we faltered."

"And your father never knew?" Arthur Kirk asked.

Ann shook her head. "We were afraid to tell him. She'd have only denied it and then punished us for telling. We knew we just had to bear up under it."

"And the religion!" Nellie suddenly remembered. "What a fanatic she was about that! Everything was a sin. You couldn't do this or that, couldn't look in a mirror or down at shiny shoes, always having to cross ourselves. Everything was bad and evil. God, I used to have nightmares all the time about going to hell. I was afraid to breathe."

"I think she must have been an ex-nun," said Ann.

"She was certainly as strict as any I ever knew," Josie agreed. "Maybe that's why she gave all her money to that French church when she died."

"She didn't leave any to your father?" Ted asked.

"No, she died after they divorced."

"When was that?" Art asked.

"Let's see," Ann said, pursing her lips in deep thought, "Da married Marguerite in November of 1898. That's when he took us out of the orphanage and brought us here to Gary to live with him. I was 12 then and you, Josie, must have been 13, and Nell was only 10. Then Marguerite and Da got divorced in 1903 and she died about four years later — so that must have been 1907, just four years ago. Of course, Josie and I went into service back in 1900 when I was 15 and Josie had just turned 16."

"And you, Nell, what happened to you?" Ted asked.

"I stayed there until they divorced. I was 15, so that's when I went into service, too. Fortunately, I ended up with a good family, so it wasn't too bad. But anything would have been better than living with Marguerite. She was horrible. I still have dreams about her."

Arthur looked at Nell with compassion. "Sounds like your father made a bad deal all around. Everybody was miserable: you girls, your father, and Marguerite."

"Ah, hindsight," said Jimmy. "If only we'd known then what we know now. But back then, Jack thought it was a good deal. All he ever wanted was to get his girls out of that orphan asylum. When he saw his chance with this woman — and not a bad looker either — with some money, well, he took it, didn't he? How was he to know it would turn out to be such a calamity?"

"But aside from providing that house, and clothes, nobody ever saw hide nor hair of that money. Da certainly never got his hands on any of it. Nor us either," said Annie.

At the far end of the table, the older generation was deep in conversation as well.

Bridget confided in her sister, Alice. "I'm going to miss Johnny, but I'm really sad for those girls. Now they'll never have a chance to put things right with him."

"I think they'd probably given up on that a long time ago. He hadn't exactly been too steady on his feet these past few years."

"I don't think Jack was ever the same after Ellen died," Harry offered.

"Yes, of course, but I think it was the accident that finally did him in. It was like all the life got crushed right out of him," Bridget said.

"I don't think he ever forgave himself for putting those girls into St. Joe's. Blamed himself entirely," Alice suggested.

"Well, it was pretty awful for them," Bridget said, "but, if it weren't for the drink, he might have been able to hold on to a job and get them out sooner, instead of having to marry that woman, just for her money."

"And marrying her never brought him any good anyway," Alice said for emphasis. "Lord knows, we all tried to help him, each of us. Even Mary tried, getting him a job at the Yacht Club."

Mary turned her head at the sound of her name. "What's that?" she said. "Did I hear someone mentioning my name in vain?"

"I was just saying, Mary, how we all tried to help poor Johnny. You even got him a job at the Yacht Club."

Mary nodded. "He couldn't hold on to it though, could he? He never missed a day of work, I'll give him that. But dark and brooding all the time, he was. Always looking for a fight, it seemed."

The conversation brought back the memory of her boss, informing her one day that he couldn't put up with John's surly attitude any longer, and he'd have to give him the boot.

"That was the trouble with him," Mary recalled, "he'd come into work drunk or hung over and looking to get up into somebody's face. You couldn't talk to him or tell him what to do without a challenge."

"I know," said Harry, "it was the same when my brothers and I hired him at the meat purveying business, before I went into real estate. He'd be three sheets to the wind and unable to do the work. Then if you took him to task, you were no good friend of his. If he didn't get fired from every job he had, it was only because he'd quit instead."

John F. nodded. "I kept him on as long as I could because he was Bridget's brother, but after a while, I couldn't take it anymore. He'd changed. He was no longer the friend we used to have. That accident did him in for sure. He just wasn't the same Jack we'd always known." He turned to his wife. "Now tell me if I'm wrong," he said.

"No," Bridget agreed, "you're not wrong. You did what you could and I never blamed you for letting him go."

"I think he was out to destroy himself," Maggie said. "He had already lost everything, so why bother? Why not just put an end to it all?"

Al Bressler, a brawny, heavyset man, added to his wife's comments. "I don't mean no disrespect to your brother, I never knew the man, but I see plenty of people like that on my job as a cop on the beat: losers, drunks, beggars, petty thieves, on the street all the time. They're hopeless. There's nothing to be done for them. It's almost better to put them out of their misery. From what you're saying, it sounds like he's better off dead."

"Albert, how can you say such a thing?" his wife exclaimed. "That's my brother you're talking about. And he was no loser nor petty thief, either. He always worked, or tried to, anyway."

"I'm not saying ..."

Harry jumped in. "It was Jimmy," nodding to his brother at the other end of the long table, now laden with food and more drinks, "who kept getting him odd jobs, like with the Democratic Party, or whatever, handing out leaflets."

"Or breaking up Republican rallies," John F. said with a smirk.

Harry smiled. "Yeah, he busted a few heads in his day, as well as getting involved with some other shenanigans."

"Got arrested for it at least once, didn't he?" Maggie asked. Bridget nodded.

"More than a couple of times," Harry concurred. "I'd call some people or Jimmy would, and we got him out soon enough. But that was Jack, ready to do anything to earn a dollar, to keep himself going."

"To keep himself drinking, you mean," Alice said. "You know, it's like they say, God helps those who help themselves. We all tried, but the truth is, he'd given up. I don't know if he was ever ready to admit it, his heart just wasn't in it anymore — that accident coming right after Ellen's death."

As the luncheon progressed, some of the diners moved around the table between courses. So it was that Bridget ended up between Maggie and Kitty, while Arthur Kirk sat down between his wife's two uncles, John F. and Harry O'Hara. The three men immersed themselves in a discussion of whether the hard-playing Cubs would be able to catch the New York Giants and advance to the World Series to face the Philadelphia Athletics, the probable winners in the American League.

Jimmy took Alice's seat next to his brother, Harry, while Alice sat down on his chair between Ann and Nell.

"How are you two holding up?" Alice asked her nieces.

"All right, I guess," Nell said. "I feel sad, of course, like it's the end of something. I'm done wishing it could be different. It's over now, that part of our life, isn't it? No more wondering if he has a job or a place to hang his hat."

Alice agreed. "There was that — the worrying. But he was extraordinarily proud, wasn't he? I think that's why he hardly ever accepted any of our invitations, always making some excuse. I think he was ashamed of what he'd come to."

"You're probably right, Aunt Alice," Annie said, shaking her head, "but it always made me angry to realize he'd rather be off by himself, probably in one of those dingy saloons down by the mills, than be with us. It always made me wonder — don't we matter to him at all?"

Kitty leaned in toward her sister. "I know, I've felt that way too. But then when Da would show up, like this last July Fourth at your house, Aunt Alice, and he would be so loving and affectionate, full of old memories and stories, I knew he loved us. It wasn't for lack of caring that he stayed away."

Nellie's eyes welled and she groped frantically in her purse for a handkerchief. Alice put an arm around her niece. Josie, who had been talking to her husband, asked what was the matter.

"Nothing," Nellie said, "just remembering things about Da."

Jimmy came back and stood behind Alice, just as the next course was being served. "Sorry to interrupt, ladies, but I'm not done yet with stuffin' my face."

After a few minutes, Nellie addressed her three sisters. "I was just remembering when we were at St. Joseph's, those Sundays when Da or our aunts came to visit, how we looked forward to them."

"I also remember that there were plenty of Sundays when no one came," Annie said. "When we'd be sitting on our beds in that huge dorm in our clean uniforms, waiting and waiting, watching the other girls get all excited and giddy when someone was there to visit them."

"Or when one of the girls got adopted — we'd be happy for them and sad at the same time, having to say goodbye, knowing we'd never see them again."

"I mostly remember a grayness," Josie said. "It's as though there was no color at all, only drabness. Like all the life got washed out of everything."

170

Kitty added, "The nuns in black, the nurse in white, the teachers in their dark dresses ..."

"Even in those sewing classes, we never had any colorful material to work with — only that gray, striped cotton we used to make everything out of," said Nellie.

"I remember the laundry," said Annie. "Do you remember that? God, I hated that laundry."

"At least it was warm there, and in the kitchen," said Nell. "I used to look forward to working there in the winter. At least I'd be warm."

"Not me," said Ann, "I hated those work details. There was nothing I liked about being there: the food, the nuns, those stupid classes with — what? — 50, 60 girls in a classroom? No wonder we didn't learn anything. I'm surprised you two came out knowing how to read," she said to Nellie and Kitty.

Jimmy listened to these recollections and finally joined the discussion. "It's true what you say, but they did the best they could. I remember going once with your da and Bridget to talk with the superintendent. I think they had something like 168 children, almost all of them girls under eight years old."

"That's right," Josie said, "Annie and I were always just about the oldest ones there."

"And almost all of us Irish," Annie added.

"I'm just saying," Jimmy continued, "they had all these young children and babies, like the two of you," he said, nodding to Kitty and Nellie on his left, "and very little staff. I think they only had four teachers."

"And two cooks," said Josie, "and two dressmakers."

"Precisely," Jimmy agreed, "hardly any staff at all to care for so many little ones. Oh, it grieved your da, it did, that he had to leave all of you there."

"Still," Annie said, "as bad as it was, being there and feeling forgotten, it was even worse living with Marguerite."

Jimmy sighed and shook his head, "Like I said before, darling, it seemed like a good idea at the time. How was he to know? He wanted to do right by you. He wanted to make it right, like before your ma died. He wanted to put everything back together again."

"But he couldn't do it, could he?" Josie said.

"Aye, and it broke his heart."

"Broke ours, too," Annie added.

6

Ann and Fred
1912

The following Sunday, there was a knock at the door of the flat where Ann, Nellie, and Kitty lived together. Ann smiled when she saw her fiancé, Fred Wilhelm, holding a small bouquet in his hand.

"I was hoping it would be you," she smiled as she noticed the flowers. "Oh, Freddie, how sweet of you."

As he leaned toward her and gave her a kiss on the cheek, Ann flushed in embarrassment and mouthed to him to stop. Then she turned and yelled to her sisters, "It's Fred. We're going. See you later." Grabbing her parasol and purse, she stepped out of their flat into the stairwell and closed the door behind her.

Later, over tea and pastry in a café, Ann leaned closer to him. "Fred, I've been thinking about the discussions we've had about getting married." He raised his eyebrows and a worried look spread over his face. "No," she said, "I haven't changed my mind." She was pleased to see relief soften his eyes. "Just the opposite. I would like for us to get married as soon as we can."

"Oh," he said, "why the change? I thought you wanted to wait."

Ann paused for a moment and glanced out the window. Then she inhaled deeply and straightened her back. "It's mostly because of Mary Ellen," she said. "Ever since my father's funeral, I've been thinking, remembering my own time in the orphanage, how miserable I was, feeling abandoned and forgotten. I don't want my daughter going through that any longer."

Fred reached his hand out to hers. "Annie, sweetie, that's just what I've been telling you these past months. You know how I feel about her being there, you only getting to see her once a week. It's not right. But I thought we agreed to wait until we had more money saved."

"No," she said, shaking her head, "I don't want to wait any longer. We'll just do with less. We'll get a smaller place, or one farther out on the Southside or west where the rents are lower."

Fred lowered his eyes. "What about religion? I know you want to get married in your church, but we can't do that unless I convert. Your priest isn't going to marry you to a heathen."

"I know," she nodded, "but you said you'd think about that."

Fred let out a long sigh. "I guess I don't have much choice, do I? If you're going to marry me, I guess it's something I'll just have to do."

Ann looked at him, her eyes brimming with tears. "You'll do it?" Fred nodded. "You promise?"

"Yes, of course. I said I would."

"Oh, Fred, I'm so happy. When will you look into it?"

"As soon as I can. But I'm only doing this so we can get married. Don't expect me to go to church with you every Sunday, kneeling, praying, all of that."

"I understand. But at least we can go ahead and make preparations. Oh, Freddie, I'm so happy."

"Me too, sweetie. I've been looking forward to this for a long time, having a home. I mean a real home. A family."

"It's been a long time for you, hasn't it?"

"Almost 22 years now since I ran away from home. Aside from the care I got from Mr. Kellogg, I haven't had any family since I was a boy of 11. Actually, come to think of it, I guess I never had any real family."

Ann grasped his hand. "We'll make a fine family together, I know we will."

"I know I won't ever be like my father was. You can count on that, Annie. I won't be knocking heads and hurting anyone. I'd sooner die than be like that."

"I know, Freddie. You wouldn't harm a soul. That's what I love about you, your gentleness." She fell silent, remembering how her mother castigated her father for being too soft. Well, she was strong enough for both of them. "We'll do just fine," she said. "I know it."

"I hope I can be like Mr. Kellogg. He was a stern man, strict in a lot of ways. He wouldn't stand for any nonsense, if you know what I mean. But he was generous and bighearted. At least he was to me, taking me in and letting me stay with them, getting me some schooling and a job so I could earn my keep."

"You'll be a good father, Fred. I see it when we visit Mary Ellen, how you are with her, how she takes to you."

"She's a good kid, Annie. I'm glad you decided we should go ahead and get married. I can't wait 'till we have our own home and that little girl with us where she belongs, instead of in that damned orphan asylum."

Ann and Fred had their small church wedding the following summer on June 26, 1912, at the Church of the Holy Nativity. Nellie was her maid of honor and the best man was Nellie's future husband, Billy Moore, who worked as a salesman at the Armour Meat Packing Company. Kitty and Arthur Kirk — who had been married on February 12th — attended, as did Josie and Ted Arcand.

Immediately after the service, Ann and Fred had their wedding pictures taken at the Fox Photography Studio at 50th and Indiana Avenue. In one of them, Ann is seated in a chair, holding a bouquet of flowers in her lap. Her high-necked, short-sleeved gown reaches to her ankles, not quite covering her high-laced black shoes. A long lace veil cascades down to drape over her arm. Her dark auburn hair, worn in the popular pompadour style, frames her square, pug-nosed Irish face, which she and her sisters inherited from their mother. Nellie, just turned 24, her tightly curled hair parted in the middle, is at Anne's side, half-sitting on the arm of Ann's chair. Fred stands smiling behind his bride, looking dignified with his hands clasped behind his back and a boutonnière proudly gracing the lapel of his new dark suit. Billy Moore, the tallest and fairest of the group, is centered behind them all, his high celluloid collar supporting his serious, handsome face.

After the picture taking, Josie and Ted treated everyone to lunch at one of their favorite restaurants. As the oldest, Josie assumed the role of mother on these occasions, and felt it was her duty to see that her sisters had a proper celebratory launching into married life.

The next morning, a staff person sent by the Mother Superior came to fetch Mary Ellen Delpha Powers from her class. Delpha, as she was usually called, quivered with fear at being summoned to the Office of the Superintendent, Mother Superior herself. What had she done wrong this time? Then she saw her mama standing there with Mr. Wilhelm. Everybody was smiling. Her mother reached down to hug her and Mr. Wilhelm himself hoisted her up and held her against his chest. Everybody beamed and clasped their hands. Mother Superior herself planted a kiss on her cheek and said, "God bless you, child."

To the five-year-old girl, everything was buzzing and incomprehensible. She clung on tightly and hid her quivering lips in Mr. Wilhelm's neck.

Miss Brown, one of the disciplinarians, handed Ann a paper bag with a few precious belongings in it. Everyone said goodbye and waved as Ann and Mr. Wilhelm said over and over again, "We're taking you home now, Del, honey. We're taking you home with us. You're going to live with us now. Forever."

Delpha could only ask herself: *Can it all be real? Blink your eyes, Delpha. Are you sure it's not a dream? Wake up or you'll be in trouble and then you'll be sorry!*

Much later, as an adolescent, Del would look back on the time spent in the orphanage as an existential nothingness, like the black pages of a photograph album in which old pictures are pasted — only there were no snapshots, no memories at all. The pages remained darkly and resolutely blank. Living with her mother and father on the Southside was like being born at the age of six. She arrived into her mother's life fully formed and aware, but with no history. Nothing existed until that miraculous day, and then everything bloomed at once.

The following June, Ann and Fred's first child, Josephine, was born on Friday the 13th. Delpha had turned seven just a month earlier.

Ann and Fred rented a flat on South Wabash with two small bedrooms, one of which was shared by the two sisters. Ann was enchanted with her new little girl — a baby conceived and born in wedlock, the birth eagerly and proudly anticipated. Although Delpha was delighted to be reunited with her mother — and to have a father who loved her — she was exquisitely sensitive to her mother's feelings about Josephine. A fierce jealousy flourished toward this interloper, one she wouldn't outgrow until her late teens.

Kitty and Arthur Kirk also had a child in 1913 — a son, Arthur Jr. The family lived on the Southside as well, and Kitty and Ann often met in a nearby park to wheel their baby buggies when the weather allowed, or sometimes at each other's flat. They took it for granted that their husbands would support them and their children, just as their own father had tried to do. After all, how could they possibly be expected to work as maidservants now that they had a home and family of their own?

Fred left the flat for his milk route before dawn six mornings a week, and Ann enjoyed staying at home as a mother and a housewife. She delighted in all of her homemaking chores: cleaning, cooking, shopping, and caring for the baby. She was proud, too, of having electric lights and indoor plumbing, and living in a neighborhood with paved streets and sidewalks — conveniences her family had often lacked, but her wealthy employers always enjoyed. Even more significant, being married legitimized her and Mary Ellen. She was no longer an unwed mother; now she was Mrs. Fred J. Wilhelm — as respectable as anybody!

To her dismay, Ann gradually became aware that Fred had a problem with alcohol. She attempted to make him reduce his consumption, appealing to his common sense and his own frugal nature. But despite his sincere promises, nothing worked. One day he returned from work early, shamefaced. With a bowed head and subdued voice, he told Ann he'd been fired for being drunk on the job.

"Drunk on the job? My God, Freddie, you've been drinking at work?" He shrugged his slim shoulders without raising his eyes from the floor.

Ann's first thought was of her father losing his job for punching someone, and how difficult it was to survive on his reduced wages. They had been forced to move to smaller quarters. And now history was repeating itself. The shame! What would people think? Fred Wilhelm fired for being drunk on the job? Would they have to move? From this lovely apartment?

"Fred Wilhelm, how could you do such a thing?" Her temper flared and she slapped him across the face. Ann was immediately appalled by her own action, but Fred barely flinched.

"Jesus, Mary, and Joseph, I don't understand you!" she ranted. "How could you do this? To us? To yourself? Have you no pride? No sense of decency? Is this how it's to be, then? You drinking away our money, losing one job after another because of your damned foolishness? Selfishness! That's all it is, pure selfishness. Not giving a thought to me or your daughters, only to yourself. Didn't I tell you that your drinking was getting out of hand? That it would lead to trouble? But no, Mr. Know-it-all couldn't be bothered listening to his shanty Irish wife. What are we to do now?"

Beside herself, she turned away from him. She needed to be far away from this bearer of catastrophe.

Fred shrugged his shoulders. Taking off his hat, he scratched his head before risking a peek in her direction. Across the kitchen she somehow loomed large, all five feet of her, arms akimbo, glaring.

"I don't know. I'll look for another job. I'm sure I'll find something. We'll make out." Then he reached for a chair and clumsily sat down. "I'm sorry. I don't know how it happened. I didn't ..."

"Don't know? Saints preserve us! What do you mean you don't know how it happened? You drank, Fred. You drank on the job. While you were working. How could you be so stupid?"

"I didn't mean that, Annie. What I meant was, I didn't think I'd get drunk. There was only a sip left in the bottle. Really, it didn't seem enough to get drunk on. I never intended that, Annie, I swear. If I'd thought it would have affected me, I never would have touched it, not even a drop. You have to believe me, Annie. I thought I'd just take the chill off — you know how cold it is before the sun comes up. I never thought I'd get drunk. I don't know how it happened. Maybe I'm getting sick or something."

"Oh, Jesus! You're sick all right. And if you aren't, you will be when I'm through with you. Stop lying to me, Fred. Stop lying to yourself."

Fear and outrage welled up as the reality set in, and she collapsed and surrendered to tears.

"I'm sorry, Annie. I'll make it up to you, I promise. And it won't ever happen again. Never. I've learned my lesson, I swear it."

Ann wiped her eyes and blew her nose. How pitiful he looked. How sad, how like a little boy. Her rage spent, she suddenly felt drained. Images from childhood flashed before her and she imagined her own two girls playing in those same muddy streets, using the dilapidated outhouse behind the flat on South Carpenter. The cold days and nights shivering without heat, the endless bowls of watered-down cabbage soup, the choking smoke from trains that rumbled by every few hours carrying squealing pigs, cattle, and sheep to the stockyards. And the hysterical fear that, if they were going fast enough, the trains could suck you under their wheels.

Oh, God, she cried silently, *is that what I have to look forward to?* She remembered her mother, short-tempered, tired and worn out. She remembered young Josie providing some sense of direction at barely a year older than Ann. Dear Josie. Maybe she would know what to do.

Fred left the flat shortly afterward, to look for a job. With Del at school for the day, Ann met Kitty in the park. Still flaring with fury every time she thought of the potential consequences, Ann spat out the sorry tale of Fred's folly.

"What will you do," Kitty asked, "if Fred can't find work?" She saw the tears in her sister's eyes.

"Do you remember when we lived down on South Carpenter?" Ann asked.

Kitty slowly shook her head. "Not really," she said, "a couple of images of Mama holding me on her lap, is all."

Ann nodded her head forcefully, assuming the authority of one older and wiser. "Well, I remember. It was hell, Kitty. You can't imagine how dirty it was, how cold and hungry we were. You cried all the time. That's all I can think about, having to live like that again, one step from being on the street."

She peered into the baby carriage, her sweet Josephine sleeping quietly under the blanket. "Oh, I swear I could kill him. I really could."

Kitty hesitated to ask Arthur if he could help Fred get a job at Montgomery Ward. What if Fred turned up drunk for work there? Would it affect Arthur's prospects? He was so set on moving up in the company and his bosses thought so well of him, she didn't want to do anything to spoil his chances.

"What about Uncle John?" she asked. "He might be able to help. Maybe he needs a driver for one of his routes."

Ann thought for a moment. "Yes, that's a possibility. I'll get in touch with him and Aunt Bridget and see if they can help. Fred's a good worker, really. This has never happened before. He's never missed a day until now. It really wasn't fair of them to fire him at the first sign of a weakness."

"Maybe if he goes back and explains, you know, and promises?"

Ann regarded her sister. "No, I don't think so. And, furious as I am, I wouldn't want to put him in the humiliating position of having to crawl on his knees to those stuffed shirts. No, a fresh start is what he needs. I know he's learned his lesson."

When a week passed with no prospects, Ann and Fred both lost whatever optimism they had managed to summon. John F. had just cut back his staff, citing increased competition from larger dairies. Albert Bressler, although keeping his eyes and ears open on his beat, could think of no one who was hiring. Ted Arcand could have gotten Fred a job at Armour, but Ann put her foot down. She would not have her husband — and herself and the girls — subjected to the abuses of the meatpacking industry, repeating the hardships she'd endured when her father worked there.

Even Uncle Harry couldn't come through. He employed supers in his apartment buildings, but there weren't any openings — and, he said with some discomfort, "Do you really want Freddie hauling other people's trash, at their beck and call to unclog their toilets and God knows what?"

When hope had all but evaporated, Jimmy came knocking at their door.

"Open up in there," he yelled, "it's the police and I know you're in there!" Ann opened the door prepared to defend her nest. She was shocked to see her uncle standing there, hat in hand, a mile-wide grin on his ruddy face. He roared with laughter when he saw the astonishment on her face.

"Gotcha," he said.

"Yes you did you old war horse. What a terrible joke. You're lucky I didn't greet you with a skillet in my hand, ready to do you in."

"How are you, my darling?" he asked, stepping inside the flat and giving his niece a hug and a kiss on the cheek.

"We're hanging on, Jimmy. It's been a tough couple of weeks. I don't know if you've heard," she said, taking his hat and coat.

"Precisely why I've come. Harry mentioned Freddie's predicament and I've been asking around. Seems a friend of mine works for a big dairy down south near West Hammond. Actually, it's just over the line into Indiana. He assures me he can give Freddie one of their routes. But it has to be done quickly. The spot just opened up, and they need to fill it quickly."

"Hammond, Indiana?"

"Don't get upset, now. It's not that far. It's only 15 miles or so, but you'd have to move down there. It's a pleasant little town, surrounded by countryside. A lovely spot for you and the girls and a chance for Freddie to get back on his feet. What do you say, lass? Isn't it the good news you've been praying for?"

Annie's thoughts jumped nervously from one thing to another. A job! Money to pay the rent, return the loans from her sisters — but they'd have to move. She'd be alone with no family around, no more daily visits with Kitty. But a new start for Fred, away from his drinking cronies and no slanderous gossip to live down — and nobody knowing about Delpha.

"Yes," she said, "yes, we'll do it. Fred's out now, but I'm sure he'll jump at the chance. Oh, Jimmy, how can we ever thank you? You're salvation itself."

"No need, sweetheart. I'm always glad to help out. You know that. It's what your father would have expected me to do." Jimmy gave her all the information and enjoyed a cup of tea with a little something extra in it that he brought with him, knowing that Annie wouldn't keep any alcohol in her home.

Uncle Jimmy had long since departed when Fred trudged in, dejected from another day of frustration, and was greeted with the promising news.

They moved within two weeks, with the help and financial support of the O'Haras and John F. Powers. Kitty cried saying goodbye to her sister, but everyone breathed a sigh of relief; it looked like the Wilhelms would rise from the ashes. Hopefully, there would be no more such calamities. Ann and Fred rented a little bungalow at 1620 South Van Buren Avenue, two blocks east of the Illinois border and only five blocks west of Calumet Avenue, where the trolley ran all the way north into Chicago.

Aside from missing her family, Ann was in heaven. They had a private house similar to the one she remembered at 3768 South Emerald Street, which she associated with the only happy memories of her childhood. This one had bigger rooms, more space outside, a covered front porch — all at the same rent they paid in Chicago. But permeating her joy was an absolute sense of relief that she would not be forced to relive the shameful deprivations of that sorry mud hole on South Carpenter.

Maybe, like Da, I'll plant some flowers around the house and my girls will play stoop-tag or play house with their dolls outside in the sun, and I'll watch them while peeling potatoes as my own mother did. We might even get a dog. Life is good. God bless Uncle Jimmy. Now, if only Freddie will conquer his demon.

And so he did — for a while. During the next three years, life progressed unevenly. There were good times when Fred was sober, or very nearly so, and Ann's spirits were high. She made friends with neighbors and women from church, and took pride in her home. With Fred's modest wage, they were living up to the lace-curtain heritage and dreams of her mother.

It was Delpha's job to dust the new furniture — the bowl purchased at a yard sale, which Ann claimed was genuine Waterford crystal ("It's famous the world over and it's where your grandparents were from"), a silver-plated tray, and other recent acquisitions. Ann skimped on expenditures, including things for herself, in order to create the home her own mother had wished for.

But then Fred would go on a binge, drunk for days at a time — although he was true to his word and never drank on the job. During those times, Ann lashed at him relentlessly (though not so loudly that the neighbors would hear).

If left to himself, he was a happy drunk, wanting only to be affectionate or sing and laugh. But the only way he could endure Ann's rage was to curl into a ball and escape into sleep. The next morning when Ann or Del awoke, he would be off to work — and maybe, by the time he returned, he might be his sober self again.

Delpha, shy and introverted, had difficulty making friends. A voracious reader, she was an excellent student and a favorite of the nuns at school. She relished privacy. Every time she went into her room — her own room! — she marveled that she was no longer in a dormitory where nothing was safe and nothing sacred. At the orphanage, the only privacy was obtained by withholding thoughts and feelings from public scrutiny, by withholding oneself from others.

Apprehensive of her mercurial, volatile, and unpredictable mother, she quickly came to trust Mr. Wilhelm, who she called Papa. She had come to adore everything about him, especially that he was so unlike Mama: He was taller and thinner with no Irish lilt to his voice and no constant references to God or church or sin. There were no fierce, glaring stares to burn right through her, no constant scolding. He was completely non-threatening. She liked the scent of his cologne mixed with pipe tobacco and chewing gum, which — she realized later — he used to hide the smell of whiskey. But mostly she liked the affectionate way he laughed and tickled and hugged her, or when he asked her to read to him.

She didn't care what Mama said about his drinking. *I love him,* she thought. *Besides, what's so terrible about getting drunk? He's funny and sweet. Why does Mama always have to be so angry, yelling such hateful things to him? Why can't he have a few drinks after work to relax, like he said? It makes him even more loveable. What's wrong with her?*

On a close par with Papa was their black-and-white mutt, Skippy, who loved all of them — even Josephine. Del resented the baby; it was bad enough that Skippy made a fuss over Mama, but Josephine? There was no accounting for a dog's taste. Still, she loved him with all her heart and the feeling was mutual.

Delpha also enjoyed the occasional long trolley rides up to Chicago to visit Aunt Kitty, who was so loving and demonstrative. They would stay over at least one night, maybe two or three, leaving Papa home to fend for himself and Skippy. Del suspected Mama was glad to have an excuse to be away from him — or maybe it was a way to punish him for another bender. Del also liked Uncle Art, who laughed easily and took time to talk to her about what she was reading. Although she missed her papa and felt sad for him on these visits, she couldn't deny that she felt right at home at Aunt Kitty's house.

And it was fun to help take care of Aunt Kitty's baby, little Arty, who was not like her sister at all. Sometimes Aunt Josie or Aunt Nellie came to visit, and that was always a happy time, almost like a party. Mama was usually in a good mood then and Del never got punished when her aunts were visiting.

At home in Hammond, it was a different story. It seemed to Delpha that her mother took exception to everything she did. She was likely to be punished for wasting time reading, looking at herself in the mirror, doing a poor job with the dusting and floor scrubbing, or not attending to Jo when she was crying.

Never a word of praise — she was more likely to hear disappointment. "What a bad girl you are. Aren't you ashamed of yourself? How can you be so thoughtless?" And the dreaded: "What will the neighbor's think? Do you want them to think shanty Irish live here? What kind of mother will they think I am? I only hope that some day when you have children of your own, they'll bring you as much misery as you seem to delight in bringing me."

Delpha soon realized it didn't make much difference whether she tried to be good or not, so she might as well indulge herself. Punishment was swift for her exploits: skipping mass to walk along Calumet Avenue looking in the shop windows (after making sure to put the designated money in the poor box); (deliberately) tipping Josephine's carriage into a snow bank; pinching the baby until she cried; eating the soft inside from a loaf of bread fresh from the bakery, leaving only the dry crust (she knew she was bound to be found out, but couldn't stop herself).

Of course, such misbehaviors regarding food inevitably led to insults about her weight. "Just look at those piano legs of yours. You're going to grow up to be a fat lady in the circus if you don't watch yourself, young lady!"

Ann was eight months pregnant in December 1916. Fred, who would turn 37 on Christmas Eve, was looking forward to the birth of his second natural child — although in every way he considered Del, now 10, his own. Because of her advanced pregnancy, Ann could no longer withstand the long trolley ride to see her sisters, so they all traveled to Hammond for the Christmas holidays: Josie and Ted Arcand and Teddy Jr.; Nellie and her friend Billy Moore ("Are they ever going to get married?"); and Kitty and Arthur Kirk with their son, Arty. Kitty, too, was pregnant with her second child, but not as far along as Ann, and therefore able to travel.

Aunt Bridget and Uncle John F. Powers, their daughter, Margaret, and Aunt Maggie and her husband, Albert Bressler, also made the trip. Aunt Alice and Uncle Harry found it impossible to come (Alice having given birth again — number 11) and sent their regrets. Ann was delighted to have her family visit her home, but was realistic enough to know that in her condition, 17 people for dinner was plenty. God forbid Alice O'Hara and her clan, too — enough was enough! And of course, Aunt Mary couldn't come because she still worked at the Yacht Club during holidays.

Delpha was responsible for cleaning the house and helping in the kitchen, but she didn't mind. She looked forward to seeing her extended family. This would be the happiest Christmas yet, she was sure of it.

Fred's workweek ended on Friday, the 23rd, and he stopped off after work to have a few with his friends and co-workers. There was much to celebrate — the upcoming holiday, his birthday, and the imminent birth of his child. When he finally came home that night, he was as happy as King Midas. No one was richer than he. Entering his dark house, he stumbled over a piece of furniture.

Must have been left there by Annie, probably rearranging things to accommodate the coming crowd. How come everything's so dark? Where is everyone? he wondered. Reaching for the lamp, he lost his balance and crashed into the table. *Annie would kill me if I broke her lamp,* he thought. Before he could get to his feet, he saw his wife standing over him, tying the belt of her robe, her long red hair hanging loose over her shoulders.

"Hello, beautiful," he said. "I saved the lamp."

"Is that the tack you're taking, then? That you're a princely hero I should be thanking and singing God's praises for? Just returned from the front lines in France, have ya? Is that where you've been to all hours?"

He held the lamp up, as if making a peace offering. Taking the lamp from him, she continued her scolding. "You're home late, Fred Wilhelm. You're home late from work and you're stinking drunk."

"Only a couple, sweetheart, to celebrate, you know ..."

"You dare come home, stumbling and falling down in front of your own wife and children?" Fred glanced toward the hallway, but didn't see Del and Jo cowering. "Did you at least bring home your pay, Mr. Wilhelm, or have you drunk it all away?"

"No, sweetie, I've got it all right here." Trying to rise, he paused to search his pockets, becoming distracted by bits of paper he found.

"I don't see any pay envelope, mister," she scolded, replacing the lamp on the end table.

Fred made the extra effort to pull himself clumsily to his feet. "Ah, here it is, right here where I put it," pulling the envelope out of his pocket and handing it to her.

She took it wordlessly and counted the contents. "And how did you manage to get this drunk without spending any of your own paycheck?"

"Oh, the boys were wonderful, Annie, because of Christmas and my birthday and the baby coming. How could I refuse?"

He leaned forward to kiss her, but she pushed him away. "You smell like a brewery. Don't think you're coming near me smelling like that. I won't have it, Fred. You can sleep it off on the sofa."

"But, Annie, it's almost Christmas Eve and it's my birthday. Come on, have a heart ..."

"No. I've told you a thousand times if I've told you once, I won't have a drunk sleeping in my bed. Look at you, slurring your words and weaving all about. You can hardly stand up. Sleep it off — tomorrow, I need you sober to help Delpha and me put up the tree. And don't forget, my family is arriving Sunday." She regarded him sternly, lips pursed, "Fred, I need you sober this weekend. Please."

"Don't worry, my love, everything will be fine," he slurred. "I promise."

"Just see that you are," she said, drawing herself up to her full five feet and tightening the belt of her robe. "And assuming you are fit in the morning ... well, we'll see about a nice birthday breakfast."

Fred attempted another kiss, but she brushed him away once more. "How's the baby?" he asked, placing both of his hands on her protruding belly.

"The baby is doing fine, thank you very much."

"Is it kicking? I don't feel anything."

"It's just sleeping, same as you should be. Now goodnight," she said and returned to their bedroom, shutting the door behind her. Fred fell on the sofa and pulled his coat over his shoulders. He didn't even bother to turn off the lamp.

Christmas morning, Mary Ellen was the first in the living room, with Josephine right behind her. Hearing their daughters, Mama and Papa were soon up and about, still pulling on their robes. The girls couldn't wait to open their presents. Josephine still believed in Santa Claus and, although Del was dying to burst her balloon, she knew there would be hell to pay if she did.

Both girls got new outfits: coats, hats, shoes, a dress, underwear, socks, gloves, and little purses. Josephine also got a doll. Thrilled with her new outfit, Del hugged both her mother and father, and was pleasantly surprised to receive a warm embrace back from her mother.

Ann usually attended mass on Christmas morning, and this year, because she was unstable on her feet due to the advanced stage of pregnancy, wanted Fred to join her. But Fred was adamant in his refusal.

"Just this one time, Fred Wilhelm," she implored. "It's Christmas and it won't do you any harm, especially considering how you've been behaving." She made a little gesture of tipping a glass to her lips.

"Annie, sweetheart, it's the one thing I won't do," Fred held his ground. "I'm sorry for everything else, and you're free to go with the girls if you'd like, but I've told you — the only way you'll get me into that church is feet first."

She pouted and muttered and banged around in the kitchen, but when she saw he meant what he said, she decided to leave Josephine home with him and take Del to church. Ann had gained a lot of weight during this pregnancy and she felt the pain in her knees and lower back. Climbing the front steps of the church was not something she thought she could do on her own. Fred's fierce determination to stay out of a Catholic church annoyed her, but she was glad to get out of the house. She enjoyed the short walk through the neighborhood to their parish church, in spite of the snow on the ground and brisk bite in the cold air.

Delpha was in an especially good mood and looked pretty in her new outfit. Ann had a sudden memory of shopping in downtown Chicago with her own mother, and a smile softened her face. She and Del even enjoyed a laugh together as her daughter recalled some silly event from school.

Family started arriving in the early afternoon. Aunt Bridget and

Aunt Maggie took over in the kitchen and the men gathered in the living room. Del was assigned to watch over Jo and Arty. Josie, Kitty, and Nellie ended up in Ann's bedroom oohing and aahing over preparations for the new baby. Gifts were exchanged with much chatter and confusion over who gave what to whom. Ann watched the men nervously, but was finally distracted by everything else going on in the crowded little house.

By early evening when everyone began to leave, the men were slapping Fred on the back and exchanging wisecracks. They wished him a happy birthday and good luck with the baby. Finally the door closed behind them and, for the moment, the house was peacefully quiet, full of lingering warmth and affection. Fred approached his wife from behind, putting his arms around her and kissing her neck.

"It was a grand party," he said. "The best I've ever been to."

"We had a nice party when we got married," she said.

"True, but it wasn't in our own home, with our own children around, and on my birthday, besides."

"I'm glad you enjoyed yourself. I had a wonderful time too. It made me feel grown up to have my aunts and uncles here. Thank you, Freddie. It's been a very happy day."

"For me too."

"But," she wagged her finger playfully, "the party is over. You must promise me: No more drinking. I understood about today, but now it's over, right? I need you to be sober for me, for us, for the baby."

"I know, sugar. I'll be there for you. I promise. Everything will be fine."

Less than two weeks later, Virginia Wilhelm was born on January 5, 1917. Josephine was delighted with her new baby sister, but Del was even more enthusiastic. As angry as Del had been at Josephine's intrusion into her domain, she was equally happy to have a new sister. She became a second mother to the baby, and was often scolded by Ann for spoiling her with too much attention and affection.

Fred kept his word and remained on the wagon until that summer when he fell off — jumped off — with a terrible vengeance. It started with the concurrence of July Fourth, Del's and Josephine's birthdays, and their fifth wedding anniversary. Fred felt that he had a lot to celebrate, including six month's of near total sobriety.

He came home late for dinner the evening of July 3rd. "Just a little celebration with my friends," he said. But the next morning, Ann saw him rummaging around behind one of the bushes in the backyard and adding whiskey to his coffee from the bottle he'd retrieved.

Around noontime they took the trolley up to Chicago to visit Aunt Alice. The O'Haras were hosting a holiday party, in part to celebrate their son's graduation from Loyola University. The whole family attended, and it was a joyous affair. The men celebrated the landing of U.S. troops in France the week before, but the party was dampened a bit when young John O'Hara announced he had enlisted in the Army. Alice turned pale at the unexpected news, but managed to bite her lip and express pride in her son's decision.

Ann lost track of Fred early on. When it was time to leave, she found him out back with the other men, thoroughly drunk. All the way home on the trolley, he attempted to lead the passengers in a sing-a-long. Ann was mortified. She was further infuriated that Delpha and Josephine thought he was funny and joined the fun, while she had her hands full with Virginia. Walking home from the trolley stop, Fred lost his balance and fell down twice. Delpha tried to keep him steady.

Ann made him sleep on the sofa that night, but when she awoke he was gone. She presumed he'd left for work early, but later that afternoon a wagon pulled up in front of their house and two men, both in high spirits, helped Fred down and half carried him to the front door. Ann took one look at them and, without uttering a word, opened the screen door and pointed to the sofa, where the two men lowered him carefully down.

"Thank you, fellas," Fred managed to mumble, before dropping into unconsciousness.

Ann sat silently for a long while, contemplating her husband. Later that afternoon, after getting Ginny up from her nap, she was astonished to find the sofa empty. She called for Fred, but got no answer. Later that night, after dinner had been eaten without him, two policemen came knocking on the door, propping him up between them. They explained that he'd been causing a disturbance in one of the local taverns and he was lucky they hadn't locked him up.

For two more days, the pattern continued. During that time, she discovered bottles he'd hidden all around the house. Short of tying him up, she didn't know what to do. He was long past scolding and seemed to not take her threats seriously. At times he was so incapacitated she was sure he could not navigate his way out of the house — but when she turned her back he'd disappeared again. She had no idea where he was getting money to drink.

In the early hours of Sunday morning, a policeman knocked on the front door. "I'm sorry to inform you, Mrs. Wilhelm, but we just got a call that Mr. Wilhelm is in Cook County Hospital in Chicago. Seems he's fallen and cracked his skull on a curb."

That morning, Ann brought the three girls up to Kitty's in Chicago and then went to the hospital to see Fred. She was shocked to find him in a straightjacket, locked up in a padded room.

"He's got the DTs," the doctor explained — "delirium tremors, from sudden withdrawal of alcohol. He was hallucinating that bugs and snakes were attacking him and got violent when we tried to restrain him. He'll probably be all right in a couple of days when he dries out, but we can't let him go until then. And as long as he's like this, we have to keep him locked up. No visitors."

Ann returned to her sister's house full of rage, fear, and shame. "What am I to do, Kitty? His employer has already been by the house, saying if he isn't at work tomorrow morning he need not show up again. He's given Fred enough breaks and this is the end of the line. But he won't be out of the hospital for at least another couple of days. And I don't even know if the crack in his skull has caused any permanent damage. No job. No money to pay the rent or put food on our table. What's to become of us? It's Da all over again. I can't stand it. Why is this happening to us? Oh, I could kill him with my bare hands, I swear I could. I'll never forgive him for this. Never."

For the first time, Delpha saw her father's drinking as a real problem. Hearing her mother's rant, she worried if they would starve to death out in the cold, like in the "Little Match Girl" story she'd read. In a moment of panic, she wondered if she and her sisters would all wind up at the orphanage. For the first time, she regarded Jo as her sibling and responsibility, the same as Ginny, rather than as competition. She felt sympathy for her mother and identified with her. What would happen to all of them? And, why had Papa done this to them?

Five days later, Ann was summoned to the hospital to bring Fred home. She found him chastened and considerably thinner, a diminished version of his former self.

"Jesus, Annie, am I ever glad to see you. Please take me home. I don't ever want to come back to this hellhole again."

Prepared as she was to lay him out in lavender, she found that she could only take pity on him.

"I don't ever want to go through this again, Annie. You have no idea what it was like." He shuddered involuntarily, recalling the violent tremors he'd experienced. "I'd rather die than have to suffer through those DTs again. I swear to you, I'll never take another drink again in my whole life. I swear on you and the girls. May God strike me dead if I do."

Fred went to his former employer and, despite the man's determination to be done once and for all with Fred Wilhelm, he was so taken with Fred's humility and contrition that he gave him one more chance.

"But one more incident, Fred, then that's it. I'll not let you make a fool of me again. Understood?"

As Fred explained it later to Ann, he felt like kissing the man's shoes. "I haven't been so damn grateful since Mr. Kellogg took me in that winter and saved my life."

Everyone relaxed. They would not be out on the streets (or back on South Carpenter) and, aside from having to pay off the hospital bill, there were no permanent consequences — except that Del now realized her papa had feet of clay and her ability to trust him was never quite the same. Plus, she now had one more thing to be ashamed of, one more reason to be on guard against insult and ridicule from others.

Fred was good for over a year. Then, triggered by the celebration of the signing of the Armistice — the end of World War I — he was off on another four-day bender. This time the tremors and hallucinations started at home. Ann was in the kitchen with the girls when she heard Fred screaming in their bedroom, where he'd been sleeping it off.

Entering the room, they found him standing on the bed, cursing, wild-eyed and terrified, violently swinging his arms to fight off his attackers: snakes and serpents, spiders, rats, and every kind of crawly bug. Ann was afraid to approach him; he was not even aware of their presence. She closed the door and sent Del to a neighbor's to phone for the police and an ambulance. She knew he'd have to be hospitalized again to dry out.

The girls had never witnessed anything like this, the violence, the profanity, the need for the police. It was frightening (and embarrassing) beyond comprehension — as if their father were possessed by demons. This time he was away for four days and lost his job.

Against his own better judgment, Uncle John — at Bridget's urging — agreed to give Fred one of his milk routes. But it meant having to move back to Chicago, where the rents were higher.

And so, at the end of November they moved to a small bungalow at 4156 South Wabash Avenue. It was smaller than their home in Hammond and the neighborhood wasn't as pleasant, but it was acceptable. Ann still had her lace curtains and the bowl of Waterford crystal. And she was nearer to her sisters, which was a definite advantage.

In her new school, Delpha made an immediate favorable impression on the nuns and teachers, but remained aloof and guarded with her new classmates. At the beginning of May, two weeks shy of her 13th birthday, she was told by her mother that she'd have to drop out of school upon completing the eighth grade, and find a job so she could contribute to the family income. Del was crushed. She loved school, excelled at it, and even hoped to eventually become a teacher herself (though not a nun).

But as disappointed as she was, she was not surprised. Del had been aware of her family's financial state and the problems of the past two years, since her father's first hospitalization. She understood her mother's silences, the tension between her parents, her father's constant sneaking from bottles hidden in the most imaginative of places. She knew of her mother's attempts at pinching pennies and making one do for two. She understood — but she was angry. Sometimes she blamed her father for drinking and not caring enough about them. Sometimes she blamed her mother for being a nagging shrew and driving him to drink. Sometimes she blamed God for letting it all happen. Regardless, it would be the end of her schooling and the beginning of work.

7

Delpha
1922

With recommendations from her teachers, Delpha was accepted into a training program at Illinois Bell Telephone to become a switchboard operator — an excellent job for a woman, never mind a young girl. During her training period she earned $8 a week. When that was completed, she would work eight-hour days, six days a week, and earn $8.50 a week to start — nearly as much as her father brought home working for Uncle John, and with fewer hours.

Del loved her job with the telephone company. It was a high-status job for a female. She wasn't just a shop girl, lucky to earn 10 cents an hour for a 60-hour week, or a factory girl doing piecework 12 hours a day, six days a week. She would soon be earning over 22 cents an hour, with regularly scheduled raises and bonuses in the future. Plus, not just anyone could be a switchboard operator — you had to pass a test and be accepted. It was proof you weren't a nobody.

Ann took Del's weekly pay envelope and gave her carfare and some spending money, including enough to buy her own clothes and lunches. It may have been only $2 or $3 a week, but Delpha felt grown up and independent. All of her co-workers were older, but she seemed to fit right in. For the first time, Del felt accepted as a person — but her new confidence only made her relationship with Ann more difficult.

For some time, she had been putting on makeup as soon as she left the house and had access to a restroom. Of course, before leaving for home, she'd remove it. Similarly, at work, she rolled down her stockings and rolled up the waist of her skirt to fit in with the new flapper style that was in vogue. Because she behaved more maturely and looked older than she was, the other girls asked Del to join them when they made plans to go to one of the clubs on the Southside of Chicago.

Although Ann had no idea that Del was growing independent in these ways, she witnessed the burgeoning attitude of disrespect and disobedience at home. In response, she was constantly on her daughter's back and sometimes gave her a good crack across the face when she thought it was deserved.

"As long as I'm your mother and you're living under my roof, young lady, you'll do as I say!"

Fred meekly encouraged his daughter not to aggravate her mother. "You know her temper," he nodded knowingly. "Just do what she says and don't cause any trouble."

Oh, she thought, *why can't he stand up to her and just once take my side against Ma?* Still, she recognized it was precisely this sweet softness that she loved most about him.

The next spring, after Delpha turned 14, she had her confirmation. Rules dictated that she could not choose her father as her sponsor, so she chose Uncle Art. In an ironic twist a few months before, Uncle Art had been promoted to branch manager for the Montgomery Ward department store in Hammond, Indiana, requiring that the Kirks move there. Kitty and Ann were fit to be tied that they had to be separated from each other once again.

Aunt Alice and Uncle Harry gave Delpha a party and all the family came, even Great-Aunt Mary, now 45 and the chef second-in-charge of the kitchen at the Yacht Club. And of course, the Kirks drove up from Indiana in their new car.

Aunt Josie and Uncle Ted were there. Teddy Jr. was now a tall, handsome 14-year-old. Uncle Ted was advancing in the Armour meat-packing company (a far cry from what it had been like to work for them 30 years ago). Great-Aunt Bridget and Uncle John Powers came as well. Bridget, at 51 the oldest of the Powers women, still assumed a protective, matriarchal role with her nieces and was determined that Ann and her two youngest daughters would be shielded from the consequences of Fred's drinking. Aunt Nellie — still unmarried at age 32 — arrived with Billy Moore; and Great-Aunt Maggie (still childless) and Uncle Al, now a sergeant on the Chicago police force, also came.

Del delighted at being the center of attention for the entire day. In the morning, the bishop conducted the mass and the confirmation ceremony at the church. The only disappointment was that Pa remained outside, smoking his pipe and refusing to go in. But he stayed sober and Del thought he looked handsome in his three-piece suit and fedora.

Afterward, they went to the Wood Photograph Studio on West 63rd Street, where she posed in her white dress holding a large bouquet of flowers, her confirmation certificate visible on the chair next to her. In the photograph, her long, brunette hair is tied with a large white bow and her lacy dress, with sleeves to the elbow, reaches to just below her knees, showing white-stockinged legs. Her shoes are modern white pumps with a modest heel. She has her mother's square face and turned-up nose. But in spite of her smile, the large brown eyes below her wide forehead are melancholy, as if resigned to the fact that the happiness of her day is already waning. Perhaps she was acknowledging her place in the world: *I know who and what I am. Today is just a dream, an illusion — and when I wake, everything will be the same as before.*

Afterward, the entire tribe made its way to the O'Hara home. Great-Aunt Alice had given birth to her 12th child the year before. Miraculously, all were still living and thriving. Indeed, the five oldest were married and starting families of their own. Alice and Harry O'Hara were already grandparents.

The party spilled out of the O'Hara house onto the veranda, where folding tables and chairs had been set up. At one point, Josephine asked her aunt, "Aunt Josie, was I named after you?"

"Oh heavens, no. First, my name isn't Josephine, it's really Johanna. I have no idea why Ma and Da named me that. They never used that name. It's on all my legal documents, like my birth certificate and marriage license, but I've always been called Josie. Actually, I was surprised when Ann named you Josephine. As you know, your mother and I have always had a sort of rivalry, because of our closeness in age, I'm sure. But I was pleased. Even though our names are different, I felt as if her naming you Josephine was an affectionate reaching out to me. So I've always had a special fondness for you because of that."

Delpha, overhearing the exchange, bit her lip and looked away for a second. "Mama said she gave me the name Delpha because of the nurse who took care of her when I was born. Is that true?"

"Yes, as I recall, it was. Your mother had a tough time with your delivery. There were complications, and she was very appreciative of the care this nurse gave her, so she named you after her — well, your middle name." After a moment Josie went on, "Of course, I had just given birth myself to Teddy Jr. a few months before, and Ted and I had our own place here in Chicago, so I wasn't living at home when Annie had you. And Da, your grandfather, well, he and Marguerite were divorced by then. She died the following year, so you never met her — horrible woman. So your mother was in a Catholic home, you know, for unwed mothers, and she went through her pregnancy and your birth all on her own. It wasn't easy for her, even though she was a grown woman by then."

"How old was she?" Del asked.

"Don't you know?"

"No, Ma refuses to discuss her age with me. Every time she has a birthday and I ask her how old she is, she gives me some smart answer, like it's a big mystery."

"Well, then, it's not for me to say. But figure it out, she's less than a year younger than I am and I was 18 when I married Mr. Arcand in 1903." She looked directly at both girls and said firmly, "Now that is privileged information and you never heard it from me! Don't you dare, either of you, let on to your mother that I told you. Ever. Agreed?"

Both girls nodded solemnly, although Delpha was already doing the calculations in her head. All this was way beyond seven-year-old Jo's comprehension and her attention went swiftly elsewhere. Who cared what age old people were?

Delpha continued working at the telephone company switchboard for another two years. Josephine, now nine, was beginning to take an interest in her older sister's clothes, and the simple outreach helped the two grow closer. Del was surprised to feel so much affection for the person her sister was becoming. As Jo developed into an adolescent, Del accepted her as a friend, not merely a sister. Josephine's even-tempered personality made her naturally outgoing and friendly; and she had a knack for making others feel happy to be with her.

With Delpha off to work every day, it was natural that Jo and Ginny also became close. Virginia, now five, was solidifying her spot as the spoiled baby of the family. With her red hair, green eyes, and porcelain skin, she was like a beautiful doll, a perfect angel, and no one in the family could resist indulging her every whim.

Fred continued working for Uncle John despite engaging in episodic drunken sprees — although there were no more bouts of DTs. Aunt Nellie finally married Billy Moore early in 1922 and promptly gave birth to Billy Jr. The Wilhelms still saw a lot of the extended family, including Aunt Kitty and Uncle Art and their two boys, Arty and Kenneth, who were the same ages as Jo and Ginny.

At the end of summer, Great-Aunt Alice gave birth to her 13th (and last) child, a healthy baby boy named Timothy. Alice was 50 and the family's reaction ranged from shock, admiration, and embarrassment to pride. Uncle Harry expressed great joy, but lines of stress and fatigue were discernable around his mouth and eyes. Aunt Alice was surprisingly robust, although she too sometimes appeared weary. No wonder! The only daughter she had at home to help was nine-year-old Bridget, although they also had hired help. Thank God Uncle Harry was doing so well in real estate and had multiplied his investments numerous times by playing the stock market.

"It just keeps going up!" he observed. "You can't lose. If it weren't for the children, I don't know what I'd do with all the money."

I have some ideas, Ann thought, but didn't say anything.

One day during lunch break, Del's friend mentioned having attended the funeral of her grandmother, and the thought elicited a long-buried memory that, until that moment, Del had completely forgotten. That evening, as she washed the dishes and her mother sat at the kitchen table mending, Del asked her, "Ma, who was that woman you brought me to visit that time when I was at St. Joseph's?"

"Now, what woman would that be?"

"You remember. She lived in a big house. You took me from St. Joseph's and we rode on a train to get there."

"I have no idea what you're talking about," Ann said quickly. "I never took you on any train ride. Besides, the nuns wouldn't let me take you out except for just a short visit, maybe a walk through the park to the lake, or maybe for an ice cream."

"But I remember it," Del pressed. "Some girls were talking today about their grandmothers and it made me think of this old woman. I remember the house was very big, with lots of windows and a big lawn and so many bushes and trees that I thought it was a park. I remember holding your hand as we went up the steps onto a big porch. When the woman came to the door, you left me there alone with her and I wondered why you didn't come in with us. I was afraid you were going to leave me there," she paused. "And then she led me up a grand, wide staircase to the upstairs of her house. There was a playroom with a little table and chairs and a tea set. We stayed there, just the two of us, and pretended we were having tea together. Don't you remember? I must have been about three, I think."

"You're daft," Ann tried to sound casual. "It must have been a dream. You've always had an imagination, probably from all those books you read."

"No, I don't think so, Ma. It really happened. I know it. Was she my grandmother?"

"You know your grandmother died when I was just a little girl. That's why me and my sisters were sent to St. Joseph's in the first place."

"No, I don't mean your ma, I mean my father's mother."

"Do you mean Mr. Wilhelm's mother? You know very well that he ran away from home in Pittsburgh when he was just a young boy. He hasn't had anything to do with his parents since. They're probably dead anyway, the way he tells it. Besides, what's so important about grandmothers? I never got to know either of mine and I'm none the worse for wear."

Delpha knew she shouldn't pursue it. She saw her mother's stubborn denial, the flush in her tensed cheeks and jaw. But she found herself pushing ahead. "Who was my father, then, if not this lady's husband or her son?"

"You just watch that fresh mouth of yours, missy." Ann bit off a thread with her teeth and then, stealing a quick glance toward the front room where Fred and the two younger girls were listening to the radio, took a deep sigh and looked at her daughter.

"If it's his name you're asking, it was the same as yours."

"What do you mean, the same as mine?"

"Powers. That's your name isn't it? I mean the one you used until Mr. Wilhelm and I got married."

"My father's name was Powers? How could that be?"

"Why couldn't it be? It's a common enough name. You just need to look to your Uncle John to see that. We weren't the only Powers family out here in Chicago and Gary."

"Gary! I thought that's where it was, why we had to take the train. That's where my grandfather lived, wasn't it? I mean your father."

"We all lived there, except for Kitty, after he married Marguerite and took us out of the orphanage."

"And that's where you went to work as a housemaid?"

Ann glanced at her and then continued with her mending. "All of us did, even Kitty when she turned 15. I was just a young girl, like yourself, only not so bold. I was still only a girl when the young master of the house had his way with me. There was nothing I could do, was there? Of course, once it was clear that I was carrying his child, she went and fired me. I was still wet behind the ears, foolish enough to believe he'd marry me. I was 16, pregnant, and without a job. Of course I had to go back and live with my da and that witch."

Del froze for a moment. *16? That can't be right.* But she didn't say anything.

"That's enough," her mother snapped. "You know enough, more than you need to. I only told you now because you're out in the world, earning a wage like a full-grown woman. You have a right to know what can happen."

Then she shook her finger at her daughter. "So let this be an example to you. You can't trust men. None of them. Ever. They think only of themselves and don't ever forget it. Not my own father, not even that man in there," she said, tilting her head to the other room. "There's none of them who won't think of themselves first. So be forewarned, girl, because if you ever get yourself in trouble, don't come running to me. I've got more than enough to take care of as it is, without taking on another bastard, too."

Delpha turned her face away. How embarrassing for her mother to talk like this! Not that she didn't know what Ann was referring to. Even in an all-girls Catholic school — and at work! — that's all the women talked about.

"You hear me, miss?" Ann said through gritted teeth and a cold, deadly glare.

"I hear you, Ma. You don't have to worry about me. I'm not *that* kind of girl. Besides, nobody wants to go out with me anyway."

"Take that as a blessing, then. There'll be plenty of opportunities for you when you're older."

At 16, Delpha was big boned, and in heels she gave the impression of being taller than five feet, two inches. And her attitude — self-contained and bristly, perhaps even haughty — conveyed the impression that she was older. Of course, she was lying to her mother about her plight. At the dance halls with her girlfriends from work, plenty of men paid attention to her — and not just Irish men, but Italians and Poles and Germans, too. But Ann didn't need to worry. Her daughter was wary and her flip, sarcastic manner served as effective insulation, protecting her from would-be rogues — though she did have an eye for the Italians.

She'd also learned the morality tale of her cousin Henry, Great-Aunt Alice's oldest boy. A stellar student in high school, after graduating very near the top of his class he attended Loyola University on Chicago's Northside. Henry intended to go to medical school, but he got a girl pregnant and had to get married, drop out of college, and go to work in his uncles' meat purveying business. The whole family was ashamed — and it served as a lesson to all of the cousins and second cousins: Don't let this happen to you!

Despite her mother's concerns, Delpha loved to go dancing. New jazz clubs were sprouting up all over the Loop and the Near Northside, up and down Wabash Avenue and State Street, and especially farther southwest, in Cicero, not far from her old Hammond neighborhood. The impact of Prohibition had not slowed the spread of these clubs. In fact, speakeasies provided the thrill of adventure and a place to dance to live music. Cicero had more speakeasies than you could shake a stick at. Twice a week, sometimes more, Del and her best friends from work — Rose, Bea, and Anita — and some of their male friends or brothers took the trolley (or drove if one of the young men had access to a car) to one of their favorite clubs.

Invariably, when Del arrived home, Ann would be waiting for her with a harangue. She'd follow her daughter into the bathroom and then into her bedroom (which she shared with Josephine and Ginny), not caring in the slightest whether she woke up everyone in the house. Ann hounded her daughter with scathing pronouncements of the no-good end she'd come to with such brazen carryings on. "You're not behaving at all like a well-bred Catholic girl, but just like some shanty Irish trash who was raised on the streets and didn't know any better — ignoring your own God-fearing parents who worked and slaved to put a decent roof over your head. And this is the thanks I get!"

But Del was too big to smack around anymore, and she knew that as long as she turned most of her paycheck over to her mother, nothing more could be done to her. Pa hunkered down in the bedroom out of the line of fire, while the two younger sisters curled up under the covers, faces to the wall, feigning sleep.

In a moment of weakness, Ann risked embarrassment and confided her anguish and shame to Kitty. "My own daughter, my own flesh and blood, has been going to speakeasies. Speakeasies! Can you believe it, Kitty? Delpha is drinking alcohol and smoking cigarettes. She's not listening to music like she'd want me to believe. Oh, no! That would be bad enough, what with her only being 16 — still a girl, a child after all! — but she goes to speakeasies where mobsters and gangsters like that Wop, Al Capone, hang out." Ann fumed silently for a few moments and then continued. "And, she's meeting men there and seeing them or dating, whatever they call it. She's cavorting with Italians! And Polacks! The shame of it!"

More than once, Ann tried to throw her daughter out of the house. "Out! I don't want you in this house one more minute. Pack your bag, take your things. I won't have it, your running around, shameless, with Wops and Dagos and Polacks. Thank God my own dear mother isn't alive to see this! She'd die of shame. Jesus, Mary, and Joseph, and all the saints in heaven."

But within a few minutes, she'd consider the loss of income and order Fred to tell Del she could stay as long as she'd mend her ways.

In February of 1923, Great-Aunt Maggie died suddenly of a heart attack. She had not yet turned 46. Uncle Al, a sergeant in the detective division, was grief-stricken. Everyone in the family attended the funeral. Maggie, the youngest of the four Powers sisters, had been much loved by everybody — most of all by her father, John Powers.

"It's a shame she never had any children," said her oldest sister, Bridget, "to carry on her sweet and vibrant personality." Ann agreed, and was reminded of her own daughter, Josephine, and her engaging, outgoing ways, so similar to Aunt Maggie's.

November brought a series of important political and social events: Republican President Warren Harding suffered a heart attack and died in office; he was succeeded by Calvin Coolidge. Chicago elected Mayor William Dever, who permitted the Capone Gang to completely take over Cicero. This precipitated a major war between the Capone mob and a gang headed by notorious brothers Myles and Billy "Klondike" O'Donnell. During the following year, more than 200 people would be murdered in a turf war for control of Cicero and Chicago's Southside.

This period of violence stirred Ann's fears to frenzied heights. Even Fred became more forceful in his warnings to his daughter. But it didn't stop Delpha and her friends from living life at flapper speed. At almost 18, she knew her own mind and paid her own way. And hadn't the 19th Amendment been passed just four years ago giving women the vote? This was a free country, damn it, and she didn't have to listen to her mother if she didn't want to.

Del's friend Anita had a cousin named Charlie — and Charlie's friend Gianfranco (or "Johnny Frank"), a member of the Capone gang, sometimes bought them drinks when they were in Cicero. Charlie's girlfriend, Megan McCarthy, hit it off with Del and her friends and often joined them when they went dancing. Megan agreed to call for Del at her house and tell Ann they were going to get a bite to eat, then go back to her house to listen to records. Ann would behave approvingly (a nice-looking Irish-Catholic girl, after all) and compress her lips into a semblance of a smile, although she didn't believe a word of it.

Meanwhile, Ann attempted to ensure that her younger girls, now 11 and seven, would not traipse down the same sin-strewn path of their older sister. The poor example of Mary Ellen Delpha Wilhelm was raised at every turn: "I'm sure you don't want to turn out like her. She'll be spending eternity in hell for sure!" Ginny made sure to never displease her mother in any way, but Jo secretly admired her older sister's spunk. Jazz, make-up, dancing, boys — she couldn't wait to get older.

On their lunch break in the employees' cafeteria one afternoon, Del and Rose were joined by Anita. "Did you hear the news on the radio this morning?"

"What news?" asked Rose. With her dark hair and dark complexion, Rose Donleavy looked more Italian than fair Anita Albanese — but in fact it was the other way around. Rose had a flippant, wiseacre attitude that Del guessed was acquired from spending too much time with Megan and Charlie's crowd.

"It was in the papers, too," said Anita, "a shooting down in Cicero last night. I can't believe you didn't hear about it. Well, anyway, it was a friend of Gianfranco's — and he called Charlie to say they'd better lay low for a while. The news said it was probably Klondike Billy who did it."

"I heard about a shooting on the radio," said Del, "but since they neglected to mention that it was a friend of Charlie's or Gianfranco's, I didn't pay that much attention. God, there are shootings down there almost every night. One more or less isn't exactly news — but there'd be real hell to pay if my mother knew that's where we went."

"Same here," said Anita, "but my old lady doesn't understand English, so she doesn't go crazy the way yours does."

Rose turned to Anita, who had sat down at their table and removed the chewing gum from her mouth, preparing to eat her soup. "So, does that mean we won't be seeing Charlie for a while?"

"Um hmm." Anita swallowed her soup. "He called me early this morning and said Gianfranco told him to get out of the city, so he said he's taking a vacation."

"Don't say anything to Megan," said Del. "She'd be upset."

"Well, we're still going out, aren't we?" asked Anita.

"Sure," said Rose. "Why not? Nobody wants to shoot us."

"We can always go over to Wabash or State Street," said Anita. "We don't have to take the trolley all the way to Cicero if we don't have a ride."

"Or we can go across the river to Division Street in Old Town. I heard there's some great spots up there," Del offered.

"Whatever," said Rose, "as long as the music and the men are hot." And the three of them laughed.

That night, the girls — including Megan McCarthy, who was despondent over Charlie's disappearance (probably to St. Louis or Kansas City) — took the elevated train across the Chicago River into Old Town on the Near Northside to go dancing. During the course of the evening, three different young, good-looking Irish men came to their table to ask if Megan knew where her boyfriend was.

"All I know is he told me he was taking a vacation," she sulked. "The bum didn't even ask if I wanted to go with him."

All of this attention made the group nervous, and they decided to go home early.

"I think those guys are working for O'Donnell," one of the girls said. The reality of the violence was now suddenly closer — involving someone they knew and cared about. For the first time, the fear was tangible, and they decided to stick to places closer to home for a while. Sometimes there could be too much excitement, too much adrenalin, and then it smelled like fear — or maybe gunpowder.

In the fall of 1924, Great-Aunt Mary died, leaving only Bridget and Alice of the original Powers immigrants. Aunt Mary had been wedded to her job at the Yacht Club and was seen only at family gatherings. Ann and her sisters were sad, but no one had felt as close to Aunt Mary as they had to Maggie. Mary's passing was symbolic of the changing times, an indication of the ending of an older era. It felt like everything was changing too quickly, without time to get one's bearings.

Prohibition was still in effect (and would be for another eight years), but 1925 saw less violence. Cicero and Calumet City ("Sin City") were still exciting hot spots to go to on Saturday nights, when the girls could sleep late the next morning. Del continued to work for the phone company, except for a brief period when her easily bruised feelings and hot temper led to a fight with her supervisor and she quit on the spot.

That same day she went downtown and got a job manning the switchboard at one of the big hotels on Michigan Boulevard. But a few months later, when she heard that her old supervisor had been fired, she went back to work with her old friends.

8

Delpha and Joe
1926

D el had dated a few young men, but no one seriously. Getting married wasn't high on her list of priorities. But soon after she'd turned 21, she was with Anita and Bea at one of their favorite speakeasies on South State Street when a young man, one of Anita's neighbors, approached the table. Anita introduced him to Del.

"Del, this is Joe Rio. Joe, this is Del Wilhelm, a friend I work with at the phone company."

Joe and Delpha hit it off right from the start. At 22, Joe was tall, maybe five feet ten, with a wide congenial face, dark wavy hair, and a thickset body build. He was a smooth dancer. When it became clear after a few weeks that they were going to see each other steadily, she stopped hiding the friendship from her mother. He came to her house on South Wabash one Saturday night to pick her up.

Ann was coldly polite as she regarded the tall, muscular man, with his oily black hair brushed straight back. She limply offered her hand before absenting herself to the kitchen, her habitual place to steam and stew. Fred, now 48 but older looking with his thinning gray hair, was more cordial with the polite young man. He inquired what Joe did for a living and was shocked when the husky fellow said he played violin for the Chicago Symphony Orchestra. Fred was incredulous.

"Yes, I've been playing since I was a young boy," Joe explained. "It's all I've ever thought of doing."

"Does anyone else in your family play?" Fred asked.

Joe gave a deep belly laugh. "My father wishes he were a singer," he said, smiling at an old family joke, "but, no, no one else plays an instrument — although back in Italy, my grandfather did. I guess the love of music runs on my father's side of the family."

"And what does your father do?" Fred asked.

"He and my uncle have a barbershop. Sometimes, he puts opera records on the gramophone and sings along with the tenors. Actually, he's not that bad, but we tease him about it. We call him Caruso Grosso because he's even bigger than Caruso," Joe said, inflating his cheeks and patting his belly.

Fred puffed on his pipe. Not to be outdone by the youngster, he reported that the dairy delivery company he worked for was doing so well that it had just purchased a whole fleet of trucks. "What do you think of that?" he asked.

Meanwhile, 14-year-old Josephine offered her sister's beau a snack while Del finished getting ready. Ten-year-old Ginny followed her mother's lead and retreated to the kitchen. From then on, Del's relationship with the young Italian man was barely tolerated by Ann — who was free with her insults, digs, and half-muttered innuendos when the young man was not within hearing range.

A few weeks later, in July, Joe invited Delpha to his house for Sunday dinner. Meeting Joe's family was an important event, and she was both excited and nervous. Ann, of course, made a futile attempt to prevent her daughter from going. Fred appeared neutral, but succeeded in giving Delpha little winks and signs of encouragement on the sly. Josephine was actively involved in helping her sister pick which dress to wear, and accompanying jewelry, cloche hat, shoes, lipstick, and purse. Even Ginny got caught up in the excitement, despite her mother's mutterings and clanging of pots and dishes in the kitchen. Ann ranted and blamed every speck of dust or dirt on her disgraceful daughter. "You're a lazy ingrate who'd rather go out gallivanting with greasy guineas than help your own mother keep a clean, lace-curtain, Irish home."

On the way to his home, Joe told Del about his family. The Rios lived on Indiana Avenue, near 67th Street, in a three-story brick home in a modest neighborhood on Chicago's Southside. He and his two younger brothers, Mike, 16, and Frank, 14, lived with their parents, Rosie and Vincenzo, on the second floor in a three-bedroom flat.

Aunt Rina and Uncle Tony Capriolli, his mother's brother, lived upstairs. Rina and Tony had just given birth in April to their first child, Irma.

Rina had immigrated to the United States in 1921 at age 30, along with her youngest sister, Maria. The two sisters had lived in New York with her oldest brother, Salvatore, until Rina met Tony. After the couple married, they moved to Chicago to be with his sister, Rose, and her family. Downstairs, on the first floor, was the barbershop owned by Vincenzo, and Uncle Tony.

Joe confessed that he'd never brought a girl home to meet his family, so he had no idea how they would react. Del wondered what they would think of an overweight, pasty-skinned, uneducated Irish girl; thank God they didn't know she was illegitimate! Before opening the door, Joe squeezed her hand and reassured her that it would be all right.

The door to the Rio apartment entered into a hallway. Immediately to the left was the kitchen. Across the hall was a dining room with a large table of polished dark wood with matching chairs. Heavy drapes accented a feeling of stuffy, but formal elegance. It was much more than Delpha expected from a working-class immigrant family (even though Joe and his brothers had been born here). She felt her anxiety mounting and feared she might stammer if she attempted to speak — an affliction she occasionally suffered when she felt under scrutiny.

Joe led her down the hall and ushered her into a large, sunny parlor. Mr. and Mrs. Rio stood up when she entered. Vincenzo Rio was a robust, heavyset man, shorter than Joe and formally dressed in a shirt with a high celluloid collar and a tie, vest, and jacket. Rose Rio was much shorter — not even reaching five feet — and quite plump, with a big soft bosom. Sensing Delpha's discomfort, Rose immediately took the girl's hands in hers. Gazing for a long moment into Delpha's eyes, she pulled her close into a warm hug.

"Welcome," she said in a thick Italian accent. Then she turned to Joe with a smile, and said in Italian (he later translated for Del), "She's beautiful. Such a nice fat girl."

Joe's father shook her hand and, in broken English, welcomed her to their home. Mike and Frank emerged from their bedroom at the rear of the flat and greeted her, then Uncle Tony and Aunt Rina, carrying Irma, came downstairs to greet her as well.

Del was too overcome to speak. She had never been in a home with such an open and profuse display of kindness and affection. Afraid to speak for fear she'd cry, she worried that her silence would make her look ignorant or, worse, rude. She had never felt so immediately accepted, except at the homes of her aunts. But here, she wasn't family; these strangers didn't have to like her — but they did. It didn't matter that she wasn't Italian, that she was overweight or hadn't finished high school, as Joe had. Eventually, she relaxed and, as she risked expressing herself, was amazed that the smiles and twinkling eyes didn't disappear.

And the food! She'd been so overwhelmed by the elegant furnishings and warm, emotional welcome that she hadn't noticed the smell of garlic and tomato sauce cooking, but then it forced itself into her consciousness. Platters and bowls were brought out as everyone moved into the dining room and sat around the large, beautifully set table. There was soup, pasta, chicken, peppers, wine, bread. It was so different from home — boiled beef, boiled potatoes, boiled cabbage or carrots or string beans. Here, at the Rios, she savored spices, emotions, spirited life. Del sat back in her chair, sipping a glass of unfamiliar red wine. Looking around the large table, listening to the chatter, she heaved a sigh of relief. This felt like home.

One hot Sunday afternoon in August, the Rio family, along with Del and the Capriollis, had a picnic in the park along Lake Michigan. Joe and his brothers were quite athletic — Joe had been a successful wrestler in high school — and were constantly running, throwing a ball, and chasing each other. Del, who had learned long ago that her thin white skin burned and blistered in the sun, sat in the shade with a long-sleeved blouse and a long skirt to shield her from the sun. Rosie and Rina had prepared a wonderful lunch of meatball or veal cutlet sandwiches on crispy, fresh Italian bread along with cheeses, fruits, eggplant, roasted peppers, and zucchini. Baby Irma slept in the shade on a blanket. Del was enjoying the outing.

Aside from occasional family get-togethers at Aunt Alice and Uncle Harry's, Del was hard put to remember such happiness at a family gathering. Vincenzo often broke into song — not only opera arias, but also popular songs of the day. Sometimes, though not on this occasion, Joe would take out his violin and play for the family and Vincenzo would sing along. Joe had been right: As a tenor, his father wasn't bad at all.

As the eldest son, and the most accomplished, Joe was the pride of the family. To Rosie and Vincenzo, Joe could do no wrong. He was their prince — and he was Delpha's prince. She admired his athleticism and enjoyed watching him play ball with his brothers. In contrast, she felt clumsy and awkward, having never been athletic. In spite of his entreaties, Del absolutely refused to run around with them. She was sure she'd make a fool of herself, and didn't want to risk losing their acceptance.

After lunch, the boys decided to go swimming. Rosie told them to wait a bit, but Joe kissed her cheek and said she worried too much. Laughing, the boys chased each other into the lake. The rest of the family watched leisurely from the shaded grass at the edge of the beach, relaxing after their small feast. Del turned her attention to Irma, who slept so peacefully, totally undisturbed by the events around her.

Suddenly, Vincenzo stood up and ran toward the water. Tony immediately followed. The two men gazed far out to where the three young men had been swimming.

Rina picked up the sleeping baby and the three women hurried to the water's edge.

"What's happening?" Del asked, feeling a rising panic. The two men shushed her, unwilling to break their focus out on the water. Tony said something to Vincenzo in Italian and then to Rina and Rosie. There followed a rapid, unintelligible exchange among them in Italian.

Del grabbed Rina by the arm, "Tell me what's happening!" Rina, who had worked outside the home while living with her brother in New York, spoke much better English than Rosie.

"It's the boys," Rina said in her halting English. "We see only two. One is missing."

Just then Vincenzo yelled out and pointed. The two boys were swimming back to shore, pulling the third with them. When the swimmers got closer to shore, Tony and Vincenzo waded chest-deep into the water to help them. As they emerged, the group saw that it was Joe they were carrying. Rosie began sobbing in Italian. Del was certain she must be praying — and found herself doing the same.

On the sandy beach, the brothers laid Joe down and began to pump his chest. Soon, water spurted out of his mouth and he began coughing. The mother and aunt crossed themselves and Rose fainted dead away, dropping like a stone. Vincenzo, unaware of his wife, cradled Joe's head against his chest while he continued coughing, spitting out water and regaining his breath. Mike and Frank had collapsed onto the sand, exhausted and overcome by what they'd just done.

Del knelt beside Vincenzo, repeating Joe's name. Tony embraced the two younger boys, speaking softly in Italian.

When Joe was finally able to focus, he smiled sheepishly at his father and then at Del. "I guess Mama was right. I should have waited another half hour."

"What happened?" Vincenzo asked his son.

"I got a cramp, Pop. It was so sudden and so sharp that I couldn't breathe. I couldn't even yell out to Mike and Frank. I just sank like a lead weight. I could hardly even hold my breath. God, it was terrifying. I thought I was dead for sure. I didn't think I'd ever see any of you again."

As Vincenzo and Tony helped Joe to his feet, his mother, now conscious, covered him with kisses, murmuring in Italian and crossing herself. Similarly, Vincenzo, Tony, Rina, and Joe's brothers enveloped him in hugs and kisses and expressions of affection. The family was physically and emotionally as one.

Despite the looks Joe gave her, Del felt excluded and walked back to the blanket to get her things. Soon Joe hurried after her.

"Hey," he said. "What's the matter?"

"Nothing. Why, do you see blood?"

"No, of course not. You seem annoyed." He attempted a joke, "You mad that I didn't drown?"

"No. I was scared to death. We all were. Your mother fainted. But obviously, this is a time for you and your family to be together. You don't need me here. I'd just be in the way."

"What are you talking about? You're not in the way. Hey, you're my girl, right?"

"Am I?"

"Of course you are ..."

"You could have fooled me."

"What?"

But by then everyone else had caught up with Joe and saw Del with her shoes on and purse in hand. Rose said something to Joe in Italian.

Del understood enough to answer her. "I've got to go. I had a great time, but you need to be together now." She gave Rose a kiss and a hug. "I hope you're all right," she said, "thanks again," and she nodded courteously to the men. She gave Rose another brief hug and ignored the confused look on the woman's face.

"Delpha, don't go," Rina said. "We're all going back to the house now. Please come with us."

But Del stubbornly declined; she gave Rina a brief hug and started walking across the park, headed for a bus stop. Joe hurried after her, but to his entreaties she said only that he should call her when he had a chance — if he wasn't too busy.

"Hey, come on, babe, don't be like that."

But she kept walking. Mike appeared at his side and handed him a towel to dry off.

"What's the matter with your girlfriend?"

"Ah, forget it," he said, watching her walk away without looking back. "She often gets huffy for no reason. She'll get over it."

That autumn, after eight years at the telephone company, Del was promoted to supervisor on the late shift, 3:00 to 11:00. In addition to the sense of pride and validation, she had achieved a new salary level with a bonus structure. Although she increased the amount she gave to her mother, she was also able to start a savings account of her own. Del looked forward to the time when she would be financially independent and not beholden to anyone.

The downside was traveling home alone late at night. Joe quickly volunteered to meet her each evening outside the telephone building, accompany her on the bus, and watch her climb the steps to her house. He understood that her mother's prejudice was such that it was better if he didn't come inside.

Del felt badly about this, but pushing Joe into her mother's face was asking for trouble. Delpha also felt guilty for not inviting Joe to her home for holidays and family occasions. She wanted him to be part of the celebration, to have Thanksgiving or Christmas dinner with her relatives, to understand what her life was like and who she was.

But she imagined Ann's cold stare, the pursed lips, the half-muttered insults. It wasn't worth it. There was also the possibility, she realized, that Pa would get drunk and cause a scene, and she didn't want to embarrass him or anyone else in her family. And so, much of the holiday season, like so many Sundays, Del was at Joe's house — more than likely in Rose's or Rina's kitchen, learning how to make tomato sauce, chicken cacciatore, meatballs, or soups and desserts in the southern Italian style.

But all was not always so rosy for the young couple. Del and Joe sometimes clashed like steel striking flint. In his house, in the comfort of his family, Joe expected things to go his way. Everyone catered to him and he expected the same from his girl. But if Del felt she was being taken for granted or treated as an inferior, her eyes would blaze and she would cut him to pieces with her no-holds-barred insults. Then the tempers would be on display: his loud and volcanic, hers vicious, steely cold, and cutting.

Rose would hold her breath for the duration of the commotion. Del quickly learned that Joe's mother had developed fainting into a fine art. The rest of the family — having ascertained that she had not hurt herself in the fall — usually ignored her until she "decided" to rejoin the activities. Joe often referred to his mother as "the Italian Sarah Bernhardt."

If Vincenzo were present when Del and Joe were fighting, he'd intervene loudly: "*Basta*! Stop it. Now." And they would. But if he wasn't there, the yelling would likely end with Del crying and storming out the door (muttering the same epithets her mother used). After Del's departure, Rose and Rina would berate Joe for behaving like a stupid peasant with eggplant for brains.

"That's no way to treat a woman," they'd harangue him. "Do you see your father or uncle behaving so disgracefully?"

Joe would tell them to shut up and mind their own business — they didn't know what they were talking about. Later, he'd apologize to Delpha, who would give him the cold shoulder — and relent after a while. Del flared up quickly, but didn't hold a grudge for very long.

One Friday night, when Joe met Del outside the telephone building after her shift, he saw she was carrying a small overnight case. He jokingly asked if she was planning on running away from home. She raised her eyebrows in mock surprise, "Oh, I didn't know you were clairvoyant in addition to all your other gifts."

"I've got a million of them," he said, waving his fedora and imitating Jimmy Durante's gravelly voice. "No, seriously, babe, what's with the suitcase? You do some shopping today?"

"No," she said plainly, "you were right the first time. I'm running away from home."

He held her arm, forcing her to stand and face him. "You're serious?"

"I can't take it any more, Joe. My mother and I had another battle this morning. She told me to pack my bag and never come back. I know she was just letting off steam, but I can't be her punching bag whenever anything goes wrong. So I'm taking her at her word. Let's see how she likes doing without $10 a week."

Joe was speechless as Del continued.

"Let her pick on her little princess for a change. I'm tired of it. You want me out of your life? Then that's what you'll get. So I told her it'll be a cold day in hell before I set foot in this house again, and I shoved a few things in this suitcase."

"But what're you going to do? Where are you going to live?"

"I rented a room at the YWCA," she told him resolutely.

"You're actually moving out? What about your father? Your sisters? You can't be serious ..."

"Why can't I? I'm free, white, and 21. I won't be treated like that anymore. Not by anybody. I'm not dirt under her shoe. Don't you understand?"

"No. I mean, no, you're not dirt. And yes, I understand. It's just so ..."

"Final? Joe, don't you realize she's wanted me out of her life since I was born! I'm nothing but aggravation to her."

"Oh, come on, that's not true."

Fire flashed in her eyes. "Don't you dare tell me what's true and what's not. You don't have to live with her. I do."

"But why would she want to get rid of you? You're her daughter for God's sake, her own flesh and blood."

She jerked her arm away and continued walking. "It doesn't matter. Just believe me when I tell you it's true. She's never loved me, never

218

wanted me. Well, now she's got her wish. I won't trouble her any more."

Del had no intention of telling him about spending the first six years of her life in an orphanage because she was illegitimate.

They walked silently for a while. "Can I at least carry that for you?" he asked. Without looking at him, she let him take the valise.

"So, you're intending to stay at the Y tonight?"

"That's what I said, didn't I?" she snapped.

After a few more minutes of walking in silence, he said, "Listen, let's stop in the coffee shop on the corner, all right?"

"Sure," she said, and let herself be ushered inside and to a booth. He ordered pie and coffee for them both.

"I've been thinking a lot about this for some time," he started slowly. "I mean, it's not just what happened today, your leaving home and everything. I actually have been thinking a lot about this for quite a while and, what I mean is — why don't we get married?"

"What?" she laughed, "oh, you're a card all right. You really do have a gift for getting me out of my moods."

"No, I'm serious. This is the perfect time. I've been planning to ask you, only I didn't know when." He was smiling now, getting past his nervousness. "I thought, maybe Valentine's Day, maybe your birthday. I was going to ask Ma and Aunt Rina what they thought, when I should ask you. They know how much I love you."

He reached out and took her hands in his. "Do you know how much I love you?"

She didn't answer. Her lips were trembling and she was afraid of making a fool of herself. When the waitress brought the pie and coffee, Del took the opportunity to retrieve a hanky from her purse. She wiped her eyes and blew her nose, as daintily as she could.

When Del had regained her composure, he asked again, "Babe, do you know how much I love you? I want to marry you. I want you to be my wife. What do you say?"

Afraid of stuttering and blubbering, she could only nod her head and attempt a smile. "I love you too," she mouthed, barely audible.

There. It was out. She had never allowed herself to say those words out loud to anyone, but now she realized how true they were. She did love him. She did want to be his wife, to be with him always.

Suddenly overcome with a wave of fear, she felt completely defense-less. What would happen now?

"Oh, Joe, what are we going to do?"

"What do you mean? We're going to get married. Let's do it tomor-row!"

"Tomorrow?"

"Why not? I'll meet you down here, at the Y — early, before City

Hall opens. We'll have breakfast and then go and get hitched. Then we'll tell my family that they have a daughter. How's that?"

"But what about work? Don't you have rehearsal and a performance tomorrow?"

He shook his head and laughed. "As long as I get to the hall by 12:30, I'll be fine. You and I will be married by then!"

"But your parents, won't they be upset that we're doing this without talking to them?"

"No," he said, shaking his head, "they'll be surprised, of course, but they'll be thrilled. I know it. Of course, Mama will faint, but they'll be ecstatic."

Del imagined the joyous faces of everyone in his family and knew he spoke the truth. She had sometimes allowed herself to think of the possibility of getting married, but had always concluded it would never happen, that they were both just having fun, playing at romance, being part of the jazz age. After all, who would want her? But she knew in her heart that he was right — his family loved her and would be happy to have her as a daughter-in-law. To them, she wasn't an uneducated, over-weight, pug-nosed, Irish bastard. To them, she was perfect.

Delpha also imagined her mother's reaction — the self-righteous indignation that her daughter was embarrassing her by marrying a greaseball. Pa would be happy for her, and sad to have her gone from the house. Ginny and Jo would miss her and she would miss them. Ginny would passively condone Ma's disapproval, and Jo would applaud the triumph of romance. Del worried that Ma might make Jo her substitute scapegoat, but then realized her mother harbored an anger for her alone that could never be transferred to Josephine or even to Pa.

"OK," she said, her brown eyes shining, for once, without a trace of melancholy. "Giuseppe Rio, I will be proud and honored to be your wife."

"Yahoo!" he yelled and threw his hat in the air.

The waitress smiled, "I didn't know the pie was that good."

Joe started making plans. "What I've been thinking is that for now we'll stay with my parents. You can move in with me; my bedroom is big enough. And with our two incomes, we'll be able to save enough money and get our own place in no time. What do you think?"

It made sense — she could help Rose with the household chores and contribute to the family income. She loved the emotional, nurturing Rose, as well as the rest of the family. It would be wonderful to be with them all of the time.

"It's a good idea," she agreed. "I love your family. Oh, Joe, I'm so happy. I never thought this would actually happen. I love you so much."

On Saturday morning, Joe waited for Del in the lobby of the YWCA. He wore his dark suit, a white shirt with a high collar, and a burgundy tie. He had even shined his shoes. A carnation peeked out from the lapel of his dark wool overcoat, and he held a small bouquet of flowers. When his fiancée came down the stairs, he approached excitedly, extending the flowers to her.

Del's dark winter coat had a narrow fur collar, and a woolen beret covered her short bobbed hair. Under her coat, she wore a two-piece lilac dress, and a strand of fake pearls graced her neck. She smiled nervously and, without a word, they quickly left the lobby.

"I'm too nervous to eat," she said once outside. "Even for coffee."

"Me too. Why don't we go straight to City Hall?"

"That's what I thought," she said, locking her arm in his. She smiled as she contemplated the flowers — how sweet he was to think of getting them.

I'm lucky, she thought. *My God, I'm actually going to get married.* Del glanced over as they walked rapidly down the street, just to make sure he was really there and she wasn't dreaming. She squeezed his arm and he flashed his wide, dimpled grin.

"Happy?" he asked.

"If I were any happier, they'd have to lock me up." Then she added, "I was so excited, I hardly slept."

At City Hall, they filled out forms for the marriage license and, after paying a fee, were directed to another office where the ceremony was performed, for another small fee. Two clerks in the office served as witnesses (another small fee), and within two hours they emerged into the brisk February day, husband and wife.

"Now," said Joe, "should we get something to eat or go directly home and tell my mother?"

"I'm still too excited to eat. Why don't we go tell your mother? We can have coffee and some breakfast with her. I'd like to do that."

When they entered the Rio apartment, Rose was in the kitchen with Rina and Irma.

"Who's there?" she called out uneasily when she heard the door open. There was no immediate answer, only the unexpected sound of footsteps and then Giuseppe and Delpha appearing in the doorway.

"What's this?" she cried. "Isn't Giuseppe supposed to be at Orchestra Hall, preparing for this afternoon's program?" Then she noticed Delpha, all dressed up.

"Ma, Aunt Rina," he beamed, "we got married this morning. We just

221

came from City Hall. We came right here, first thing, to tell you." He looked at Del, who was beet red from blushing. "This is Mrs. Giuseppe Rio, Ma, your new daughter-in-law."

"Married?"

"Yeah, just now. You're the first to know, the two of you." Rose's hand went up to her mouth, her eyes rolled into her head, and she slid limply to the floor.

Within seconds, Rina and Joe had her revived. Tears filled her eyes, and she held her son and his bride to her short, chubby body. "Oh, I'm so surprised! Why you don't tell me, before? We make a nice party, a nice occasion."

Aunt Rina, too, was on her feet and, shifting Irma on her hip, kissed her nephew and his new wife.

"I'm so happy for you," she said to each of them.

"I had no idea," Rose said. "I thought maybe it's a burglar come in the house to rob or maybe something wrong with Mike or Frank. I never think it's you." And turning to Del, "And you, all dressed up, looking so beautiful, I never expect. Oh, what a wonderful surprise! But Joey, you scare me like that. You shouldn't do. Not good for old lady get all scared like that."

Aunt Rina chimed in. "Joe, did you tell your father and Uncle Tony?"

"No, when I looked in, the shop was full, so I didn't want to make a big scene. I'll tell them later."

"He'll be so pleased. I know he was hoping you'd marry Delpha. But he'll be disappointed that there's no wedding, no celebration. He'd want to invite all the friends and family."

"Well, Zia," Joe said to his aunt, "we can always do that. But we only just decided last night to get married this morning."

"But why? Why so quick?" Suddenly Rose brought her hand up to cover her mouth and she looked at Delpha's belly.

"No, Ma. Don't even think that. We didn't have to get married, we just wanted to. Del had another big fight with her mother and we decided to get married. She's going to move in with us, into my room. I figured it would be all right with you and Pop."

"Of course, is all right." Rose looked at her new daughter-in-law. "You belong here. This your home now. We your family, right?"

"Right," Del said, giving Rose another big hug, and then one for Rina.

"Ma," Joe said, "we haven't had breakfast yet …"

"Of course, of course. Come, sit. Take off your coats. I make whatever you want. This a special day. You tell me and I make. Oh, my children, you make me happy so much."

222

After breakfast, Joe suggested that Del come to the matinee program. Then, they would go collect her things from her parents' house. His presence would hopefully inhibit her mother and, besides, he said, she'd need him to help carry her things. So, off they went to catch the bus to the ornate Orchestra Hall, the home of the Chicago Symphony Orchestra.

It wasn't the first time she'd heard Joe play, but it was the first time she heard her *husband* play. As she surveyed the audience, and realized how enraptured everyone was by the stirring music, she was filled to overflowing with a sense of pride.

At her house on South Wabash, Del knocked and then let herself in with her key. Ann was on her way to the door when Del opened it, and the two women stood staring at each other.

"I brought Joe with me, Ma, to help me get my things. I'm moving in with him and his family."

Ann's eyebrows jumped into her hairline. "You're what?"

"We got married this morning."

Visibly deflated, Ann looked away and then went slowly into the front room and dropped into a stuffed chair. Del waited for some sort of reply, but her mother merely gazed out the front window at the traffic passing by.

After a minute, Del motioned to Joe and he followed her into the bedroom she had shared with her sisters. He looked questioningly at his bride, but she shook her head, indicating that there'd be plenty of time later to talk about her mother's behavior. As Del was packing clothes and Joe was putting them into the valise, they heard a door close. "She's gone into her bedroom," Del whispered. It was obvious from her clenched mouth, watery eyes, and abrupt movements that she was very upset, but Joe said nothing.

Waiting for the bus, the dam finally burst. "That bitch!" Del exclaimed. "Can you imagine that? I'm her oldest daughter and I just got married. I'm leaving home for good and she has nothing to say? She doesn't give a damn. I'm nothing to her. I told you she'd be glad to be rid of me. Now you can see for yourself how she is. I can't even begin to imagine your mother behaving that way."

Joe chuckled. "Ma? Are you kidding? She'd be on her knees pulling out her hair, calling on all the saints in heaven to punish her for being such a poor mother that her son could possibly do such a thing. And Pop, he'd beat the crap out of me. Where was your father?"

"He works on Saturday, same as everybody. My sisters usually take the bus down to my Aunt Kitty's on Saturdays, so I didn't expect them to be there. Jo's going to be upset, I know. And Pa, he'll be shaken, but he'll be glad for me too." She looked at her new husband. "Not everybody in my family is like her. My aunts and uncles and all my cousins, you'll like them when you meet them. They're fun and warm and I know they'll like you. Ma is the most narrow-minded of them all — and I had to be stuck with her. I wish I could have had someone like Aunt Kitty, or your mother, for mine."

"But if you had mine, then we never would have fallen in love and gotten married."

She smiled sadly, her eyes still filled with tears. "That's true," she said, "but it would have been nice to have an older brother."

Joe laughed. "Well, no chance of that now."

When Vincenzo came upstairs that evening, Del was in the kitchen with Rose and Joe was in the front room reading the paper. Mike and Frank were lounging on the sofa and listening to the radio while waiting for dinner. Vincenzo took one look at his oldest son and immediately erupted, "Giuseppe, what are you doing home? There's a performance tonight — how come you're not where you're supposed to be?"

Joe couldn't help but allow a smile to spread across his face, knowing he'd be teasing his father with it.

"Well, it's been a hectic day, Pop, so I decided to take the evening off."

"What? You're telling me you're too tired to go to work?"

Joe laughed, anticipating his father's reaction. "No," he said, drawing it out, "I got married."

"What? What are you talking about? What do you mean, you got married?"

Joe approached his father. At almost five feet ten, he was taller than Vincenzo by several inches. He put his hands on his father's shoulders. "Del and I got married today."

"What is this, a joke?" He turned to his younger boys. "Mike, Frank, you know about this?"

"No, Pop, nothing. We're as surprised as you." By now, Rose and Delpha had entered the room.

"It's true?" Vincenzo asked his wife.

"Si, Vincenzo, they surprise me this morning. They just decide last night."

224

Mr. Rio looked at Delpha, who stood nervously next to her mother-in-law, and then at his son, who still stood before him, beaming.

"Nothing's wrong, Pop. We didn't have to get married. Del had another big fight with her mother and decided to move out. I thought it was as good a time as any for us to get married. I wanted to surprise all of you with the good news. Del is going to live here with us, in my room. Ma said it was all right."

A smile slowly spread across Vincenzo's face and he reached up and pinched his son's cheek.

"You play a joke on me, right. You make me think you're a bad boy, missing work, and then you give me this wonderful surprise. Eh?" He gave Joe a playful slap on the cheek. Then he turned to Delpha and opened his arms.

"Come here. Give me kiss." He turned to Rose, "Hey, Mama, finally you have the daughter you always wanted." Vincenzo sent Mike downstairs to the cellar to retrieve a few bottles of wine. Frank was dispatched upstairs to get Rina and Tony.

Overcome with emotion, Del's eyes filled with tears, her lips trembled, and her face and neck flushed. She excused herself and retreated to the bathroom to regain control. Recalling her own mother's reaction, she shook her head in despair.

She wished her father and sisters could be here to share this warmth and affection. Pa would be treated with respect by the Rios and made to feel important for once. Josephine would respond enthusiastically to the emotional openness, although poor Ginny would be scandalized by so much touching and hugging and kissing.

Emotions flowed like olive oil in the Rio household and Delpha's sensitive nature fit right in. Rose was loving and generous with her affections, wanting to feed the world, but she was quick to worry and fear for the worst. Vincenzo, her emotional rock, was more stable — a traditional "man of the house." As the boss, he made the decisions, gave the orders, and demanded respect, but was also good-humored and kind.

Del had a good sense of humor and enjoyed playing practical jokes, but as Joe had noted, she was also thin-skinned and took offense easily. Her biting temper could sometimes turn vicious.

Joe, as the "prince" of the household, magnanimously bestowed his charm and grace on everyone. He was affectionate and helpful to his family and especially protective of his new bride. But he felt entitled to their adoration and expected exceptions to be made on his behalf. When they weren't, he devolved into insulting those around him.

From time to time, feelings got hurt, but despite the turbulent squalls, most days were warm and comfortably sunny.

Mondays through Saturdays passed in a fairly routine way. Vincenzo rose early to open the barbershop. Rose and Rina made breakfasts for their husbands. Mike had quit school and was driving a delivery truck. Frank, at 15, was a star pupil and athlete and had been promised an invitation to West Point if he stayed on track. Although her workday started later, Del was up with the rest of the family, admitting that she had difficulty sleeping. The remainder of the morning passed with the women doing household chores, food shopping, and laundry, and then enjoying a leisurely lunch. All three women participated in the care and feeding of baby Irma. Later in the afternoon, Del would leave for work while Rose and Rina prepared dinner, stopping for a rest whenever Irma surrendered to nap time.

After a 12-hour day, Vincenzo and Tony would close the shop and come upstairs to wash up before dinner. Most nights, the two households ate together as one big family. Joe met Del after her shift to accompany her home on the bus. If he had a late rehearsal or performance, Mike would be sent in his stead. Once home, Del and Joe would retire to their bedroom. Usually, by that time, everyone else was already in bed. Del and Joe sometimes made love — but quietly and wordlessly, for both of them were embarrassed by any sounds they made (as if no one knew what they were doing).

The men ate heartily and Rose and Rina cooked prodigiously; everyone, except for the young Mike and Frank, was overweight. Del was introduced to plenty of exotic vegetables — different kinds of peppers, zucchini, eggplant, and artichokes. They ate pasta most days, and cheeses like mozzarella, ricotta, gorgonzola, and parmesan, and loaves of crisp, freshly baked Italian bread from the bakery two blocks away. All this, in addition to meats, cold cuts, various kinds of salami, veal, chicken, and beef.

Perhaps it was the food — the sheer quantity! — that resulted in Delpha gaining weight. Maybe it was it due to the *"mangia, mangia"* attitude in the family. Rose was pleased and Joe didn't mind, but Del was annoyed that her clothes were getting tight.

Then, by June, she knew she was pregnant. She told Joe one night in bed. He wanted to wake everybody to share the happy news, but she giggled and restrained him and they made love to celebrate. At breakfast, they told the family.

Rose clasped her hands and blubbered in Italian before swooning to the kitchen linoleum. Mike and Frank looked at their brother questioningly. Del wasn't sure how to interpret the look, but it appeared to be approving. Vincenzo beamed proudly at the young couple. Del would always remember it as one of her happiest moments.

Everyone in the family, except for Mike and Frank (who kept out of it), urged Delpha to quit her job and stay home, now that she was pregnant.

"You don't want to take a chance," argued Rose. "You must be careful not to lose the baby. Stay home."

Vincenzo took a different tack. "Giuseppe is going to be a father. It's his responsibility to take care of his family. You make him feel ashamed if you continue to work now. You must stay home."

Joe, who knew better than to push her, was practical. "So it'll take a little longer for us to save for our own place. So what? What's another few months? Really, babe, it's fine with me if you decide to quit the phone company. We'll be fine."

But Del dug in her heels. "I'm perfectly healthy. I'm not a lazy good-for-nothing. I've always worked and there's no reason for me to quit a job I love. I'm a supervisor. I make good money. I won't give it up until I have to."

And for the rest of the summer, things continued as they had. Rose and Rina sewed maternity outfits as Delpha continued to grow into her pregnancy.

"*Mangia, mangia,*" Rose urged, "you eat for two now." And so she did.

Over a period of time, Del gradually became aware that Joe was less attentive to her. She automatically assumed that getting fat had diminished his desire for her. When she confronted him with the reduced frequency of their lovemaking, he attributed it to the summer heat and to feeling washed out after work, and denied that her pregnancy had anything to do with it. "It has nothing to do with you, babe. I'm just exhausted, that's all."

On those Sundays when Joe wasn't at a performance, they still went to Lake Michigan. Now, Joe spent more time with her lying on a blanket than playing ball with his brothers. And despite his having been a strong swimmer, he rarely ventured out in deep water. Mike and Frank said he was turning into an old married man. When they were alone, they teased him that he was wearing himself out with too much sex.

By the end of October, Del was six months pregnant and 50 pounds heavier. She finally gave in to the entreaties of her new family and stopped work. Now, she joined Rose and Rina in their daily routines, although she was not permitted to strain herself. They carried the baskets of laundry and did the shopping, while she performed only those tasks requiring less physical exertion.

It would have been impossible to determine who was most excited about Del's baby. Everyone was sure she was carrying a boy. Rose eagerly anticipated her first grandson and was already jealous she wouldn't be able to nurse him herself. Vincenzo was the proud grandfather-to-be, entertaining fantasies of his grandson carrying on the family traditions, the family name. Joe was thrilled at the prospect of being a father, teaching his son things his own father had not been able to teach him.

But Delpha, already in love with the growing life inside her, eagerly awaited the bond, flesh against flesh, eyes locked on eyes. She imagined nursing him, her baby, a part of herself, a love connection that could never be broken, need never be questioned or doubted. This relationship would be completely different from the one she'd had with her own mother.

Del stopped work at the end of October and 10 days later, on November 6, 1928, voted for the first time in a presidential election. She happily cast her ballot for Democrat Al Smith, the first Catholic ever to run for the presidency. The next day, she and the Rios were disappointed to learn that Smith had been defeated and Herbert Hoover, a Republican, had won handily.

She doubted that her mother had exercised her right to vote, as neither Rose nor Rina had. It made Del even more proud to be one of the relatively few women who had voted. The newspapers characterized the women's vote as *unimpressive*, meaning lower than expected. Well, she was impressed with her own vote, even if it had accomplished nothing more than establishing her as a legitimate voter. Del liked the sound of that and smiled as she repeated it to herself: a *legitimate* voter.

With the holidays approaching, Delpha and Joe made an effort to visit some of her family. As she had anticipated, everyone took to Joe. How could they not, with his engaging personality, infectious dimpled smile, and wavy black hair? Del's relatives appreciated his knowledge of arts and culture without putting on airs about it, instead presenting himself as being of the same humble origins as everyone else.

At one of the visits to Aunt Josie's house, she encountered her parents and sisters. Facing her mother was awkward for Del, but Ann was polite and her embrace was unexpectedly intense and sincere. From that moment, Del hoped all was forgiven. She was surprised to feel such a sense of relief — a lightness and freedom as her resentment suddenly melted away. She had thought she didn't given a damn about her mother, but now realized that hadn't been true. She had been hoarding her anger and hurt feelings. Del barely glimpsed the truth that she still sought her mother's love, before quickly immersing herself in an embrace with her father and sisters.

At Aunt Josie's that Sunday were Uncle Ted and cousin Teddy Arcand with his wife, Violet, and their baby daughter; and Aunt Nellie, Uncle Billy Moore, and Billy Jr., now seven years old but already entering puberty, with an oddly low voice and premature sprouting on his upper lip. Although not especially tall for his age, Billy was unusually developed for a seven-year-old, and Aunt Kitty quietly informed Del that Nellie and her husband were embarrassed by this "freak" of a boy-man, apparently the result of hormones gone wild.

"The pituitary or something or other, I think she said. Anyway, he's got the strength of a grown man, they say. Nellie refuses to give him a bath anymore ..." Kitty raised her eyebrows and indicated with her fingers the reported size of Billy Jr.'s penis.

Kitty's husband, Art, was there along with their three children — 16-year-old Arthur Jr., 12-year-old Kenneth, and two-year-old Helen Catherine, already an engaging enchantress. None of her mother's aunts were at the gathering.

On the way home, Joe shared how much he had enjoyed talking with young Ted Arcand, who was the same age as Joe; and with her father and uncles. Del was pleased; it meant she would be able to raise her new son as part of this large and happy side of her family.

And reconciliation with her mother meant that her son would benefit from the attention of two grandmothers, one Italian and one Irish. In fact, Del had been shocked by her mother's happy reaction to her pregnancy and revelation that she was looking forward to Del's visits with the baby. Ann told Del that she missed sitting in a rocking chair, gently swaying back and forth with a baby snuggled in her arms. It brought tears to Del's eyes and they hugged again.

When they arrived home, Joe went into the bathroom and Del heard him vomiting.

She rushed in. "What's the matter?"

"I don't know." He attempted a smile. "Maybe I'm not used to Irish food. At least I know it's not morning sickness." He laughed and then bent over to retch some more.

"It's just my stomach," he said sheepishly. "It's been upset lately — probably a touch of flu or something."

Del was worried, but he washed his face, combed his hair, and looked as good as new.

He kissed her. "Don't worry. I'm fine."

9

1929

D el's son was born in the hospital on January 30, 1929, after a long and difficult labor. He emerged into the world with something of a head start — weighing in at a whopping 13 pounds, 12 ounces! Four days later, mother and son were brought home by the proud father and his ecstatic parents. Joe's reign as crown prince immediately came to an end, as all attention was now directed to the newborn heir apparent. He was named Vincent, after his paternal grandfather.

Unfortunately, Del was unable to nurse, which meant that Rina, who was still nursing Irma, served as a wet nurse.

As Vinny grew and flourished under the care of the women, Joe lost some of his luster. Frequent arguments flared with his parents and brothers over issues that once would have been ignored. The family accused him of being irritable and temperamental, "even for a musician." Joe defended himself by blaming it on fatigue.

"Always you're tired," his father complained. "Your stomach hurts, your chest hurts, always you need to rest. What's wrong with you? You're not a boy like Mike and Frank. You're 24 — be a man! What's the matter with you, eh? Your wife don't let you sleep at night?"

True, sometimes Del had trouble sleeping and he'd wake to find her reading in bed. And although he awoke often, warm and sweaty, pajamas damp with perspiration, he usually fell right back to sleep. Still, he seemed always to be tired and suffering from various maladies — nausea, stomach pains, headaches.

He tried to minimize his lack of energy, certain he'd feel better soon, pushing himself to do his share and trying to maintain his usual good humor and high spirits. Still, everyone noticed his malaise.

"You're not your usual self, Joey," they'd say.

"I'm just a little tired," he'd explain.

In early May, his symptoms were attributed to spring fever ("When the iron in your blood turns to lead in your ass," said Del). In the summer, it was the heat and humidity. But by September, when the sky turned deep blue and the weather cooled to crystal clearness, it became increasingly difficult to deny that something was wrong.

Unlike everyone else (except for Delpha, who was on a diet), Joe was losing weight. He didn't eat as much as before, which worried Rose.

"You're a man — don't worry about being too big. Look at your father. Del wants to get her girlish figure back — you need to eat more! That's why you're tired so much, not enough food."

Del finally prevailed upon Joe. "Go to a doctor and find out what the hell's going on. You haven't been yourself for months now. Your father thinks you're spoiled and lazy. And we never make love anymore, even though I've lost more than 20 pounds since Vinny was born. You don't even play with him like you used to. He'll be walking before you know it and running rings around you if you don't snap out of it."

Joe finally relented. He'd see a doctor, although he didn't expect it to do much good. He didn't believe anything was wrong with him.

Neither the Rios nor the Capriollis made much use of physicians, but they did occasionally use Dr. Sussino. Joe went one day when he had no rehearsal. Dr. Sussino took a medical history and then examined him. Although still a large man, Joe admitted to having lost weight during the past months.

"Maybe a few pounds, I don't know. I don't keep track, but yes, my clothes are looser. The truth is, I just don't have the same appetite I used to. I guess I'm not a growing boy anymore. Actually, I know I could stand to lose a few more pounds, but my mother would probably faint if I did."

In response to Dr. Sussino's questions, Joe went on to describe more of his symptoms — all of which he attributed to benign causes: night sweats, because the apartment was too warm; tightness in his chest, due to a mild cold; some vomiting and nausea, in all likelihood because of something he ate.

"I have a slight cough," he admitted, "maybe an allergy, nothing to be concerned about; after all, I'm not a singer like my pop."

And yes, he agreed, he had noticed a slight swelling in his neck. "I assumed it was due to playing the violin, probably irritating something — between practice and performance, I play at least eight hours a day. With all this extra flesh, I haven't paid that much attention to it, but yes, maybe the swelling has been increasing. It doesn't hurt, so I haven't really paid attention to it."

Finally, the doctor asked him about the lumps in his armpit.

"No, I haven't noticed those little lumps before this; just never paid attention. Aren't they normal? Maybe they've always been there. Really, doctor, the only problem is feeling tired all the time."

Dr. Sussino, without much comment, wrote out some prescriptions for lab tests and blood work. Joe took a bus to the hospital to have the tests taken. The following week, he returned to the doctor.

"You have Hodgkin's disease, Giuseppe. It's a form of cancer." He'd probably had it for at least a year, maybe longer. There wasn't much they could do: medication to relieve some of the symptoms, changing his diet might give him more strength. Avoid alcohol.

But the reality was: There was no cure, and he would get progressively worse over the next couple of years.

Joe was aghast. How could the man sit across from him like that and give him a death sentence? At 24? Joe looked down at his hands, his feet. *I'm not an old man. I'm a young man, big and healthy, strong. I'm married, with a son. I'm still living with my own mother and father, for Christ's sake. I haven't even lived my life yet. I'm not sick, just tired sometimes, some indigestion. How can you tell me I'm going to die? I'm in line to become first violinist. You're full of shit, you moron! What do you know? You don't know what the hell you're talking about. Goddamn jerk. Imbecile. Quack. No wonder my family never comes to you. I never should have come. That's what I get for listening to my silly wife.*

He sat in silent turmoil, a whirlpool of confusion carrying him helplessly in a downward spiral. Finally, he asked the doctor, "What about a second opinion? Shouldn't I see a specialist?"

Sussino agreed that made sense. "Maybe there's something new I haven't heard about. Here, I'm giving you three names. They're all good men. Bring these lab results with you when you go. Have whoever you consult call me if they wish. I'm sorry, Giuseppe. If there's anything more I can do ..."

Joe left the office. *I need a place to sit down and think.* He didn't want to go home right away. He needed to digest the news. He needed to be alone. *Cancer. Only a few more years, maybe only two or three. Shit. What will Mama say? Pop will kill me for this. And what about my wife and my kid? Jesus Christ, how can this be?*

They were almost done with dinner when he came in. "Hey, Joey, where you been?" Mike shouted when he saw his big brother enter the dining room. His father glared silently.

"Come, Giuseppe, sit down. I save a plate for you, just in case," Rose said as she got up to fetch his dinner.

Del looked at him, her eyes filled with anxiety.

"Where you been, honey? We've all been worried. Nobody knew where you were."

"I went to the doctor like you wanted me to," he said, sitting down at his place next to his wife.

"I thought you went last week. You said it was a waste of time, that he had nothing to say, that there wasn't anything wrong."

Joe nodded and sighed. He studied the plate of macaroni and meatballs in front of him. He had no appetite, not for any of it. The thought of food made him nauseous.

"And what did he say?" Del asked.

Rose held her breath, glad that her daughter-in-law was asking the question she'd never have had the courage to ask. Everyone else sat suspended, waiting anxiously.

"So ..." she pursued into his silence.

He licked his lips and looked around the table. "He'd wanted me to get some tests done, some blood work. I went back today to get the results. Then, he wanted me to go see a specialist. And the specialist wanted more tests. So it's back to the hospital and then back to the specialist. I've been on the damn buses all day. I'm exhausted, just plain exhausted."

Del knew evasion when she saw it. She felt herself growing fearful; dread grew like a lead lump in her stomach, and the floor fell from under her. He was avoiding something.

"So, what did the specialist have to say? He tell you you're pregnant?" she tried to joke. Wisecracks and sarcasm were a good first line of defense. Anger and hopelessness could come later.

The laughter broke the spell and everyone exhaled. "No," even Joe smiled, "he said I have Hodgkin's disease."

"Hodgkin?" somebody said. "What kind of disease is that?"

Joe and Del's eyes remained locked on each other. Without letting go of his visual hold on her, he said quietly, "It's a disease of the blood, the white blood cells."

"So," Vincenzo broke in, "did he give you the medicine you need? I bet he charged big bucks for it, eh?"

Joe took Del's hand in his but turned to look at his father, studiously avoiding his mother's face.

"Yeah, Pop, I got some medicine. It'll help me feel better, make my blood stronger, so I won't be so tired all the time."

"Fine. Good, then. It's good that you went. Now you'll be your old self, not like an old married man before his time." Vincenzo turned to Tony and Mike and Frankie and they all laughed and sipped their red wine.

"I'm sorry. I don't feel so good," Joe sighed. "I'm really tired. I'm going to go lie down for a while."

"But you haven't eaten. Not even a bite."

"I'm sorry, Mama. Maybe later."

Del squeezed his hand. "I'll go with you."

"OK," he said.

They walked hand in hand down the hall and into their room. Everyone remained silent at the table.

"It's going to be all right now," Vincenzo pronounced. "The specialist gave him the medicine. He'll get well. He'll be his old self. Everything *va bene. Tutti va bene.* You'll see. I know I'm right about this. All you have to do is look at him, for Christ's sake. Anybody can see, a young man like that, big and strong, not even in the prime of his life yet. How could anything be wrong?"

In the privacy of their room, Del made Joe tell her every detail. He kept his eyes on the floor, trying at first to minimize the implications, but she succeeded in dragging every last bit of information out of him. He had her feel the swollen lymph nodes in his neck and armpits.

"It's not from playing the violin, like I thought. It's the goddamned cancer."

They sat in silence for a long time, quietly weeping in each other's arms. They agreed not to tell any of the other family members until it became clear he wouldn't have much longer to live. That might not be for a year or more. All they needed to know now was that he had anemia, weak blood; he tired easily and couldn't work too hard, his stomach got upset easily, he'd run a fever sometimes. All of that, his parents and brothers and the Capriollis could deal with.

It was then that Del decided she would return to work. If Joey was going to die, she couldn't expect Vincenzo and Rose to support her and Vinny forever. Maybe she'd wait until after the holidays. By then she'd have lost more weight and look more presentable.

On October 24, 1929, the bottom dropped out for everyone. They called it Black Thursday. The stock market fell like a mountain climber who lost his grip. It was the headline story in all the papers. That evening, everyone talked about the precipitous drop of almost 13 percent! Would it go back up? Was it the beginning of the end? Billions of dollars of wealth were lost. The next day was almost as bad as people panicked, and the market plunged an additional 12 percent.

Still, hope prevailed. Perhaps over the weekend, everyone would rethink, take advantage of the new bargains. But Monday saw another abysmal decline, and Del followed the stampede of people withdrawing their savings from the bank early the next morning — Black Tuesday. The line of nervous depositors reached around the corner. People prayed that the bank would not run out of money and close before they could claim their savings. After Del had secured her $400 — more than five month's wages — the bank did shut down.

No one in the Rio household was immediately affected, but it soon became apparent that the stock market crash would have widespread ramifications. During the Great Depression, one out of every four adults would be unemployed — and that would affect everyone.

The Chicago Symphony Orchestra received fewer subscriptions and smaller donations. Before long, Joe's salary was significantly reduced, and he was grateful that he still had a job. In fact, he felt it his duty to inform the conductor of his condition, and they agreed that when he could no longer perform as a full member, he would continue as a substitute violinist — though still permitted to rehearse with the orchestra.

The first week after the crash, Del applied for her old job and was rehired based on her superb record.

Business slowed in the barbershop as men opted to shave themselves, wait longer between haircuts, or have their wives cut their hair. On one of her newly instituted weekly visits to her parents, Del learned that Uncle Harry had suffered the biggest loss in her family. He held out hope during that first disastrous weekend that the market would rebound — but it didn't, and he lost a fortune. In addition to his losses in the market, tenants in his apartment buildings were unable to pay their rent. Harry found himself scrambling to pay the mortgages on his buildings, and was forced to sell some of them at substantial losses.

To make matters worse, his brother had died from a heart attack that horrible October weekend. Uncle Jimmy was 65 years old. Harry's oldest brother, Ed O'Hara, was the only one still in the meat purveying business. He, too, saw a decline in business and was forced to lay off workers.

Uncle John F. Powers' business also took a hit. Many customers either canceled their deliveries or reduced their orders. New customers were scant. He, too, laid off workers and, although he kept Fred on as an employee, had to cut his wages by 10 percent. At 50, Fred was grateful he still had a job. Where else would he find work?

Thankfully, the Illinois Telephone Company didn't cut their workforce, so Del's job was safe, although she did have to work longer hours as the company cut back on hiring new operators. Consequently, the Rios and the Wilhelms were forced to tighten their belts and live more frugally. The increased financial stress did, however, distract most of the family from Joe's growing lethargy and weight loss.

Without being aware of what was happening, both Rose and Del started paying more attention to the baby. While the two women were afraid that paying too much attention to Joe would reveal the depth of their fear for him, there was no such danger in showering Vinny with unreserved love and attention.

When Del wasn't home, Rose hovered over him, feeding him, holding him, singing to him in Italian. She did her household chores with one arm while she hugged him possessively to her hip. Perhaps she had done the same with Joe, her firstborn — but Del did much the same thing when she was home.

When Joe felt well enough, he'd initiate lovemaking with Del and then it was alternately passionate and desperate or tender and languid, as they savored every moment, every sensation; as if by committing it to memory, they could deny the end they knew was coming. Although the frequency declined due to his fatigue and abdominal discomfort, Del was determined to have another baby with him. When she missed her period, she held off making any announcements until another month had passed.

She miscarried during Thanksgiving weekend. Bearing the disappointment, discomfort, and grief alone, she hid the news from everyone.

In January, she missed her period again, only to have her hopes dashed by another miscarriage in early March. These two blows physically and emotionally exhausted her. Discouraged, she became despondent and lost interest in everything except Joe and Vinny. In June she became pregnant once more. When she missed her second period without incident and felt herself ripening, she felt sufficiently confidant to tell Joe. He was euphoric and couldn't wait to tell the family. It was only during their celebration of the good news that Del confided that she had suffered two miscarriages in the preceding months.

On Labor Day weekend, Joe and Del and little Vinny, now over a year and a half old, went to a family picnic at the park by Lake Michigan. Ginny and Jo joined in the festivities. Adoring aunts, the two teenagers had great fun playing in the water with Vinny. It was a beautiful day and, for a brief time, everyone felt relaxed and content, despite Joe's illness and the tight financial times. The sunny day brightened everyone's mood; they talked of names for Del's new baby and of the upcoming season for the Chicago Symphony Orchestra, which Joe was very excited about. Tony and Vincenzo shared ideas about increasing business and bringing in new customers. There was an air of hopefulness, if not outright optimism. After a day of laughter and joking, Joe played the violin and Vincenzo led them in singing old Neapolitan love songs.

That night, Del had another miscarriage.

On her next trip to her mother's, Del earned about a terrible accident that had just occurred. While Kitty and Nellie were visiting Great-Aunt Bridget, Billy Moore Jr., not knowing his own freakish strength, had pulled little Helen Catherine across the lawn by her legs.

"And wouldn't you know," Ann exclaimed, "he pulled her leg right out of its socket. Right out! Poor Helen Catherine — that sweet child who is always smiling and laughing — lying there in the grass howling with pain. And Billy Jr. standing there, still holding her foot, not comprehending what he'd done." She shrugged for emphasis. "Well, none of us did. I've never heard of such a thing. They rushed her to the hospital. She was there a week; still in a cast she is, but they say she'll never walk right again. Can you believe it? And her being such a pretty angel."

Del listened, aghast.

"Billy Jr. hasn't been right since," her mother went on. "Crying all the time for what he did, Nellie says. He's afraid he's going to hell for sure. He really has a sweet disposition. He loves Helen Catherine so much. It's like something you would have done to poor Josephine when you were that age — only you would have done it deliberately. I know how much you hated her then." She gave a little smile to indicate that all of that was now in the past.

Picturing little Billy Jr. and Helen, Del tried to remember being so hatefully jealous of Josephine's claim on her mother and new father. She had, indeed, tried to harm her sister — and she now smiled gratefully at how much her feelings had changed. She glanced to where Jo and Ginny were playing on the floor with Vinny. Her sisters were so generous with their love — not at all like she was at their age. She felt grateful that Vinny was surrounded by so many people who loved and cherished him. Her life had been so different. As she sipped her tea and watched her mother gaze adoringly on her grandson, she realized that Ann had not had an easy childhood either. She was glad her mother was mellowing with age, as maybe she was herself.

Just before the holidays, the Rio family received another blow. Seventeen-year-old Frankie was in his senior year at high school and Vincenzo had, through the help of one of his customers, obtained an invitation for Frank to attend the West Point Academy upon graduation. The family had been eagerly anticipating his acceptance for a few years.

But then scandal broke: A girl in his class was pregnant and claimed that Frank had forced himself upon her. The outraged parents called upon Rose and Vincenzo, demanding that Frank do right by her or they would have him put in jail. It was agreed that Frank and the girl would get married right away, but continue living with their own parents until they graduated. Then the parents would help set them up in an apartment.

West Point, or any other school for that matter, was out of the question. The whole family was crushed. Vincenzo and Rose (who fainted at the news) couldn't be consoled. Even Joe was so angry at his brother that he threatened to beat him up.

"Now look at yourself. Instead of a distinguished career, you'll be driving a truck like Mike, who never cracked a book in his life. You're so goddamned smart, how could you let this happen?"

Vincenzo apologized to his customer, Johnny Frank, who had obtained the West Point invitation from a local congressman.

"What can I say, Mr. Johnny? He's a young bull. He doesn't realize that what you do today determines what happens tomorrow. But we are all grateful for what you tried to do for him."

The remainder of 1931 passed like a rainy day shrouded in gray mist. Del had a fourth miscarriage. Frank was married in a joyless civil ceremony, with only grim parents and intimidating in-laws in attendance. His graduation was an anticlimax that, in spite of academic awards, brought no pride — only the shaking of heads and grumbling frowns from his parents and family. Business in the barbershop got worse. Tempers frayed.

Joe's deterioration was steady. When he could no longer attend rehearsals or practice for more than a few minutes at a time, the family became resigned to the fact that he was dying. And then, with an inaudible sigh, Joe fell into a precipitous decline. One day he had color and the next day he was pale and deflated, quietly complaining of pain and nausea.

"Maybe another month," the doctor told them. "Pray. Make him as comfortable as you can."

On February 10, 1932, one day before his third wedding anniversary, he succumbed.

The wake was held in a local funeral parlor on Friday and the service, which was well attended, was the following day. Most of Del's family came, as did customers from the barbershop, Del's co-workers from the phone company, symphony orchestra members, as well as many friends and neighbors. Three-year-old Vinny was sullen, but whether he was responding to everyone else's grief or actually understood his own loss was not clear. Mother and son were inseparable; the other women, including Ginny and Jo, attended them protectively. It was the first — and only — time that Ann and Fred Wilhelm met the Rios.

10

Delpha

C aring for Vinny saved Rose and Del from sinking into terminal depression. Keeping him happy and occupied forced the two women to put on a brave face and go on with their lives. Del was grateful for her job, to which she returned the Monday following Joe's funeral. Rose had only Vinny to fill her days with purpose — and his flashing dimpled smile, his curly black hair, his happy personality filled the Rio apartment with a much-needed affirmation of life.

But at night, with Vinny sleeping peacefully in his crib, Del would find herself in tears. Unable to read, she'd let the book fall onto her belly and give herself over to overwhelming emptiness. Watching her sleeping son, her arm reached automatically to the empty place next to her, as if expecting to find Joey's emaciated, sweaty body there.

The world is an empty place. Or rather, it holds no place for me. Vinny is here in his father's home, his father's room, with his grandmother and grandfather. He belongs. But this is no place for me. I'm not needed here. If it weren't for him, they wouldn't want me here. They don't need me. And Vinny doesn't need me. He's got his father's family. I'm 26, a fat Irish bastard widow with no education and a three-year-old boy. Who will want me? I'll be like my Aunt Mary, who died an old maid. I might as well be dead now. Nobody will miss me. Vinny has his father's family. Now that Joey is gone, nobody even cares if I'm alive or not.

Although Delpha never acted on these feelings, they became a habitual way of thinking. She lost her appetite and interest in life. She dropped weight without even trying. True, she continued to work and contribute to the household, but most of it was done mechanically, and without personal investment.

Her girlfriends were occasionally successful in getting her to go out with them. But except for rare moments when the music carried her away, the excursions were joyless and she went home early.

Delpha floated through the rest of 1932 with a grin-and-bear-it attitude of resignation. Even the election of Franklin Roosevelt in November didn't do much to brighten her spirit. Indeed, the holiday season of 1932 was melancholy in the Rio household (and the country, for that

245

matter). Except for the delightful and chubby children, Vinny and Irma, everyone plodded through the brittle, unforgiving months of a typical mid-western winter.

Toward the end of April of 1933, Rina received a letter from one of her brothers in New York City.

"My older brother, Umberto, wrote that as a graduation gift he is sending my nephew, Gerardo, here to Chicago for the opening of the World's Fair."

Over dinner, Rina explained that since she'd left New York in 1926 after marrying Tony, she hadn't seen any of her family, so she was looking forward to her nephew's visit in June.

During the ensuing discussion, Rina recalled that her older brother, Umberto, and his wife, Iffigenia, had three children — a boy and two little girls.

"The youngest is named after me, only she spells it R-e-n-a. She must be about 16 now. Although I lived with my other brother, Sal, and my sister, Maria, we were often at Umberto's. Their son, Gerry, was always either reading or out with his friends. They went roller-skating all over the city, hitching rides by holding on to the backs of trolley cars. Where they lived was called Hell's Kitchen. It was very rough, but Gerry was used to the neighborhood and knew how to take care of himself."

"So that's who's coming to visit, Aunt Rina? That kid, Gerry?"

"Yes, only now he's grown up, like you. He's 20 and already graduating from college."

Tony took a sip of wine and cleared his throat. "I was just thinking, Delpha, maybe while Gerardo is visiting, you might accompany him to the Fair, help make him feel welcome. You know, show him around."

Del stopped eating. She looked at Rose and Rina and then Vincenzo, and what she saw was encouragement — and perhaps some awkwardness. At first she was puzzled, but then realized they were concerned about her. This was their way of saying: *Go on, get out of the house a little. Get on with your life. Live a little.* And, of course, they would pitch in to help cover her expenses — after all, she'd be doing them a favor.

"If Gerry is your nephew," Mike asked Rina, "and Frank and I are your nephews, that means that Gerry is our cousin, right?"

"Yes, of course," Rina said.

Del piped up, "Well, if Joey was your nephew's cousin, and I was married to Joey, then I guess that means I'm his cousin too, by marriage."

"Whoa," said Frankie, "this is getting too weird and complicated for me."

They laughed, and it was agreed that when cousin Gerry visited in June, Delpha would accompany him to the Chicago World's Fair and show him around the city. She thought Mike and Frank would probably do a better job of hosting this visitor, but she didn't complain.

What the hell — at least I'll get to see the World's Fair. And that was the last she thought about it.

On June first, Mike and Frank went to the Greyhound terminal to greet Gerardo's bus from New York. The Rio brothers were both happy to discover that they were considerably taller than their wiry cousin, who seemed energetic despite the 24-hour bus trip. The three young men immediately hit it off. Although Gerry was a college graduate, he didn't lord that over them. Friendly and outgoing by nature, he was genuinely interested in what their lives were like.

He remembered hearing stories about Joe's violin playing and expressed deep sadness at the loss of their older brother. "Such a shame," he said. "I heard that he was quite talented and a truly good person with a good heart."

By the time they got back to the house, all three were on excellent terms.

Aunt Rina couldn't do enough to make her nephew feel at home. For his visit, they had converted the sewing room into a spare room, and borrowed a bed from friends. As soon as Gerardo had greeted his aunt and put his suitcase down, the brothers took him to the barbershop to meet Vincenzo and his uncle. Tony took great pride in introducing his nephew to the customers in the shop.

"Our nephew, from New York City," he beamed. "He just graduated from Fordham University, and he's only 20 years old!" Although no one said anything directly, Frankie must have felt some pangs of remorse. Here, his cousin was a college graduate, and Frankie — the object of his father's pride — was driving a truck instead of studying at West Point.

Rina and Rose put on a big feast that night, and Gerry said he had never eaten so well. "My mother never cooks like this," he said. "She's a very simple cook and a very simple person, really. And my father couldn't care less about food. All he's interested in is his business."

Rina confirmed what he'd said about his parents. Meanwhile, the women's eyes were wide with delight as they watched him consume the meal with such gusto. While the Rios and the Capriollis peppered Gerry with questions about his family, Del had an opportunity to learn about this new "cousin" of hers.

In addition to his parents, Gerardo also had two aunts and an uncle living in New York. His father's younger brother, Salvatore — who, at

47 was still a bachelor — lived with his youngest sister, Maria, now 27.

"Si," said Rina, "Maria and our oldest sister, Concetta, came over with me in 1921."

"Oh boy," Gerry laughed, "Aunt Connie is a real piece of work. She's an old maid who lives by herself a few blocks from us and works as a seamstress in the garment district. Every time she comes to visit, she goes through a whole bottle of wine all by herself. She's a cranky old woman to begin with, but the wine makes her even more miserable. I think of her as one of those old hag witches from Shakespeare."

Through the ensuing conversation, Del learned that Gerry's father had two older brothers still in Italy, in a town called Contursi, in the province of Salerno. The oldest of his father's nine siblings was also named Gerardo, after their father, who had been responsible for bringing the first railroad to their town.

Del was intrigued to learn that Gerry's mother — also from the Salerno region near Naples — was one of three sisters named for characters in Greek plays: Iffigenia, Gerry's mother; Artimus (Aunt Arty); and Elektra, who remained in Italy. Aunt Arty's husband, Conrad, and her bachelor brother, Leo, also ran a barbershop in Jersey City, New Jersey.

"No kidding," said Vincenzo, "they also have a barbershop? Like ours here?"

"Very much like yours," Gerry confirmed. "It's also on the first floor of an apartment house and they live upstairs, with my cousins Johnny and Matilda. We see them about once a month or so. I think the only person my mother really cares about is her sister, Aunt Arty."

Del's first impression of Rina's nephew and godson was that he was, even if only as tall as she was at five feet two, a handsome young man. It was obvious that he was intelligent, but she was surprised at how much fun he was. She confirmed her impression in the days and weeks ahead as she accompanied Gerry around the city.

In addition to going to the World's Fair a few times, they walked all over the city. Gerry admitted he was an inveterate walker, covering five to 10 miles a day back in New York. They walked to Lake Michigan and along the beaches and parks that lined its shore from the Southside (where her old orphanage, St. Joseph's, still stood) past the Loop, the Science and Art Museums, past the ritzy North Shore, and up to the Northside and Old Town.

She showed him Orchestra Hall, home of the Chicago Symphony Orchestra, where Joey had played. And she pointed out some of her favorite speakeasies on South Wabash Avenue, as well as Minsky's Burlesque.

"Maybe you'll want to go there with Mike and Frank," she said boldly.

She showed him the stockyards where her grandfather had once been employed, and some of her uncles and cousins still worked. She showed him The Fair, a department store owned by Montgomery Ward, and the elevated train that ran around the Loop. And they visited her old house, where her parents and sisters still lived.

Unlike when Del had introduced Joe Rio to her parents, her mother was cool but polite. Perhaps Ann was more accepting because Gerry was introduced as a cousin of the Rios, briefly visiting Chicago to see the World's Fair, rather than as someone Del would be dating. Maybe it was his friendly, respectful manner or his small stature — shorter than either Ginny or Josephine — and so unlike the robust, classically Italian Joe Rio.

Eventually, Del introduced him to her friends and they all went to clubs to listen to jazz and dance together. Gerry was a good dancer, as Joe had been, and Del was transported. She felt alive again. Initially, she simply enjoyed Gerry's company for what it was — someone to have fun with, seeing the city through new eyes, hearing about New York, talking about books, listening to him play the harmonica.

The fact that he was almost seven years younger than she was initially precluded her thinking about him as anything but a friend. But as they spent endless hours walking the city, delving into discussions about authors, religion, and politics, she began to experience him quite differently. Gerry was not simply carefree and adventurous, with an exuberance for life, he was also the most serious person she'd ever met — not somber, but deeply thoughtful. For 20, he was unusually wise and mature.

She learned that although he had attended public school ("... because my father was too cheap to pay the tuition at the Catholic school ..."), he had attended the Jesuit-run Fordham University with the intention of becoming a priest. "In fact," he told her, "I used to make a novena every week for years. To do that, I walked a couple of miles to take the 42nd Street Ferry across the Hudson River to Jersey. Then, I'd hike up a steep hill to the top of the cliffs overlooking the river, and walk another two miles to the monastery in Union City. And then, of course, I'd reverse the process to come home again."

But while taking one of his many philosophy courses at Fordham, he'd read Nietzsche, which was forbidden by the Jesuit faculty at the time.

"When I read him, I had an epiphany," Gerry enthused. "He put all my own thoughts into words, and I knew for certain that everything I'd been taught about religion and Catholicism was nonsense. Now, just on principle, I won't go into a church."

Gerry was the first atheist Del had ever met. No one she knew —

especially herself — even admitted out loud that they had any doubts. Although she was a little frightened by this, she also admired his courage and principle — but she didn't dare mention it to anyone in her family.

Originally, Gerry had planned to stay with the Rios for two weeks. But two weeks stretched to four and then six. During that time, Gerry and Del became quite close, and saying goodbye was difficult when the time finally arrived. Rina and Irma accompanied Del and Vinny to the Greyhound bus terminal, and both children saw their mothers wiping their eyes while waving goodbye to the man in the bus window.

Soon, Del and Gerry began writing to each other. Gerry confided that he had never had as much fun with anyone else and that he enjoyed their lively discussions — and sometimes arguments, for Delpha didn't hesitate to speak her mind. Back in New York, he didn't have those kinds of stimulating discussions with anyone outside of the classrooms.

Gerry explained that, in September, he would be starting a graduate program at Fordham, where he'd be studying for his master's degree in psychology and philosophy, and that he planned on becoming a teacher at the college level.

Del, too, missed his company. She had never felt so comfortable with anyone — even with Joe. They hadn't had the occasion, as she had with Gerry, to discuss books and religion and current events. Every day, she looked forward to his letter; if one didn't come, she immediately worried that he was no longer interested in her friendship. The next day two letters would arrive, and she'd be ecstatic, reassured that he really did care for her.

Inevitably, their expressions of affection grew stronger and more passionate. Finally, Gerry wrote and asked her to come to New York to pursue their relationship. Del was excited, but torn. How would it be possible?

One evening at dinner, Del broached the subject. She confirmed what everyone had suspected — that she and Gerry had fallen in love. She wanted to go to New York to be with him, but he would be in school for another two years. Del would have to work to pay rent and living expenses. How could she do that and take care of Vinny?

Now the family understood the root of her recent moody irritability. Tony offered, "I have a niece, my sister's daughter, in New York. She is also a widow, but, unlike you, has no children. Perhaps you could stay with Mary?"

Rose reached out to touch Del's arm. "Sweetheart, why don't you leave Vinny here with us until you get settled? He would be no bother. You know that. This is his home. It's all he knows and he'll have all of us, even Irma, to keep him company until you're ready to send for him."

Del looked at Vinny. Recalling her own childhood apart from her mother, she shook her head. "No," she finally said, hugging her son to her, "thank you for the kind offer, but I couldn't."

"Well," Vincenzo offered, "I'm sure we'll think of something. Anyway, like you say, Gerardo will be in school for the next two years, studying for his master's degree. He won't have much time for a social life."

"I'll write to our niece, Mary, and see what she has to say about you living with her. At least we can find out about that," Rina said.

Del wrote to Gerry about the conversation. He knew Mary Cleavenger — the Capriolli and D'Alessio families had been friendly back in Italy and Mary now lived on 64th Street, not far from where he and his parents lived on 50th Street. He was sure she would be glad to have a roommate to share expenses, given how difficult the Depression was proving to be. He also thought it made sense to leave Vinny with his grandparents in Chicago, as Rose had suggested, until Del was sufficiently settled to send for him.

"He'll probably be better off there anyway," he reassured her, "since he knows everybody and has Irma to play with. New York City is really no place for little kids."

His comments served to start her thinking again about leaving Vinny with his grandparents. It was obvious that they would love to keep Joe's son with them for as long as possible, but she didn't want to be away from him. After Joe died, she often consoled herself with the thought that her life had not been a complete waste. She had produced a beautiful, legitimate son. Even if she was a failure, Vinny validated her.

With Gerry in her life, however, she felt alive again. It was a miracle, but this man actually loved her, desired her, wanted her. And she loved him. She couldn't bear to give that up; she had to pursue their connection as she pursued her next breath. But to leave Vinny behind, even for just a few weeks, felt wrenchingly impossible. The very idea of separation from him let loose a terror from some dark void deep within her. She belonged with him and he with her. God forbid he should ever feel abandoned. She'd never forgive herself. She wrote to Gerry of her torment.

"Delpha, my love," he answered, "this first year in graduate school is going to take most of my time. But whatever time I have that won't be consumed by school, I want to spend with you. I have no doubt in my mind that if you come to New York, we'll get married as soon as it's possible. It's the only logical conclusion I can come to. How could it be otherwise? You have no idea how much I miss you, how lonely I am without you. There's no one in my family (other than Uncle Sal) I can talk to, not even my sisters — certainly not my parents. You're the most intelligent woman I know — and besides, you're beautiful and wonderful in every way. Come. Leave Vincent with his father's family and give us the opportunity to start our life together. Please say *yes*."

Yes to getting married? Of course. Yes to leaving her son behind? She felt herself wavering. Mary Cleavenger had written to Rina that she'd welcome Del as a roommate for as long as she wanted, so Del knew she had a safe place to stay. But she was still unwilling to leave her son behind, no matter how briefly.

She talked to her parents and sisters about her conflict. Ginny and Jo were excited about her being engaged again.

"Of course we'll visit Vinny and have him stay over with us," they said. "We'd love to do that. You'd be doing us a favor."

Her father was more practical. "A bird in hand," he said, drawing thoughtfully on his pipe. "How many young men would be willing to raise another man's boy?" (*Was he giving himself kudos here? Did Delpha make the connection that he had done that very same thing for her?*) "And, this D'Alessio fellow is going to be a college professor, you say? Well, I'd hate to see you give that up, that's all."

Del interpreted her mother's silence as another negative judgment of her: *You married one guinea and now you want to marry another? What can you expect, except some sort of trouble?*

At work, she confided in her girlfriends and they all agreed: a few weeks without mommy wouldn't hurt the boy. After all, it's not like you're leaving him with strangers. And think of the life you and your son will have, married to a university professor in New York City. My God, Del, who would pass that up?

Still, Del fretted: *What if something happens to Vinny while I'm away? A thousand miles! He's all I have. I'm his mother. I'd never be able to live with myself if something happened and I wasn't there for him.*

In the end, her heart won out. No doubt her passions and loneliness contributed to her decision. But first, with the help of her supervisors, she arranged for a position with the New York Telephone Company — so when she arrived in the big city, a job would be waiting for her.

Early one chilly Sunday morning in September 1933, Del went to the Greyhound bus terminal accompanied by Rose, Vincenzo, Vinny, Rina, Uncle Tony, and Irma. Josephine and Ginny met them there.

"We couldn't let you go without saying goodbye," they said. "Who knows when we'll see you again?"

Despite the brave smiles and attempts at humor, four-year-old Vinny must have sensed the solemn mood of the occasion. As Del hugged her family, she was unable to conceal her emotions. Finally she held her little boy, who also had tears in his eyes.

"I'll only be gone for a little while before I come back for you," she promised. "You'll be having so much fun playing with Irma and your Aunt Ginny and Aunt Jo, and Aunt Rina and Uncle Tony, you won't even have time to miss me. And of course, you know Grandma and Grandpa will take good care of you. Grandma Rose will cook all your favorite foods for you. I'm going to miss you so much. I love you to pieces."

Vincenzo reached down to pick up the boy and Delpha tearfully boarded the bus. They watched as she found a seat next to a window so she could wave as the bus pulled out. Vincenzo told Vinny, "Wave bye-bye to Mommy and blow her a kiss." And Rose told her sobbing grandson not to worry, that she'd take care of him until Mommy came back. Meanwhile, Rina shook her head and confided to her husband that she couldn't imagine ever leaving Irma.

"I don't understand how a mother can leave her own child," she sighed. "I mean, I love Gerry and I know Delpha will make a good wife for him — but still, I don't know how she can actually leave her own son. It doesn't feel right. "

As Delpha sat in her seat, wiping her eyes and blowing her nose, she tried to put on a happy face for them. Watching the tableau — Vincenzo holding her son, his other arm firmly around Rose's shoulders; Rina with Tony holding Irma; and her sisters, both beautiful young women now — she told herself that she'd be back soon. It wasn't as if she were going on a long ocean voyage, after all. Still, she gazed at them intently, burning the images of her family into her mind — their smiling faces, her little boy waving and blowing a kiss as the bus revved its motor and slowly backed away.